ANTIQUES
OF
AMERICAN
CHILDHOOD

The Christmas Tree.

The Christmas Tree. Demorest's Young America, *December, 1872.*

ANTIQUES
OF
AMERICAN
CHILDHOOD

by

Katharine Morrison McClinton

Bramhall House • New York

For
Catharine and Chase Ashley
Joyce and Kim McClinton

CONTENTS

ACKNOWLEDGMENTS

Special thanks go to John Mackay Shaw, whose unique collection, "Childhood in Poetry," in the library of Florida State University, has been the source of much of my research. I also want to thank him for writing the chapter on Story and Poetry Books, and for his valuable notes on collecting.

When I first came to Tallahassee in September of 1967, I had outlined the contents of this book and had completed considerable research. My sources had been The New-York Historical Society, The Museum of the City of New York, The Museum for the Preservation of New England Antiquities, The Shelburne Museum, The Henry Ford Museum, and Old Sturbridge Village, all of which have excellent collections for study. However, in Tallahassee I found a mine of additional material in the Shaw Collection at Florida State University and in Tallahassee's state and county libraries. Mr. Shaw's "Childhood in Poetry" stacks have provided particularly fruitful research because of the availability of books and magazines hitherto unfamiliar to me. Especially valuable have been the illustrations of toys in the early books and the advertising pages of nineteenth-century children's periodicals. I also wish to thank Dr. N. Orwin Rush, Director of Florida State University Library, for his interest in my work.

Katharine Hagler, Assistant Researcher of Decorative Arts, The Henry Ford Museum, has again been most helpful, especially in locating the Hair Album. Janet Byrne, Associate Director of the Print Department of The Metropolitan Museum of Art, introduced me to Album Amicorams and other rare albums in the Museum's collection. Eleanor Fayerweather, Curator of the Costume Center, Rhode Island School of Design, gave information about children's kerchiefs, as did the Textile Department of Cooper Union.

Sally Luscomb has generously furnished photos of buttons from her collections "Just Buttons." Mrs. Margaret Whitton and Barbara Whitton have also supplied photos from their collections, as have The Seamen's Bank for Savings, New York City; F. H. Griffith, Otto Wasserman, Ginsburg & Levy, Inc., Tillou Galleries, Milton Bradley Company, Parker Brothers, and Mrs. William Liebowitz. Mrs. Malcolm Johnson made available the old issues of *Harper's Bazaar*.

Girl in Dog Cart on Cliff House beach, San Francisco, California. J. Fruebis, 1890. California Historical Society.

The Early American Child

eager records provide little information about early American children. There are few diaries or books of childhood reminiscences to tell us how the child thought, but we do learn much from the books they read, the games they played, and the old treasured toys that are preserved in museums and private collections. There are also many children's portraits that picture how they looked and what they wore. However, it is impossible to understand the child of colonial America without understanding the importance of religion and moral teaching in the Puritan background.

The Seventeenth and Eighteenth Centuries

Although children were greatly desired, and large families were eagerly welcomed, the pleasure of having children was always tempered by religion and the sense of duty. Strict rules in the training of children began as soon as the child drew breath. Regardless of the weather, all children had to be baptized in the meetinghouse within a few days of birth. Cotton Mather's child, born in July, 1699, at 1:00 A.M., was baptized in the afternoon. "I baptized my Son and in Honor to my Parent, I called him Increase." Another child was born in April, 1711. "I called the child's name Jerusha to admonish her if she lives, that she should walk in the steps of Piety, which were taken by my deceased Sister of that Name." Names that indicated a virtuous trait of character such as Temperance, Patience, Hope, Submit, Amity, Thanks, and Supply were common, as were the well-known Bible names Ruth, Mary, Esther, Sarah, and John.

11

The life of the child of early America was often short, and almost half of those born never saw five years. Medicines were scarce, and such remedies as the anodyne necklace were relied on to relieve not only the pains of teething, but such ills as violent convulsions and fevers. Prayer was depended upon in place of medicine. Such was the child's early training that he lived in fear of God, and in thoughts of the next world. "Child, don't you forget every Day to go alone to pray as I have directed you." (From the diary of Cotton Mather, February, 1705.) Mather also obliged each of his children to retire and ponder on the question, "What should I wish to have done if I were now dying?" To further inculcate piety, each child had to draw up a daily prayer and show it. Even when the children were sick with smallpox, prayer seemed to be the remedy. "The little creatures keep calling for me so often to pray with them, ten or a dozen times a day."

In spite of all this piety and religious discipline, Cotton Mather was lenient in dealing out punishments. "I would never come to give a child a Blow; except in Case of Obstinacy: or some gross Enormity. To be chased for a while out of my Presence, I would make to be look'd upon as the Sorest Punnishment in the Family."

Early American children started to school in infancy. In the letter book of Samuel Sewall, 1691, we learn that his son Joseph attended a Dame School, "his Cousin Jane accompanying him, carried his Horn-book." Joseph was then about two and one-half years old. In 1695, Joseph went to Mrs. Kay's to school. In 1696, his sister Mary "goes to Mrs. Thair's to learn to Read and Knit." Mary was then five years old. Much was expected of colonial children, and it was not unusual for a child to learn the catechism and to spell at two years of age. In fact, there was a tendency to overstimulate the young minds. There were children who entered the Boston Latin School at six and one-half years, and it was not unusual for a boy to enter Harvard at eleven, or to graduate from college at fourteen.

Puritan teaching followed the child to school. Learning was made to seem a privilege and a reward, and each lesson, whether grammar or mathematics, was made a lesson in piety. Also, whatever subject was taught, the book usually contained a catechism or the Lord's Prayer, and if there were illustrations, the cuts pictured Biblical scenes. Although education was important, godliness came first, and education in colonial America was made the handmaid of religion. The following advertisement of a school for boys from the *Boston Weekly News-Letter*, January 26–February 2, 1727, gives an example of how learning and religion were combined: "It is likewise intended, That their very Recreations shall be made profitable to them, either to their Health or Understanding, or rather to both: That Virtue & Godliness shall be encouraged amongst them, and Vice discountenanced by all means possible; and that their Understanding, Judgment & Parts shall be Tryed & Improved every way."

Manners and courtesy also played a part in the child's education from his earliest years and had much influence upon the molding of

his life. The requirements of dress and posture helped to maintain a formality which the many books of etiquette put forth in their rules of behavior. After the hornbook and primers, the Psalms in verse, and the Testament, came the little books of manners. Children's books of etiquette were printed in Europe as early as the fifteenth century. Instructions for behavior at table included: "Grease not thy fingers or napkin. Spit not, cough not, nor blow thy nose at table. Lean not thy elbow on the table or on the back of the chair. Stuff not thy mouth, smell not of thy meat or turn to view the other side. Gnaw not bones at table. Drink not nor speak with anything in thy mouth." *The School of Manners,* an English book, was reprinted by Isaiah Thomas of Worcester, Massachusetts, in 1787, and traces of these old rules were continued in books of etiquette for many years. Children were also taught promptness, and respect for parents, the elderly, and the poor. A little book of manners put out by the New York Sunday School Union in the nineteenth century contains the following rules: "In silence I must take my seat / And give God thanks before I eat, / Must for my food in patience wait." There were books that also gave correct phrases with superfluities of formal politeness that helped to create the formal, stiff little children that we see in the early portraits.

SCHOOLING

The parents of colonial America were determined that their children should be educated, and most colonies assisted in building and maintaining schools in towns where there were sufficient numbers of pupils. In 1636, the governing body of Massachusetts gave money to establish the school which later became Harvard College. In 1647, a Massachusetts law ordered that every town of fifty families provide a school where children could be taught to read and write. These schools were public but not free, and were called "Latin" or "Grammar" schools and "Writing" schools. They were supported at the expense of the parents, who also provided the wood for the fireplace that kept the school warm. Such cities as Boston had better schools. There was a Free School in Boston (1635–1684). The Latin School was established in 1684, and the South Grammar School in 1713. The public school system of Boston was established in 1720. Rhode Island was the only New England colony that did not compel the building of schools and the education of children. There were also few schools in the southern states, and here children of the well-to-do were taught by private tutors or sent to school in England. A scarcity of educational advantages prevailed in Pennsylvania as well, where the Quakers and German sects disapproved of learning beyond the "three R's."

The newspapers are the most important source of information about the schools of the eighteenth century. They give us a picture of the cultural and vocational needs that existed. Robert Francis Seybolt has gleaned the newspapers of colonial Boston and recorded the notices in two important little books: *The Public Schools of Colonial Boston* and *The Private Schools of Colonial Boston*. While the public schools offered only the usual elementary instruction in the "three R's," plus the catechism, and the free grammar schools' curricula were strictly classical, the records of the private schools as found in the newspaper sources tell quite a different story. Writing and grammar remained of first importance, but the needs of commerce and the trades were also met. Arithmetic of all sorts was taught, including geometry, plane and spherical, trigonometry, surveying, gauging, navigation, and the use of globes and mathematical instruments. Commerce called for bookkeeping, shorthand, languages, and geography. History was also offered in the private schools of Boston as early as 1734. Samuel Goodrich (Peter Parley) was six years old when he attended Aunt Delight's Dame school in the summer of 1799. The children, both boys and girls, were taught reading, writing, and arithmetic, and used Dilworth's spelling book. Before reciting, each child was required to "make his abeisance," that is, bow to the teacher.

The first schools in America were built of logs. The light was dim, and larded papers served as window glass. Rude plank desks were set on pegs. There were no blackboards or maps, but, by the mid-eighteenth century, pencils were available, as were slates and slate pens. Paper was scarce, and copybooks were made of hand-ruled foolscap paper.

The accomplishments for boys included "Small-sword, Back-sword" fencing "with all the principal Attitudes and Positions peculiar to the Art," dancing, music, drawing, painting, and horsemanship, "An Art justly admired and counted Part of polite Education."

In large cities there were small classes where girls could be taught further rudiments of education than those learned in a Dame school. But whether girls were taught at home or in private schools, the only things that the average early-American girl learned, besides deportment and elegance of carriage, were to "sew, floure, write and dance."

Accomplishments for girls included "Reading with Elegance and Propriety," English grammar, "English Diction, Epistolary Writing" and the "polite Accomplishments, including French, vocal and instrumental music, dancing, pastry, waxwork, Japanning, quill-work, glass painting, drawing, water painting, painting on gauze and catgutt." Needlework included: "Dresden on Lawn and Muslin, and Work in Imitation of Brussells Lace . . . Shell-Work, and Flowers for the Head," samplers, "Embroidery in Gold and Silver, and all Sorts of shaded work in Colours," filigree, "Turkey-work," flourishing, "Brocaded-Work for Handkerchiefs," "Silk Embroidery's of every kind, Tambour, Feather, India and Darning, Sprigings, with a Variety of Open-work to each; Tapestry, plain lined and drawn Cat-gut black and white, with a Number of beautiful Stitches, Diaper and plain Darnings, French-quilting, Knitting, various sorts of Marking with the Embellishments of Royal-cross, Plain-cross, Queen, Irish and Ten Stitches, Plain-work & Baby-linnen of the newest Taste."

An interesting list of the articles needed to be furnished by the boy attending boarding school in eighteenth-century America is given in the following from the *Boston Gazette,* October 24, 1727: "Any gentlemen (Members of the Church of England) that are desirous of having their Sons Educated after the Method of West-minster School, may be further inform'd by applying to J. Boydell. Conditions, To find their own Bed, Bedding &c. and to bring as Entrance one pair of Sheets, six Towels, six Napkins, one Silver Spoon value 10s Sterling, one Knife, Fork, and Pewter Porringer; which Entrance on their leaving the School is not to be returned. None to be admitted but such as can read well and write; nor the Number of six to be exceeded."

Dancing schools were prohibited in New England in the seven-teenth century, but in 1713 Mr. George Brownell taught "Dancing, Treble Violin, Flute, Spinnet, etc." Singing psalm tunes or "Vocal Psalmody, Hymns, Anthems, etc.," were taught in 1743 by Mr. Peter Pelham, Jr., the son of the well-known early engraver. In 1753, John Rice, "lately from New York and Organist of Trinity Church in this Town," advertised to teach "Instrumental Musick viz Spinnet or Harpsicord, Violin, German Flute, etc." (The *Boston Evening Post,* November 17, 1753). In 1772–1773, Anna Green Winslow took danc-ing from William Turner at his fashionable "Dancing and Fencing School." Miss Winslow, aged ten, gives a report of an evening party. "There was a large company assembled in a handsome, large, upper room in the new end of the house. We had two fiddles, and I had the honor to open the minnuet . . . our treat was nuts, raisins, Cakes, Wine, punch, hot and cold, all in great plenty. . . . For variety we woo'd a widow, hunted the whistle, threaded the needle . . . play-ing of pawns." From this time on, many schools of dancing and fencing were established in Boston. Cotillions, hornpipes, and Eng-lish country dances were the popular dances of the eighteenth century.

The Nineteenth Century

In the nineteenth century, the hardships of colonial days gradu-ally gave way to increasing security and prosperity. The strict rules of the seventeenth and eighteenth centuries regarding children's behavior were somewhat relaxed. However, diligence was still ex-pected of children. In some households there were housekeeping tasks, and even in wealthy families no idle hours were allowed and little girls' fingers were kept busy with needlework. Boys on the farm helped with the harvest. There was firewood to be brought in. Boys also learned to hunt, and many of them possessed guns. At the very least, most boys had jackknives, with which they made simple household articles and carved whistles, bows and arrows, and other toys.

There was now a tendency to look upon children as children and not as small adults. One feature of the emancipation of children was the change in dress. After 1800, children's dress became more comfortable and more suited to their activities. This new liberty was looked upon as laxity by some and writers noted that children ruled the household and lacked respect for their parents. Timothy Dwight, in his *Travels in New England and New York* in 1822, comments that American children are not taught to be wise, virtuous, or useful: "Instead, the end proposed by the parents is to make their children 'objects of admiration' to be admired by visitors. They are taught music, dancing, embroidery, ease and confidence and graceful manners." He complains that too much emphasis is put on appearance, on clothes, behavior in company, and fashionable conversation for admiration, "not for thinking." However, he did find the Sabbath observed in New England "with greater sobriety and strictness than in any other part of the world." Indeed, the New England child was still governed by the rule to be seen and not heard. *The School of Good Manners,* first printed in London in 1701 was reprinted by Jesse Cochron in Vermont in 1815, and New England children were still governed by its rules, such as "Speak not at table. . . . Sing not, hum not, wriggle not." Children were still taught a profound respect for their parents, and prompt obedience. Religion continued to play an important role, with public worship twice every Sunday. Laws in Massachusetts and Connecticut forbade travel on Sunday. But to keep Sunday from being a day of gloom, there were Bible pictures, hieroglyphical Bibles, children's Sunday Books, and such games as a cut-up map of Palestine. Also, beginning with the nineteenth century, there was an endless flow of tiny chapbooks and juveniles. After the Revolution, Isaiah Thomas brought out reprints of English books by John Newbery. Although the cuts and stories of these little books afforded the child some amusement, there was always a moral, with an exhortation for obedience and goodness, and the rewards of the good child were balanced against the troubles of the disobedient child. Religion was also still a dominant feature in the storybook as well as in the ABC's. There were fairy tales with morals and rhymes for the nursery with lectures about the child's well-being and the "good parent." In the stories of Maria Edgeworth, the moralist, a gracious lady always appeared to give an award or point a moral. The Taylor Sisters still preached an omnipresent avenging God. However, though hell and damnation continued to be preached in the books of Mrs. Barbauld, Hannah More, Maria Edgeworth, and Jane and Ann

Family Group: the Hatch Family. Eastman Johnson. 1824–1906. The Metropolitan Museum of Art. Gift of Frederick H. Hatch, 1926.

Taylor, there was a gradual realization that this morbid tone was bad for children. In 1819, Washington Irving's *Sketch Book* gave children Rip Van Winkle and Ichabod Crane, and Clement Moore's *A Visit from St. Nicholas* (" 'Twas the night before Christmas") appeared in 1822. Peter Parley (Samuel G. Goodrich) was writing in 1827 and in a brief time he produced more than a hundred juveniles, which were published to the delight of both American and English children. An anonymous juvenile, *Little Dick and His Playthings*, published by J. Lumsden, Glasgow, in 1823, was illustrated with eight cuts. The story told was of bad little Dick who broke his playthings, and, of course, the moral was the dominant theme. In the 1820's the American Tract Society began publishing a large variety of children's books, including *Honesty the Best Policy*, *Active Benevolence or Lucy Careful*, *Good Boys*, *Falsehood Chastised*, *The Lost Opportunity*, and *The Premium*: all books with morals. *The Youth's Companion*, in its issue of March 14, 1832, contained an article entitled "Infant Schools in Boston." There were three schools for the children of the poor. These schools were under the direction of religious bodies, and food, clothing, and religion were handed out by religious ladies of the city. Children less than a year old were cared for.

Although the discipline of children based on religion and morals gradually changed, the change was not drastic and, through the influence of Victorian England, the pious rules of right and wrong lingered to the end of the century. Indeed, in small country towns of New England, life continued simple. The often-quoted story of *A New England Girlhood* by Lucy Larcom gives a picture of a child who worked in the spinning mills of New England. A picture of a more fortunate child is given by Emily Wilson in *The Forgotten Girl,* a small book of reminiscences of a New England girlhood in the middle of the nineteenth century. There are many parallels to child life in the eighteenth century. Emily Wilson was born in Marlboro, Massachusetts, in 1840. She attended Mount Holyoke College and graduated in 1861, during the Battle of Bull Run. She taught at Holyoke for two years and later at Mills College in California, and died in 1941 at the age of 100 years. The description of her early childhood seems unduly strict.

> Children were kept in the background to be seen and not heard. We were early taught implicit obedience, honesty and truthfulness. . . . The books for children were rather circumscribed. We had the Rollo Books and Mother Goose . . . but the two books which really influenced our lives were *I'd Be a Lady* and *I'd Be a Gentleman.* The family library included *Universalism, Examined, Renounced and Exposed;* Foxe's *Book of Martyrs;* Bunyan's *Pilgrim's Progress;* and *Watts Hymns; The Distant Hills;* and *The Shadow of the Cross.*

They also owned a bound copy of *The Youth's Companion* and several volumes of *Godey's Lady's Book.*

> Life for children was simple in the extreme. There were no movies, no card games, no telephones or electric lights, no radio, no grand birthday parties, no array of costly toys—only everyday thinking and living and the joy that comes from a happy home.
>
> Sunday was not like any other day. We did not play games nor read the same books and the long church services with Sunday School between were inevitable. We did not take long walks nor have the use of the family horse and carriage except to visit the graveyard . . . or occasionally to attend a prayer meeting at the Poor House.

This lingering Puritan influence in the life of American nineteenth-century children is reflected in their portraits and in the daguerreotype of Emily Wilson and her sister. She sits bodily upright with hair parted and pushed back behind her ears, and an overserious expression on her face.

But, though there were certain prescribed duties, children also had time to escape into their own world. Again I quote from Emily Wilson:

> For amusements we were dependent on our own ingenuity. My sister and I had the regulation rag dolls with long curls and club feet. . . . For outdoor games there was "I Spy Tag," "Blindman's Buff," "Hide and Seek" and a ball game. . . . In winter there was coasting on single or double sleds. . . . There was skating. . . . There was the never failing swing. When put to our wits' end for amusement we would sit down side by side, and with our hands clasped say: "Now let's laugh." We had many house games: . . . backgammon, checkers, fox and geese, jack straws, and stage coach, in which nonsensical jingles like the following played an important part: "Intery, mintery, cutery corn / Appleseed and apple thorn / Wire briar, limber lock / Five geese in a flock / Sit and sing by the Spring. Out."

William Wells Newell describes this last game in his *Games and Songs of American Children* thus:

> An evening amusement formerly common in Massachusetts: All present laid their hands with fingers resting on the knees. The speaker then told off the words of the rhymes, one for each finger. The rhyme being thus recited, that finger to which the last syllable fell must be quickly withdrawn, on penalty of being sharply rapped by the hand of the leader. After all had been counted out but one person, he or she was liable to the same risk for every word of the rhyme, the result of which situation is alluded to by the epithet—black finger.

Newell quotes a rhyme twice as long as that quoted by Emily Wilson.

The festive days were not many. Miss Wilson mentions May Day and May baskets, the Fourth of July, and Thanksgiving.

> The table was a picture for an epicure. The big beautifully browned turkey graced the center, flanked by the inevitable chicken pie and an array of vegetables, all served in Flowing Blue Shanghai ware. The menu ended with a succession of pies. First on the list was mince flavored with brandy and rich

in raisins. A procession of pumpkin, squash, apple, custard and cranberry followed. . . . Christmas meant little to us. That was counted an event exclusively observed by Roman Catholics. We did hang up our stockings.

Other childhood reminiscences of such well-known people as Edward Everett Hale, Samuel Goodrich, and the Beechers give a similar picture of a strict but happy childhood of serenity and gentleness shared with their parents in an atmosphere of mutual trust and happiness. Even Lucy Larcom, whose life was spent working in the mills, presented a happy picture. "There was a great deal of play mixed with it." One privilege shared by nineteenth-century children was unregimented, unpressured leisure. After the lessons were learned, the chores done, and the duties performed, the free hours belonged to the children and they could escape into a world of their own. There were the fields and the woods for fishing and hunting, and every boy owned a bow and arrow, a jackknife, and later a gun for shooting rabbits, squirrels, woodchucks, pigeons, and quail. With his knife he carved a willow whistle or some other simple toy. Little girls had their dolls, usually homemade. They had a doll's house and doll furniture, also mostly homemade, and they could escape into the world of "play house" with "calls" and "tea parties," or they could play "store." There were also mud pies made in little tin dishes or cast-off kitchen utensils. Then there were the swing and the teeterboard, and the apple tree to climb, and often there was a tree house built in the branching arms of the tree. Or the little girl, too, might escape to the world of the fields and the woods, the mountain stream, or perhaps the nearby seashore.

There were outdoor games such as hide and seek and run, sheep, run played at twilight; hopscotch or marbles and top-spinning for the boys. And there were kites to fly and stilts to walk on.

However, this cheerful picture is not reflected in the faces of the little children who sat for portraits by Joseph Stock, William Prior, and the host of unknown nineteenth-century painters. Yet much of the gloom in these portraits was due to the lack of skill on the part of the artist and the fact that the child was "posing for his picture." Instead, there was undoubtedly some truth in the picture of vitality and gaiety described by Mrs. Harriet Porter Beecher in her letter, "I never saw so many rosy cheeks and laughing eyes."

By the 1860's a new conception of child life began to be expressed in children's books. *Alice in Wonderland,* which appeared in 1865, set the precedent for fun and nonsense. The natural child with all his faults as well as virtues became the hero of juvenile literature, as first seen in *The Story of a Bad Boy* by Thomas Aldrich, published in 1870. *Little Women* appeared in 1868. Mark Twain's *Tom Sawyer,* in 1876, and *Huckleberry Finn,* in 1884, followed, and Kipling wrote his first children's book in 1894. Yet many children's books still possessed a theme of pious priggishness, as evidenced in the Elsie Books and the Pansy Books, all of them stories of girls who were prim paragons of virtue.

From the 1830's, when *Peter Parley's Annual* was first issued, there was a succession of children's magazines which provided amusement not only for children, but for the whole family, and actually helped change the family attitude toward children, increasing their importance in the Victorian household.

ANCIENT MAY DAY SPORTS

AS PRACTISED IN SCOTLAND.

DANCING ROUND THE MAY-POLE.

It is a pleasant sight, to see
A little village company,
Drawn out upon the first of May
To have their annual holiday :—
VOL. II. 6

The POLE hung round with garlands gay ;
The young ones footing it away,
The old, too old to trip it longer,
Wishing, in vain, themselves were younger

Maypole Dance. Early-nineteenth-century periodical.

1

Coral and Bells, Children's Silver, and Christening Cradles

To a Child

With what a look of proud command
Thou shakest in thy little hand
The coral rattle with its silver bells
Making a merry tune!
—Henry Wadsworth Longfellow

Coral and Bells

very rare and most interesting antique of American childhood is the silver whistle and bells. This whistle with coral and bells was the aristocrat of children's rattles. The origin of the coral and bells is rooted in religion and superstition. The ancient design relates to the scroll bells used in synagogues, and coral was regarded from early times as an amulet against evil. The color of coral was believed to indicate the state of the user's physical condition, deep red in health and pale when illness was threatened. Even the shape of the coral, often resembling a hound's tooth, was thought a protection against harm.

The coral and bells consisted of three parts. A smooth piece of coral several inches long was at the bottom, a whistle was on the top, and each was fastened to a center bulbous portion which was

Silver coral and bells, ca. 1760. Museum of the City of New York.

Emma van Name, ca. 1795. Artist unknown. Child wears small coral and bells. Collection of Edgar William and Bernice Chrysler Garbisch.

hung with from two to five, but often seven, and even as many as ten, bells. Sometimes the bulb and shaft were plain, but more often the shaft was in hexagonal or octagonal baluster form and the ends which held the coral or whistle were often ornamented with borders of scallops, applied leaf decoration, and bands of gadrooning, while the whole might be plain or chased or covered with repoussé flower and leaf designs. The bells were usually held by a simple ring, but some were attached by elaborately wrought "C" scrolls. The whistle end also varied in shape, but, as a rule, its design related to the general pattern of the whole. The whistle opening might be heart-shaped, round, or oblong. There was also a ring to which a chain or ribbon was attached to hold the whistle to the child's belt or about his shoulder. The coral and bells was given as a christening present in England, and is shown in portraits of royalty. A gold rattle of similar type was owned by Napoleon's son, the king of Rome. Many English and continental children's rattles were made in the shape of lions, seahorses, eagles, horses, birds, ships, and mermaids. These were hollow and were chased with scroll or floral designs or made of silver filigree. They had silver bells attached and were hung on silver chains. None of this type of rattle is advertised by American silversmiths or jewelers, nor are they shown in children's portraits.

The coral and bells was always an expensive item and was carefully preserved and handed down in families from one generation to another. Although mentioned in literature and illustrated in early engravings and paintings of continental Europe in the Middle Ages, it was not generally known in America until the eighteenth century. The earliest mention in American newspapers was in the advertisement of John Pennefather, goldsmith, of Charleston, South Carolina: "A child's whistle and chains" (*South-Carolina Gazette*, November 16, 1738). There were many advertisements of coral and bells in the *Pennsylvania Gazette*, including that of John Leacock, silversmith: "Chased coral and Bells" (*Pennsylvania Gazette*, January 25, 1759). However, Leacock's advertisements mention that the goods for sale were just imported from England in the "Carolina" and "Arrabella." In the *Pennsylvania Journal*, Philip Syng, Philadelphia silversmith, advertised "a neat gilt silver whistle and coral with eight bells" (*Pennsylvania Journal*, March 17, 1763). In the same newspaper, another well-known silversmith, Edmond Milne, advertised "silver whistles and bells with corals chased and plain" (*Pennsylvania Journal*, December 15, 1763). William Ball advertised in the *Pennsylvania Journal*, November 13, 1766, and again on October 12, 1772. He mentioned "whistles and bells" and also "corals and whistles," and "corals for children's whistles." Entries in the account book of William Ball provide evidence of the cost of these whistles and also the fact that the majority of them were imported rather than crafted by Ball. A shipment on the "Myrtilla" contained "18 Wissels and bells. £215/0 chased or £25/0 plain." John Carnan, a goldsmith of Baltimore and Philadelphia,

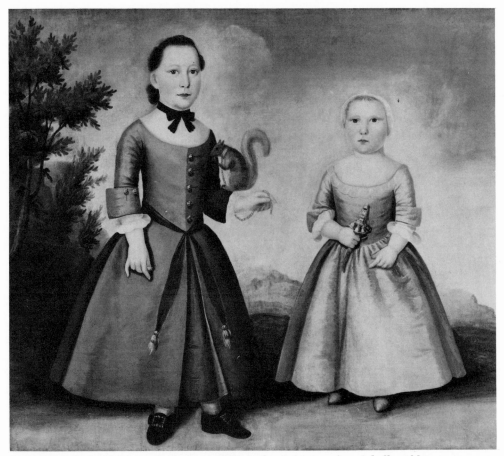

Portrait of Two Children. J. Badger, 1760. Baby holds coral and bells. Abby Aldrich Rockefeller Folk Art Collection, Williamsburg, Virginia.

advertised "silver and silver gilt whistle and bells" (*Pennsylvania Journal*, August 1, 1771). In the *Pennsylvania Gazette*, October 21, 1772, John David advertised "chased and plain bells and whistles" among articles just imported. John and Daniel Dupuy advertised "Corral and Bells" (*Pennsylvania Packet*, July 12, 1773), and Richard Humphreys listed "coral and bells for children, gum sticks for ditto" (*Pennsylvania Evening Post*, August 19, 1777). Among other Philadelphia silversmiths who are known to have made coral and bells is Joseph Anthony, whose existing bill of sale for a coral and bells made for Martha Washington in 1791 lists the price as twenty-five dollars. Account books of Joseph Richardson in the Historical Society of Pennsylvania give evidence of this trade in "coral and bells" and "wisel and bells," and a bill for a "piece of corell, Makeing 6 new bells, mend. socket." William Whetcroft of Annapolis listed "whistles" in his advertisement in the *Maryland Gazette*, May 13, 1773.

Advertisements mentioning coral and bells also appeared in Boston and New York newspapers of the eighteenth century. Daniel Boyer, jeweler, imported corals for whistles and listed them in his advertisements in the *Boston News-Letter* in 1767 and again in 1771. In the *New York Mercury*, October 26, 1761, the silversmith Joseph Pinto advertised "chass'd and plain whistles." Richard Sause, who was listed as a Philadelphia silversmith ca. 1778, advertised "Silver correls, rattles and cawls for children" (*New York Gazette and Weekly Mercury*, January 6, 1777). The well-known silversmith Daniel Van Voorhis also had "corrells and bells for children" for sale in 1797. The latest advertisement for "Coral and Children's Coral Bells" was that of Eph[rai]m Hart.

Of the existing corals and bells, none are by any of the silversmiths recorded in the newspaper advertisements. However, the silver coral and bells in the Henry Francis du Pont Winterthur Museum is by Joseph Richardson (ca. 1740), whose account books list the making of coral and bells. One made by Jacob Ten Eyck (Albany, 1705-1793), has six bells in two tiers and is embellished with simple engraving. It is in the collection of Mrs. John Emerson Marble and was illustrated in *Antiques Magazine*, February, 1951. A coral and bells in the Metropolitan Museum is by Richard van Dyck (New York, 1717-1770), and another in gold is by Nicholas Roosevelt (New York, 1715-1769). The gold coral and bells by Daniel Christian Fueter (New York, 1754-1770) is in Yale University Art Gallery, and another gold coral and bells by George Ridout (ca. 1745) is in the Sterling and Francine Clark Art Institute in Williamstown, Massachusetts. Only these gold coral and bells made by American silversmiths have come to light, and only a few advertisements mention "gilt or silver gilt" coral and bells. The following advertisement from the *Boston Gazette* points up the importance and suggests the rarity of such an item: "Gold Whistle—to be sold at public vendue at the New Auction-Room over Mr. Thomas Walley's Grocery Store . . . a very handsome Gold Whistle, with Bells and Coral" (*Boston Gazette*, August 23, 1762). However, all the known American gold coral and bells were made by New York silversmiths.

Obviously the coral and bells were rare in America and not everyone could afford them. However, there must have been a considerable number in use, for the numerous advertisements indicate that there was a demand for them. Since coral sticks were sold separately, some less-well-to-do children probably used the sticks, without the silver bells and silver holder. Coral and bells are rare and expensive today; a few are by American silversmiths, but there are also others made by English silversmiths. Coral and bells were made by John Shaw of Birmingham, England, in the eighteenth century and were made by many other English silversmiths. Although none of the known coral and bells date after the end of the eighteenth century, they were probably made and in use into the

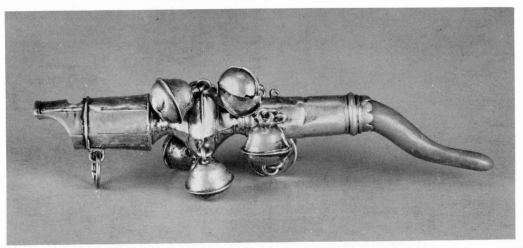

Silver coral and bells. Joseph Richardson, ca. 1740. Henry Francis du Pont Winterthur Museum.

Silver coral and bells. Richard van Dyck, early eighteenth century. The Metropolitan Museum of Art, bequest of A. T. Clearwater, 1933.

Rattle, gold and coral, eighteenth century. Nicholas Roosevelt, 1715–1769. The Metropolitan Museum of Art, Rogers Fund, 1947.

first quarter of the nineteenth century, as indicated by Longfellow's poem.

Just when the silver rattles with pearl handles were first made is not known. They were probably not made until after 1850. For years these consisted of a pearl shaft set in a silver handle with bells attached. Later, a ring of pearl had bells attached, and, about 1890, silver rattles with heads of a jester, man in the moon, Santa Claus, or Bopeep were made by Graff, Washbourne & Dunne of New York and sold at Tiffany & Co. This type of rattle is still made today. Tin rattles with whistles are included in the 1870 catalogue of the Stevens & Brown Manufacturing Company.

Three Children. John F. Francis. Baby holds late-type coral and bells or rattle. Museum of Fine Arts, Boston, M. and M. Karolik Collection.

Girl Holding Rattle made of rushes or tin (?). *E. S. Field, ca.1835.* Abby ▶ Aldrich Rockefeller Folk Art Collection, Williamsburg, Virginia.

The well-to-do eighteenth-century child, dressed in silk, satins, real lace, and plumed hats, not only had his gold or silver coral and bells, but the silversmith was also employed to make such children's articles as the rare silver nursing bottle, the papboat, the porringer, and other articles of silver. Since children were treated as "little grown-ups," it is not strange they were given these articles of fine workmanship and expensive materials. The silversmith Joseph Anthony, Jr., advertised "a complete alphabet of cyphers" (*Pennsylvania Packet*, October 4, 1783). Edmond Milne also advertised engraved gold cyphers for children's necks along with silver buttons, coral necklaces, and blue turkey beads for children (*Pennsylvania Journal*, November 8, 1764). The well-to-do child also had his papboat.

The papboat is a vessel with a long spout which was used for feeding liquids and soft foods to children and perhaps to invalids. It is usually about four and one-half inches in length, excluding the handle. However, papboats were made both with and without handles. They differ little in shape or size, although some are decorated with fine-cut designs and some with borders of beading. They were made by American silversmiths from the end of the eighteenth century to the middle of the nineteenth century. A papboat in the Maryland Historical Society was made by S. Kirk &

Baby's nursing bottle. Pewter. Thomas Danforth Boardman, 1784–1873. The Metropolitan Museum of Art, gift of Joseph France, 1943.

Papboat. Joel Sayre, 1778–1818. The Metropolitan Museum of Art, bequest of A. T. Clearwater, 1933.

Papboat. William Thomson, active 1810–34. The Metropolitan Museum of Art, Rogers Fund, 1938.

Papboat. Benjamin Halsted. Yale University Art Gallery, Mabel Brady Garvan Collection.

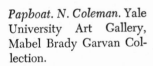

Papboat. N. Coleman. Yale University Art Gallery, Mabel Brady Garvan Collection.

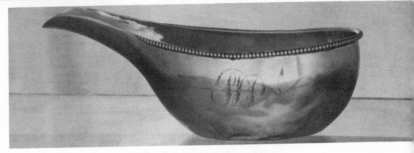

Son ca. 1850 and is engraved "August McKim from his aunt M. D. McKim." Although the papboat is seldom mentioned in advertisements of silversmith's wares, it was made by many silversmiths, and a collection of papboats could include examples by representative American silversmiths. The papboat is not an especially attractive piece, and lack of beauty, rather than scarcity, may account for the fact that there are not too many to be seen in museum collections. However, there is a papboat by Shepherd & Boyd in the Albany Institute of Art, one by Joel Sayre and William Thomson in the Metropolitan Museum of Art, and five in the Yale University Art Gallery, including one by Benjamin Halsted, one by Daniel Van Voorhis, and one by N. Coleman.

A porringer is a shallow circular bowl with a single flat handle. The shapes of porringers do not vary but they do differ in size. Although at first the porringer was not made specifically for children, it became a favorite children's piece and was made in both pewter and silver.

Porringers for children were made in the same designs as those made for grown-ups. However, the child's porringer was not more than four and one-half inches in diameter, whereas those made for adults were from five to six inches in diameter. A child's porringer with keyhole handle is in the collection of Philip Hammerslough. The handles with their pierced designs and interesting combinations of patterns offer many variations for the collector. Although the early handles are smaller and have less-intricate piercing, the date cannot be determined by the handle, nor can we say that one variety of handle came into fashion at a certain date. Pierced-handle designs of similar patterns were made by different silversmiths and all the designs of one silversmith are not alike. Generally speaking, the New York handles have simpler piercings than those made by New England silversmiths. A design formed of scrolls with a center hole which looks like a metal keyhole plate is called a "keyhole" handle. More porringers seem to have been made in New England, if we can judge from their mention in newspaper advertisements. Some of the earliest porringers made in Boston in colonial times were made by Jeremiah Dummer (1645–1718), Peter Oliver (1682–1712), Samuel Vernon (1683–1737), John Coney (1655–1722), and Edward Winslow (1669–1753). Known New York porringers were made by Benjamin Wynkoop (1675–1751), Peter Van Dyck (1684–1750), Joseph Newkirke (ca. 1716), Jacob Boelen (1654–1729), John Brevoort (1715–1775), and Adrian Bancker (1705–1772). Philadelphia silversmiths who made porringers include Joseph Richardson, Joseph Anthony, Jr., and Philip Syng, although here as elsewhere porringers were made by practically all silversmiths in the eighteenth century and early nineteenth century. However, the porringer continued to be made by later silversmiths and by silver manufacturers, and to the present day the porringer is a favorite gift to the newborn child.

Other gifts to babies of colonial days included the christening blanket. This was usually made of silk, lace-edged, and embroidered with flowers, the child's name, and sometimes a verse of Scripture. The mother was given a pincushion of silk with name, date, and a message of welcome stuck in with pins.

Other articles available to collectors of children's silver include children's mugs and christening sets which included a porringer or bowl and plate and a knife, fork, and spoons. In the twentieth century, a silver food-pusher, shaped like a small hoe, was added to the list of children's silver. Many of these articles had interesting ornamentation which ranged from embossed classical designs of dancing children and, later, nursery rhyme illustrations, simple cats, dogs, and bunnies, to such popular children's subjects as Palmer Cox Brownies, The Sunbonnet Babies, and Overall Boys. Sterling silver handmade mugs and other articles were made by Samuel Kirk & Son, Tiffany, and Gorham, and less expensive pieces were made by Reed & Barton, Oneida silversmiths, and others.

Thousands of plated and silver mugs were made by American silver manufacturers after 1850, and there are many on the market at reasonable prices.

Christening Cradles

A customary christening and birthday present in the midland counties of England in the seventeenth, eighteenth, and nineteenth centuries was the pottery cradle, ranging from four to twelve inches in length. The first cradles were made of slipware. This quaint and grotesque ware originated in Staffordshire and Wrotham and was also made in centers near London. The coarse dark or light ground was decorated with scratched designs or colored slip of white, buff, brown, yellow, or black dropped from a spouted vessel. The ornament included wavy lines, dots, herringbone, and floral designs, and an inscription including initials, and, sometimes, the date. Because of the pious nature of the inscriptions, these pieces were thought to have been made by or for Puritans, and thus some few may have reached America. Possibly some may have been made in early

Slipware christening cradle. English, seventeenth to eighteenth century. The Metropolitan Museum of Art, Rogers Fund, 1912.

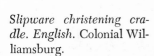

Slipware christening cradle. English. Colonial Williamsburg.

Christening cradle. English salt glaze. Colonial Williamsburg.

Staffordshire cradle, green glaze decorated with relief scenes of Aphrodite with lily of purity, and nymph dancing Cupid on her foot. D. M. & P. Manheim, New York.

Christening cradle. English delft pottery, eighteenth century.

American potteries, although none have come to light. The English cradles were also made of salt glaze and cream color pottery. The early cradles were worked up by hand and the little knobs or finials were rolled from a piece of clay. Later, cradles were cast in molds. The cradle structure was similar to the oak cradles of the era and had straight sides and a hood and was set on rockers. Late-eighteenth-century cradles were curved and had a rounded head and foot and a rounded hood. In the nineteenth century, some cradles were patterned to imitate wicker. In about 1800 some cradles were made with a dressed child in the cradle. Other cradles had the figure of an angel or a fiddler, and small white heads with black eyes hovered above the hood. A cradle in the Victoria and Albert Museum is decorated with the letters of the alphabet.

These early cradles are rare and expensive. Some were made by the well-known potters Thomas and Ralph Tofts, and other potters of the Toft School. Late in the eighteenth century, larger cradles, twelve by eight inches, were made of Pratt ware, a cream-tinted earthenware with a bluish glaze. These were decorated with classical subjects modeled in relief and consisting of scenes such as

Parian cradles used as christening gifts (?). Bennington Museum, Bennington, Vermont.

Aphrodite with the lily of purity, or a nymph dancing Cupid on her foot, all in shades of antique orange, yellow, blue, and green. These cradles were made in various Staffordshire potteries. One with a rich green glaze over a cream body has a cord edging and palm leaves alternating with a girl's head in profile. The hood and sides of the cradle are decorated with classical scenes in relief. This type cradle may have been made by Wedgwood. A similar cradle was of Pratt ware. There were also cradles of Whieldon-type tortoiseshell, and in the mid- and late nineteenth century, cradles were made of white pearlware. Some were also transfer-printed and had a cartouche on the hood where the name or initials and birth date could be painted on.

Although cradles were made at Leeds Pottery, Wedgwood, and other well-known potteries, they are rarely marked. Cradles are to be seen in the British Museum; Victoria and Albert Museum, London; the Fitzwilliam Museum, Cambridge; the Brighton Museum and the Hanley Museum, in England; the Metropolitan Museum of Art, New York City; and Colonial Williamsburg, Virginia. A few are for sale in American antique shops.

Pottery cradles were also made of Dutch delft, some dating from the eighteenth century. Small Parian-ware cradles holding one or two infants were made at Bennington, Vermont. There were also many later cheap Staffordshire tiny toy cradles, but these are in a different category.

2

Children's Costumes

n order to picture child life in early America, one must know something of the conditions and surroundings in which the early colonists lived. Colonial days in America cannot be described by any general statement, for life in colonial times does not present a composite picture. There were differences in the material wealth and the type of people in the various settlements. The Plymouth Pilgrims who came on the May-flower in 1620 were poor men and artisans and they were set back by misfortunes. The Massachusetts Bay Colony, headed by John Winthrop, arrived ten years later, in 1630. They came with wealth and they prospered. They were men of landed estates, farmers from Lincolnshire, professional men, lawyers, scholars, and clergymen. The social status and financial condition of the settlers of Jamestown and other southern colonies more closely resembled those of the members of the Massachusetts Bay Colony than of the Plymouth Colony, and the Dutch that settled in New Amsterdam were prosperous patroons. If we understand these differences we can better comprehend the variations in costume of the different colonists.

In all cases the dress followed the styles in England and continental Europe. The first outfit the child wore was for his christening. Since the christening of the New England child was of great importance, his christening blanket was usually made of silk, richly embroidered. Governor Bradford's christening blanket was a rich crimson embroidered with sprays of flowers. Some blankets were embroidered with initials and emblems, or words such as "God Bless the Babe." The child himself wore a long dress, inner and outer caps, and linen-lace mittens. The baptismal shirt was of homespun linen trimmed with lace and was low necked and short sleeved. One of the presents to the mother of a new baby was a satin pincushion, and Anna Green Winslow gives a description of one in her diary, December 30, 1771: "My aunt stuck a white sattan pincushion for Mrs Waters. On one side is a planthorn with flowers, on the reverse just under the border are on one side stuck these words, Josiah Waters, then follows on the end Decr. 1771, on the next side & end are the words Welcome little Stranger."

The list of Governor Hutchinson's furnishings in the *Boston News-Letter*, September 5, 1765, included "rich embroidered christening Blankets, Sleeves, Cradle, Quilt and Curtain, and a set of Child-bed Linen."

Few of these early infants' clothes exist today, but Governor Bradford's baptismal shirt and mittens are in Essex Institute, Salem, Massachusetts, and another infant's robe, cap, and christening blanket are in Memorial Hall, Deerfield, Massachusetts. Other articles can be seen in Pilgrim Hall, Plymouth, Massachusetts, and Bedford Historical Society, Bedford, Massachusetts, while a few pieces remain in private hands. Needless to say, there are none of these early articles of clothing available to the collector.

According to tradition, the Puritans wore "sad" colors—russets and browns, which related to their simple life. They wore doublets of leather, breeches and shoes of skins and hides, russet hose, and linsey-woolsey or homespun materials, and sometimes beaver hats. It was a dress close to nature, simple and fitting for their conditions of life. It was also the dress of the Puritans in England and Holland. A Dutch painting of the seventeenth century depicting a company of Puritans including Richard Cromwell, shows the men in russet brown coats and pantaloons, some with the stiff squared and starched falling bands, and others with small white neck cloths tied under the chin with a cravat string. A boy, who may be his grandson, is at Cromwell's knee, and is garbed in a suit with neck cloth similar in both color and style to that worn by Cromwell. An old English verse describes the average Puritan woman's dress:

The Good old dames among the rest
Were all most primitively drest
In stiffen-bodyed russet gowns
And on their heads old steeple crowns
With pristine pinners next their faces
Edged round with ancient scallop-laces.

However, the diaries, letters, and inventories as well as many other
portraits of the era do not picture such simple costumes, and the colors, though dark, are strong and pure.

Even in the first years the colonists paid close attention to their attire—so much so that there was constant preaching against "excesse in apparell." Dress as a badge of rank and dignity was followed in America as in England, and it was believed that to dress orderly and well helped preserve the morals of the individual and the general welfare of the community. There was a dress for servants and a dress for those of wealth or distinction. Sumptuary laws in New England forbade rich dress, as evidenced by the 1634 edict of the General Court of Massachusetts:

That no person man or woman shall hereafter make or buy any apparell either Woolen or Silk or Linen with any Lace on it, Silver, Gold or Thread under penalty of forfeiture of said clothes. Also no person shall make or buy any apparell with slashed sleeves other than one slash in each sleeve and another in the back. Also all cut-works, embroideries or Needlework, Caps, Bands or Rails are forbidden; also all gold or silver girdles, Hat bands, belts, Ruffs, Beaver hats are prohibited. . . . Poor folk must not appear with naked breasts and arms or superstitious ribbons on hair and apparell.

In 1639, "immoderate great breeches, knots of riban, broad shoulder bands and rayles, silk roses, double ruffles and capes" were forbidden to folk of low estate. Elizabeth Paddy Wensley, a Puritan woman of wealth and refinement whose portrait is in Pilgrim Hall, Plymouth, Massachusetts, is clothed in silks and lace. However, we know from old inventories that this dress was not the ordinary attire of Plymouth women of this era.

Children's dress followed that of their elders for the most part, but there were certain details of dress that were different. Portraits exist of a group of New England children of the mid- and late-seventeenth century, and the costumes of all these children are of the same rich materials as those shown in adult portraits. The frocks are scarlet and blue brocade or velvet, or black brightened by bits of scarlet such as linings to sleeves, scarlet ribbons, or tassel trims. Such early paintings as those of the Gibbs and Mason children, and of Mrs. Freake and Baby Mary, show children's costumes of seventeenth-century America. These pictures are closely related to English portraits of the time in both style and richness of materials and similar to the costumes of the children of Charles I, as shown in the paintings of Van Dyck. Both boys and girls wear long frocks with stomacher, an apron with bib and a cap edged with Flemish lace. Virago sleeves with slashes and puffs tied with ribbons or gathering-strings were worn by both boys and girls. This

Alice Mason: white hood tied over lace-edged cap, dark gray dress with elbow-length slashed sleeves tied with red ribbons; puffed white undersleeves. The white pinafore is edged with lace. The square-toed shoes have red soles and red bows and the two-strand red necklace is probably coral. Seventeenth century. Adams National Historic Site, Quincy, Massachusetts.

Margaret Gibbs, seven years old. American, seventeenth century, artist un-known. Elaborately dressed blond hair is tied with a red ribbon. The dress is of heavy rich material with slashed sleeves and long "hanging sleeves." She wears a wide lace collar and an apron edged in lace. The white square-toed shoes have red bows and soles. Collection of Mrs. David M. Giltinan. Photograph, Worcester Art Museum.

was a French style popular in Queen Elizabeth's day. An outer hanging sleeve worn as an ornament was also used as a rein to steady the young child. The shoes are of buff leather with square toes and are tacked to a scarlet sole. The costumes are further embellished with needlework, bow knots, and galloon braid, and several of the children wear lace collars called "whisks." Their stiff appearance was caused by stays worn so that "children will appear strait." This custom continued into the eighteenth century. "Misses and children's Pack-thread stays from one month to seven years old" were sold at the Sign of the White Stays (*New York Gazette,* February 24, 1766). The garments of these children are too stiff for comfort, too long for walking, and too rich and costly except for children of wealth.

Since the less wealthy could not afford having their children painted, we have no portraits to show how they dressed, but there are many descriptions of the dress of runaway servants in the newspapers of the time, and the coarse simple materials and costumes described are those worn by less-well-to-do people. Also, the dress of the clergy when not in the pulpit was plain and somber black, but a portrait of Cotton Mather a century later shows him in an elegant, richly curled periwig, according to the fashion of the time.

The existing portraits of eighteenth-century Americans and their children also show a richness of costume and a refined way of life. Children's costume still followed the fashion of grown-ups, and their clothes were formal, of rich materials, and elaborately trimmed. Although there was a greater freedom in children's dress, they still wore stays, hoops, and masks, and carried fans. Boys as young as seven wore costly wigs. One cannot imagine the children in any sort of play.. Indeed, much of the time was spent in learning to read and write, and in needlework and other sedate accomplishments such as painting and music.

The dress of young girls of the eighteenth century included kid gloves, masks, fans, necklaces, and silver buttons with stones. In 1761, George Washington sent abroad for garments for his stepchildren, and some of the items on the list include finery such as a coat of fashionable silk, fashionable dresses of "Long Lawn," satin shoes, silver shoe buckles, and pack-thread stays. The little girl was six years old. In the *Diary of Anna Green Winslow, a Boston School Girl, in the Year 1771,* she describes the dress that she wore to a child's party:

I was dressed in my yellow coat, black bib and apron, black feathers on my head, my past[e] comb and all my past[e] garnet, marquesett and jet pins, together with my silver plume—my loket, rings, black collar round my neck, black mitts and yards of blue ribbon (black and blue is high tast), striped tucker and ruffels (not my best) and my silk shoes completed my dress.

Catalynje Post three years old, ca. 1730. Artist unknown. Collection of Edgar William and Bernice Chrysler Garbisch.

Susanna Truax, four years old, wearing earrings and necklace. Artist unknown. Collection of Edgar William and Bernice Chrysler Garbisch.

Mrs. John Nicholson and child by Charles W. Peale, 1790. Child wears large plumed hat over lace cap. The Art Institute of Chicago.

Portrait of child with pet dog. Ralph Earl, 1776. Collection of IBM Corporation, New York.

She also wore a Heddus roll of false hair. Miss Winslow was ten years old. The portrait of the two Bowdoin children is ample proof of the richness of children's dress. The fancy shoes and shoe buckles and the girl's headdress of feathers and pearls are similar to the costume of adults.

The dress of eighteenth-century American children is shown in many portraits by John Singleton Copley, William Williams, Joseph Badger, Ralph Earl, Jeremiah Theus, Justus Engelhardt Kühn, Pieter Vanderlyn, and others, and here is evidence of the elaborateness of their attire. The paintings of Copley offer the richest field for research. Copley had a fascination for dress and fine furnishings, and his portraits show not only costumes of rich material but jewels and elaborate hairdress. His portraits of children include their pets—favorite birds, squirrels, spaniels, and toys such as dolls, coral and bells, and battledore and shuttlecock. The portrait of the Copley family is one of the most interesting of all pictures of American children. The charming little girl in the foreground in the frock of striped gauze with the sash and long streamers of pink gauze and the little cap with tiny rose pin shows the marked difference in the comfort of children's dress between the seventeenth and the eighteenth century. Little girls no longer wear dresses with tight bodices. The sleeves are also less bulky and more related to the shape of the arms.

Boys in the eighteenth century still wore long coats with ribbon sashes, low necks and fancy hats with plumes and ribbons. The coat in the portrait of Thomas Aston Coffin opens over a white satin petticoat. The neck is low-cut and there is a full white undersleeve. Boys were not breeched until they were three or four years old, and some were kept in petticoats until they were six or seven. Once the boy was breeched he was dressed in a replica of his father's coat, waistcoat, and breeches. The coat fitted at the waist and flared into a skirt at the knees. In the 1730's the skirt of the coat was stiffened and pleated at the side, and there were large pockets with shaped flaps that were trimmed with braid and buttons to match the buttons that went down the front from neck to hem. There was no collar on the coat until late in the century. The sleeves had wide turned-back cuffs similarly trimmed with braid and buttons. A long cravat was worn. The waistcoat also resembled the adult waistcoat. It reached to the knees and had buttons from top to bottom. Knee breeches were worn by boys until the end of the eighteenth century. They were buckled at the knee with buckles of silver, brass, or paste. Shoes had square toes, tongues, and buckles. The three-cornered hat was the most popular style for boys of the eighteenth century. Late in the century a ruffled shirt-collar replaced the cravat. The cutaway coat with wide lapels was worn by boys in the 1790's, together with a waistcoat and trousers. Younger boys wore a short jacket with a sash, and later the trousers were buttoned onto the jacket or frilled-collar shirt.

The Copley Family. Baby holds silver coral and bells. Doll in foreground, eighteenth century, dressed in costume similar to child's. John Singleton Copley, 1738–1815. National Gallery of Art, Andrew W. Mellon Fund, 1961.

Thomas Lodge by Tellschaw, 1745. Long coat with buttons and braid. Silver shoe buckles. The New-York Historical Society. Photograph; Tillou Gallery.

Thomas Aston Coffin by John Singleton Copley, ca. 1758. Long satin coat with low neck, ribbon sash, and buttons open over a satin petticoat. The hat is trimmed with metal braid and plumes. Pet doves are held by ribbons and a battledore and shuttlecock are shown in the foreground. Munson-Williams-Proctor Institute.

The majority of the portraits show elaborate costumes and rich colors in both the clothes and the settings. In the portrait of Mrs. Benjamin Tallmadge and her children by Ralph Earl, the children wear dresses of embroidered gauze. Mrs. Tallmadge wears a blue satin gown with a fine lace fichu and an especially elaborate coiffure of plumes, pearls, and flowers. The brightly colored figured carpet suggests a well-furnished room. In the portrait of Mrs. William Moseley and son Charles, the boy, who is three or four years old, wears a red suit with brass buttons and white ruffled collar. Mrs. Moseley's coat is dark blue trimmed with gold braid and brass buttons. She wears a white dress and a white hat with feathers. The portrait of Mrs. Noah Smith and her children shows the clothing of two girls and three boys of various ages. Mrs. Smith's dress is gold silk, the older boy wears a brown coat and yellow breeches and waistcoat; the next boy wears green, and the youngest, red. The girl wears a white dress with blue sash, and the sash of the baby's dress is pink. Mother and baby both wear caps.

Mrs. Noah Smith and children, showing costumes of boys and girls of different ages. Ralph Earl, late eighteenth century. The Metropolitan Museum of Art, gift of Edgar William and Bernice Chrysler Garbisch, 1964.

The dress of the Dutch settlers in New Amsterdam was rich in pattern and color. Inventories list cornet caps with lace and quantities of jewels, and these typical Dutch caps are seen in the colorful portraits of young girls of New Amsterdam of the eighteenth century. The most interesting feature of the girls' portraits, besides the bright color and pattern, is the pointed, high-heeled, colorful shoes which are usually shown in profile. They are similar to the shoes in delft pottery and this suggests an interesting costume item for the collector, for although the actual shoes would seldom be available, those of pottery and porcelain are found in many shops.

There is a group of mid-eighteenth-century paintings of children of the Dutch de Peyster and van Cortlandt families of the Hudson River Valley that show the rich costumes that the well-to-do patroon children wore. These paintings are in the New-York Historical Society, the Brooklyn Museum, the Museum of the City of New York, and the American Jewish Historical Society. Thomas Flexner has attributed the paintings to Pieter Vanderlyn. However, what interests us here is not the artist, but the subjects themselves and how they were dressed. In the surviving portraits the clothing is rich and colorful. The picture of the twin daughters of Abraham de Peyster was painted when they were five years old. They are dressed in red velvet gowns with trains, and wear long ropes of pearls. Katherine Ten Broeck, another Dutch child, wears pearls and earrings in a portrait painted when she was three years old. Of the boys' portraits, those of the de Peyster boy with deer, in the New-York Historical Society, and of John van Cortlandt, in the Brooklyn Museum, are the most interesting. They picture the costume of the boy of the well-to-do family in the early eighteenth century. The de Peyster boy is the younger, as shown by his skirts, while the van Cortlandt boy is breeched and wears a shorter coat and a long cravat. The costume of Abraham van Cortlandt in the Sleepy Hollow Restorations shows a later development of the waistcoat. The fancy court style of English painting is reflected not only in the costume, the poses, and the pets, but also in the backgrounds of formal masonry and foliage. Similarly rich costumes and formal backgrounds of gardens and masonry are shown in the portraits of Henry and Eleanor Darnall by Justus Engelhardt Kühn and of Charles Calvert by John Hesselius. Several other portraits by Kühn have recently come to light. These pictures show children, probably under six years of age, dressed in velvet and brocaded costumes with lace-trimmed bodice and sleeves and aprons with wide lace borders. Elizabeth Franks (ca. 1710) is dressed in salmon pink, gold, and green brocade over a skirt of salmon-colored satin. The costume is richly trimmed with lace and ribbons and she carries a black velvet hat with pink and white ostrich feathers. The child in a similar portrait by Justus Kühn carries a fan, as does Jane Bonner in her portrait in the Connecticut Historical Society. Portraits of

Charles Calvert by John Hesselius, 1761. Elaborate costume with plumed hat and silver shoe buckles. Negro servant is dressed in similar style livery. The Baltimore Museum of Art.

Elizabeth Franks, ca. 1710. Justus Engelhardt Kühn Dress of colorful brocade over salmon pink satin with trimmings of rose ribbons and lace. White apron edged in lace. Rose and white plumes at back. The Milwaukee Art Center. Photograph, Tillou Gallery.

Mary Beekman, about two years old, with pet lamb. John Durand, 1766. The New-York Historical Society.

James Beekman, Jr., eight years old, with pet squirrel. John Durand, 1766. Metal buttons on coat and waistcoat. The New-York Historical Society.

children by William Williams (ca. 1710–ca. 1790), John Durand (act. 1767–1782), and Joseph Badger (1708–1765) also depict rich costumes against formal backgrounds.

Advertisements in eighteenth-century newspapers tell us of many items of children's attire. Women's and children's fans of all sorts were advertised in the *Boston News-Letter,* January 17, 1724. In 1735, Robert Jenkins of Boston had on sale "a variety of Haberdashery consisting of xx silver lace, black silk and snail lace, children's silver Peaks and Flowers, Velvet Masks, Wiggs, Ribbands and Cauls" (*Boston News-Letter,* June 5–12, 1735). Silk hats for children were advertised in New York in 1749, and an advertisement in the *Boston Gazette,* October 15, 1751, included "Children's French Sattin Gloves and Mittens, worsted and thread hose, Russel and Morocco shoes, Pumps, hoop petticoats and stomachers." Boys and youths wore felt and castor hats in 1756, and girls' stays continued to be worn. In the *New-York Gazette and Weekly Mercury,* 1765, Nesbitt Deane, Hatter, advertised "best of beaver hats both for ladies and gentlemen and children's ware, both ruff and plain, either black, white, blue, green or red." A "hair dresser" from London cut children's hair "after the royal fashion to promote the growth of the hair in a regular form" (*New-York Packet,* May 29, 1786). "Children's scarlet broadcloth shoes and children's black, green and red Morocco shoes; cotton, thread and worsted hose, plain and clock't;" "boys' sattin Jockeys and Feathers" were other items advertised in the mid-eighteenth-century New York and Boston newspapers.

In the eighteenth century, the finer fabrics such as damasks, silks, satins, and broadcloths were imported from England and other European countries. There were also East India goods such as "China Tafities, plain, striped and flowered Persians, Chints, Flowered Muslings and Callicoes" advertised in New York newspapers. Although the materials for the fine costumes shown in portraits were imported, much of that worn by the less well-to-do was made in America. In 1753, a child of a runaway Indian servant was wearing "a double stuff gown, blue Camblet Petticoat and a striped flannel one" (The *New York Gazette and the Weekly Post-Boy,* February 5, 1753).

By the middle of the eighteenth century the Society for the Promotion of the Arts was founded to encourage spinning and weaving, and to help establish the manufacture of linen and other goods in America. The Society for encouraging Industry and Employing the Poor walked in procession to Boston Common where they put on a weaving demonstration with "near 300 spinners, some of them children of 7 or 8 years old" (*Boston Gazette,* August 4, 1753). Also, a spinning school was established in Charlestown, and William Nelson advertised spinning wheels "after the best manner." Small spinning wheels for children were of maple and similar woods. Prizes such as silver bowls, teapots, and pitchers were given for the "best specimen of woolen cloth." Family weaving in New

England, New York, and New Jersey now produced both woolen and linen goods, and checks, linens, and woolen materials were made at small factories that produced camblets, Callimancoes, Cambletees, plain, striped, and figured stuffs, Druggets, Saggathies, German serges, Everlastings, Shalloons, and serges. George Washington is known to have worn a suit of clothes made of material manufactured in the United States.

In the nineteenth century, the clothing of infants and children became more practical and comfortable. Babies still wore long dresses for several months, but in most instances stays were replaced by stiff buckram bands, and by the 1830's the stays were no more than a corded bodice of a petticoat. When the child began to walk it was put into shorter dresses with a bodice, low neck, and short sleeves. Caps and bonnets were still worn both in and out of doors. They were made with lace shirring and with a rosette of ribbon in front for a girl, on the left side for a boy.

For dressing up, little girls wore high-waisted white muslin frocks with colored sashes, trousers below the ankles, and red Morocco shoes. Sprigged cotton or nankeen was for morning wear. Boys of three years wore long frocks with low necks, puffed sleeves, and matching trousers to the ankle. At five years the boy was put into a suit with slit trousers, a high waistband, and a shirt with ruffled collar. Younger boys wore tunics over the trousers. At seven, short jackets were worn, with a tall hat. The next garment (c. 1820) was the skeleton suit, consisting of a short, tight jacket braided with silk tape and with buttons to hold the trousers up under the armpits. The low-necked blouse had a ruffle about the neck. A tasseled hat or a tall beaver hat completed the costume. At the age of twelve, boys might wear trousers and short-tailed coats like adults. High-waisted, ankle-length frocks, with pelisses, shawls, and high-crowned brimmed hats or poke bonnets tied with ribbons were worn by ten- and twelve-year-old girls. By the middle of the nineteenth century, warmer materials such as cashmere and velvet were used for winter, with nankeen or drill for summer.

In the 1840's and 1850's, boys wore tunics with drawers, often trimmed with lace, showing below, and socks and laced shoes. Girls wore low-necked short-sleeved dresses with pleated bodices and three or more flounces on the skirt, drawers showing below, socks, and button shoes. Older girls had longer drawers or pantalets, sometimes gathered and drawn together at the ankle or finished with two or three ankle ruffles. Charles Oakford advertised hats in *Godey's Lady's Book* in 1846. A straw hat for girls was turned up on one side and trimmed with a plume. A boy's hat of soldier's-cap type was made of haircloth and trimmed with a silk band, a buckle, and a silk tassel.

Plaid and striped woolen materials and velvet were the favorites in the 1860's. Young boys wore velvet dresses with velvet hats trimmed with feathers. In 1860, *Peterson's Magazine* described

*Children of William Rankin
and Abigail Ogden Rankin.
Oliver Tarbell Eddy, ca.
1838.* The Newark Museum,
bequest of Dr. Walter Mead
Rankin, 1947.

*Family group in late Empire
interior showing children's
costumes of the period. Frederick R. Spenser (1806–1875).*
The Brooklyn Museum, Dick
S. Ramsay Fund.

Child's dress of embroidered white batiste, ca. 1850. Index of American Design.

Boy's suit of black velvet with covered buttons and braid ornaments, ca. 1850. Index of American Design.

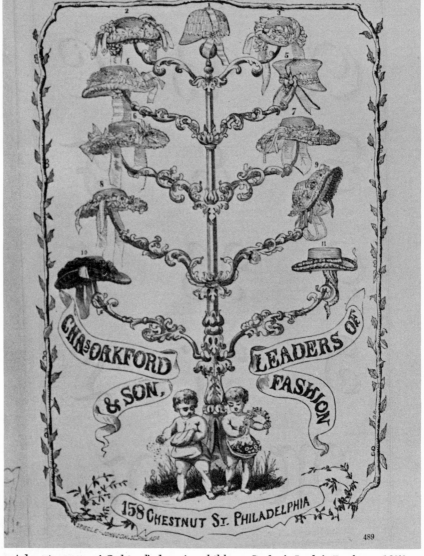

Advertisement of Oakford's hats for children. Godey's Lady's Book, ca. 1850.

Scotch suits for boys with the basque jacket cut in points and trimmed with two or three rows of black worsted braid. Due to the influence of styles set by Queen Victoria's children, a braided jacket, waistcoat, and skirt with short pants to the knees, socks, high-button shoes and a round, beribboned straw hat were thought proper for a boy of five, while little boys of two wore turbans trimmed with silk and ribbons. The Little Lord Fauntleroy velvet suit was in vogue in the 1880's.

Also, in the 1880's, hats for both girls and boys were larger and generally had turned-up brims. At the end of the century, knicker-bocker suits, full and closed at the knee, sailor suits with middy blouses, and sailor tam-o'-shanter caps were popular for small boys. Boys a little older wore reefer coats and long trousers. The Norfolk suit was also popular at this time.

Boy in jacket and pants trimmed with braid and buttons, ca.1855–1860. Arpad Antiques, Inc., Washington, D.C.

Little Lord Fauntleroy suit. Jacket red velvet embroidered in holly pattern. Pants green velvet, ca.1880's. Index of American Design.

58

Children's dresses. Godey's Lady's Book, July, 1870.

Above: *Children's fashions.* Below: *Fancy costumes for children.* Godey's Lady's Book, 1871.

Little girl with coral necklace, ca. 1855–1860. Dress trimmed with braid as shown above. Arpad Antiques, Inc., Washington, D.C.

Child's dress, blue faille moiré, ca. 1880. The Metropolitan Museum of Art, Rogers Fund, 1941.

Godey's Lady's Book is the best source of how American children were dressed in the 1870's and 1880's. Pages of fashions for children with full descriptions of the clothes shown were a monthly feature of the magazine. The illustrations in the many children's magazines of the time such as *St. Nicholas, Demorest's Young America, Wide Awake, Chatterbox,* and *The Youth's Companion* also show children's dress, and some of them have fashion pages. For small boys the Zouave jacket of black velvet trimmed with silk galloon was worn with a pleated skirt, black velvet hat with scarlet feather, scarlet and black plaid stockings, and velvet boots. Little

Costumes of Victorian era. Infant's christening dress, lawn trimmed with val-type lace.
French, ca. 1860. Left, little girl's dress, wool with soutache braid, ca. 1869. Right, girl's
dress silk bound in taffeta, ca. 1869. The Costume Institute of The Metropolitan Museum
of Art.

girls' dresses were made with double skirts trimmed with ruffles shirred or pleated. The interest was at the back where the overskirt looped up to a point and was finished with a large bow or an apron-like panel. "Imported cloth paletots for girls from three to twelve years of age are in gray, brown, and white, and are beautifully trimmed with velvet bands, fur, and elaborate cording in braiding designs." Dresses for little girls were "prettily lighted up by machine embroidery in gay colored silks, scarlet, green or blue with white." Velvet trims were in Greek-key pattern, and scallops were often cut in Gothic points. Chenille, passamenterie cords, and braids were also used as trimmings.

Harry Woodward's dress, alpaca, silk embroidery, ca. 1865. Shelburne Museum, Inc.

Not only were the clothes worn by American children similar to those worn by adults, but their accessories, such as jewelry, made little ladies and gentlemen out of the tiny tots. In colonial days the anodyne necklace was worn to ease the pains of teething, amber beads prevented croup, and coral beads were thought to ward off evil. But jewelry was also worn for adornment. Anna Green Winslow, in her diary written in Boston in 1771, describes her dress and jewelry. "I was dress'd in my yellow and black bib and apron, black feathers on my head, my past(e) comb and all my past(e) garnet, marquesett and jet pins, together with my silver plume—my locket, rings, black collar round my neck." In *Miss Leslie's Behavior Book,* published by T. B. Peterson & Bros. of Philadelphia in 1858, there are notes on "Baby's behavior." She speaks of the baby "on show" with necklace, sleeve-loops and bracelets of branchy coral and gold chains, and comments that smooth round coral is no longer fashionable, and the "day of worked caps is over."

Jewelry continued to be worn by children throughout the nineteenth century. Coral remained a favorite, and portraits of children show not only one neck strand but even as many as three. The next most popular necklace was pearls. Gold beads were also popular, as were heart-shaped lockets and necklaces of small silver daisies. Some children wore tiny gold or silver earrings, while others wore elaborate drop earrings of mosaic or enamel with borders of tiny pearls, and pins and bracelets to match. There were also brooches of silver filigree with designs of leaves and flowers. Bracelets were worn in pairs. In the 1850's and 1860's, coral beads were often given as christening presents. Crosses and gold lockets on chains were popular, as were black velvet and ribbon bracelets and necklaces. In the *Jewelers' Circular,* 1888, a style note reads: "Infants are again wearing bead necklaces. Other jewelry provided for these little folk includes a single strand of guinea gold beads, smooth amber or coral."

Collecting children's jewelry would be an interesting and unique hobby. Undoubtedly there is much to be found, but no collections are recorded. Children's clothes of the nineteenth century are available to collectors and are often on the market when estates are settled and old trunks opened. Many of these go to "thrift shops," but they are now being bought up by museums and other collectors. The Metropolitan Museum and the Museum of the City of New York have children's clothes among their costume collections.

Silver Shoe and Knee Buckles

In 1659, Pepys notes: "This day I began to put buckles on my shoes." Buckles continued in fashion for men and boys down to 1800. They were used on shoes, at the knees, and to fasten the stock at the neck.

American children of the seventeenth and eighteenth centuries wore shoe and knee buckles similar to those worn by their fathers. There were wooden shoe buckles and buckles made of copper and other metals, including silver plate, but privileged children wore silver buckles. Buckles were made by New England silversmiths, including Paul Revere, in the eighteenth century. They were also made by New York and Philadelphia silversmiths. Although many American children's portraits of the eighteenth and early nineteenth centuries show both shoe and knee buckles, the large collections of buckles in the Goyette Museum and the Metropolitan Museum of Art do not identify any as belonging to children. The only means of identification would be size. Such a collection of buckles could be assembled.

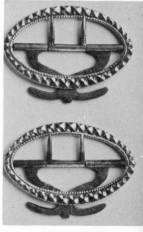

Silver knee buckles, American, ca.1800. The Metropolitan Museum of Art, bequest of A. T. Clearwater, 1933.

Portrait of Samuel D. and Sarah E. Franks. "Painted in the year 1798 in Bethlehem, Pennsylvania, by a Brother of the Moravian Society." Collection of Mrs. Harold Bellamy Starkey, San Diego.

Shoe buckles, silver and steel, Joseph Richardson, Jr., 1752 –1831. The Metropolitan Museum of Art, bequest of Charles Allen Munn, 1924.

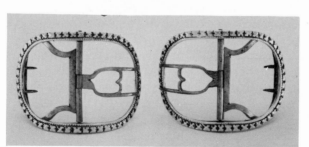

Silver shoe buckles, American, ca.1730– 1775. The Metropolitan Museum of Art, bequest of A. T. Clearwater, 1933.

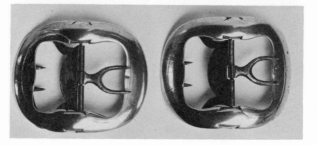

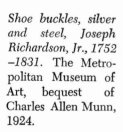

Silver knee buckles, American, ca.1770– 1810. The Metropolitan Museum of Art, bequest of A. T. Clearwater, 1933.

Children's Buttons

he portraits of early American children show a lavish use of buttons. In the seventeenth and eighteenth centuries buttons were the style, and the costumes of both adults and children had dozens of buttons. Besides the buttons necessary to fasten the garments, many were used purely as ornament. Men's and boys' coats and waistcoats sometimes had double rows of buttons down the front and four or more buttons to hold the deep cuffs in place. Buttons were used to trim pockets and to accent the flare of a coat. Knee pants were fastened with a buckle, and a row of four or five buttons continued up the side of the leg from the buckle. Girls' dresses usually fastened up the back, so the buttons there—and for comfort's sake they were usually of cloth—did not get the same attention as they did on the boys' costumes. When buttons were used on the front of the dress or the coat they were more ornamental.

The wide use of buttons in America in the eighteenth century is evidenced by the following list of buttons taken from an advertisement in the *Boston Gazette and Country Journal,* October 3, 1757: "A great Assortment of white and yellow mettle Coat and Breast Buttons, Sleeve Buttons," "White and yellow mettle coat and breast buttons, white stone and other kind of sleeve buttons," "Best double gilt Regimental Coat and Breast Buttons and a Variety of a cheaper

Silver button engraved with cypher "T D." Marked "PG" within rectangle on the back. Peter Getz, Lancaster, Pennsylvania, 1790–1810. Henry Francis du Pont Winterthur Museum.

Silver button engraved with the cypher "T G." Marked "L H" in rectangle on back. Lewis Hecht, Lancaster, Pennsylvania, ca.1760. Henry Francis du Pont Winterthur Museum.

Silver button with bright-cut star and rope twist border. Marked "T S" on back. Thomas Skinner, Marblehead, Massachusetts, 1712–1761. Henry Francis du Pont Winterthur Museum.

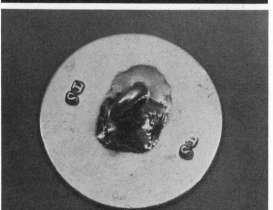

Button back showing marks and soldered loop. Henry Francis du Pont Winterthur Museum.

kind for the Country Sale, best London made Silver Sleeve Buttons, set with Brilliant Stones and all other sorts of Sleeve Buttons."

Buttons in colonial America were like those worn in England, and in the seventeenth century most American buttons were probably imported from England. However, a button maker is listed among the Irish servants arriving in Boston in 1716 (*Boston News-Letter,* June 18–25, 1716), and a button maker Thomas Thornton was reported to have died in Boston (*Boston Gazette,* April 22–29, 1728). These men probably made pewter buttons.

Since few buttons today, unless found on garments, can be identified as belonging to children, it may be questioned just what sort of buttons children wore. Surely garments of silk and satin would be fastened by buttons of equal elegance. However, there is little information about children's buttons. Only one advertisement, that of Edmond Milne, well-known silversmith, mentions buttons for children. "Chrystal and Mocoa buttons, in silver, children's do" (*Pennsylvania Journal,* November 8, 1764). In the mid-eighteenth century, many American silversmiths made buttons of silver and gold, often set with crystals. One story has it that the New York silversmith Benjamin Halsted made to order a set of silver buttons for Andrew Bowne who refused to accept the buttons when finished. The case was publicly aired in letters in *The New York Gazette or the Weekly Post-Boy,* August and September, 1764.

"Buckles, clasps, buttons, broaches, rings, and lockets, both plain and set with paste, moco, etc.," were advertised by the silversmith Nicholas Roosevelt in 1769. Many other American silversmiths, both famous and obscure, including John Coney, James Boyer, John Burt, Jacob Hurd, William Ball, Charles Oliver Bruff, Paul Revere, Daniel Van Voorhis, Elias Pelletreau, Joseph Anthony, Jr., John Pennyfeather, John Leacock, Richard Humphreys, and John and Daniel Dupuy, made silver buttons in the eighteenth century. In fact, practically every silversmith made buttons to order. Buttons were included in the inventory of the estates of the Connecticut silversmith Samuel Gray (1684–1713) and Peter Quintard (1699–1762) as well. These silver buttons were engraved either with the monogram of the owner or with a small decorative design such as a star or a cross. Buttons in the collection of Phillip H. Hammerslough and made by Isaiah Wagster (Baltimore, 1776–1793) and by Lewis Hecht (ca. 1760, Lancaster, Pennsylvania) were monogrammed. A set of greatcoat buttons by Thomas Skinner (Marblehead, Massachusetts, 1712–1761) have a gadroon edge and an engraved center star. Bristol stone and crystal were set in silver. There were also silver buttons with patterns cast in relief, but these proved too heavy, and for a few years buttons covered with cloth were more popular. Buttons advertised in eighteenth-century American newspapers include "mohair, plain and work'd"; "Bath metal, Tortoise Shell and Horn Coat and Waistcoat Buttons"; "twist and

Pewter buttons with star flower and leaf designs, 1800–1820. Collection of Sally Luscomb, author of *The Collector's Encyclopedia of Buttons.*

Metal buttons carved, engraved, and engine-turned. Eighteenth century. Collection of Sally Luscomb, author of *The Collector's Encyclopedia of Buttons.*

deathshead Buttons"; "Mathewman's and Wild's buttons; Silver basket and death-head."

Metal buttons are an important and interesting group, and many of these must have been used on children's clothes. Metal buttons of brass, copper, bronze, or tombac were made in the eighteenth century. They have loop shanks brazed on, and engraved, die-struck, hand-stamped, or engine-turned decoration in geometric patterns. They range in size from one to one and a half inches or two inches in diameter. The early ones were made in one piece with a loop shank. Philadelphia buttons made of brass and strongly shanked were made by Caspar Wistar before 1750 and later by his son, Richard Wistar. Philadelphia-type buttons were also made by several button makers in New York including Henry Witeman, or Whiteman, who served an apprenticeship with Wistar. The following quote is from Whiteman's advertisement in a New York newspaper: "He gives this Notice to the Publick that he calls those of his Make, New York Buttons" (*The New-York Gazette*, October 13, 1760). "Thomas Yates, Brass Founder and Copper-Plate Printer from Birmingham Makes all Sorts of Hand Irons, Buckles, Buttons, etc." (*The New-York Gazette*, November 19, 1759). Another English button maker arrived in Boston in 1772 bringing "over the Materials for making all sorts of gilt Buttons."

Pewter buttons were also used extensively in eighteenth-century America. Some were imported, but some were also made on hand-operated molds in the home. American-made pewter buttons were worn by the American soldiers in the Revolution. Later, pewter buttons were made by such well-known makers as the Yales and Danforths, and many a button is found with the pewterer's name on the back. Henry Grilley was the first craftsman to start a factory solely for making buttons. Pewter buttons have also been found with the following early makers' names: Aaron Benedict, Anson Matthews, Amasa J. Goodyear, and Bishop and Hemingway. Although pewter buttons are seldom mentioned in books about old pewter, the marked buttons form an interesting record of pewterers' names.

The newspaper notices of stolen goods and runaway servants give descriptions of the buttons on their clothes. For example, the description of an English servant, a jeweler by trade, who ran away from the silversmith Myer Myers, was as follows: "Had on when he went away a turned blue cloth coat with black Buttons half trim'd, small round cuffs without Buttons, an old blue lapell'd Waistcoat with Brass Buttons, the Lappels lin'd with black Velvet, a pair of black Leather Breeches with solid Silver Buttons . . ." (*The New-York Gazette or the Weekly Post-Boy*, April 9, 1753).

Pewter and metal buttons were most often found on servants' clothes. Although pewter buttons were molded, they were sometimes chased and die-stamped with initials, or were flat with simple geometric designs, stars, or flowers. An advertisement describes another type. "Taken . . . a blew Great Coat with a Cross Stampt

Pewter Buttons" (*Boston Gazette,* June 23–30, 1735). There were
also flat pewter buttons, round, small, and homemade pewter buttons, all carefully described in the advertisements. Generally, brass
and pewter buttons were found on clothes of homespun while "a fine
shirt with silver buttons" suggests a costume of a higher class, as
does the following: "Great Coat—Lost; dark blue Great Coat with
light blue velvet cape and frosted Buttons" (*Boston News-Letter,*
November 20–27, 1735).

There was great competition between the English and the American button manufacturers, and several button companies from
England set up factories in New York after the Revolution and
advertised in New York newspapers: "Cornwell and Martin from
Birmingham, Respectfully inform their Friends and the public in
general, they have established a manufactory for gilt and plated
Buttons, at Corlear's Hook, New York, where they intend carrying
on the business in all its branches" (*The Weekly Museum,* July 6,
1793). "Button Manufactory. A person well acquainted with the
manufactory of Mathewman's Hard Metal Buttons, will hear of a
very advantageous offer, by making speedy application to Shotwell
and James, No. 214 Pearl Street" (*The Diary; or Evening Register,*
August 30, 1794). "Plain, fancy, gilt and plated coat and breast
Buttons" were received by John Cauldwell and Company direct
from the manufactory in England and advertised in the *New York
Daily Advertiser,* May 15, 1797.

In the nineteenth century the button industry in America
centered in Waterbury, Connecticut. Abel Porter, a pewterer of
Southington, Connecticut, who made pewter buttons before 1800,
was later an early brass button maker. He moved to Waterbury and
his firm eventually became the Scovill Manufacturing Company.
Other early makers of gilt buttons were Mark Leavenworth and
Aaron Benedict. Benedict was associated with numerous companies
in Waterbury, and his firm eventually became the Waterbury Companies, Inc. These companies started as makers of brass and gilt
buttons. Early brass buttons were large for the greatcoat and
smaller for the waistcoat and breeches. After 1800, gold-plated
buttons appeared. Victorian gentlemen and older boys also wore
jeweled buttons with glass centers and metal rims. By the 1850's the
metal buttons on men's coats gradually gave way to cloth buttons
matching the coat or waistcoat. Little boys' costumes still required
buttons to fasten the trousers to the blouse, and the blouse itself was
buttoned up the front and often had diagonal rows of buttons
reaching from the waist to the arm pits. Women's and girls' costumes were fastened with gilt buttons well beyond the time when it
was no longer the fashion for men to wear fancy buttons. Even so,
their costumes depended more on the materials and on trimmings
such as pleats, ruffles, puffs, lace braid, and embroidery. Jewelry
also took the place of buttons. Pearl necklaces, gold beads, or lockets

are seen in children's portraits at this time. The children also wore pairs of bracelets. However, little girls' calico and sprig-printed dresses were undoubtedly fastened by the fascinating transfer-printed china buttons called calicoes. Calicoes were made in America by Charles Cartledge and Company of Greenpoint, Long Island, from 1848 to 1850. These buttons were sold a dozen on a card. Calicoes usually have holes in the center instead of a metal shaft. There were also more expensive china buttons, including those with designs from Aesop's Fables.

Although late-nineteenth-century buttons were made in a variety of materials including glass, paste, mosaics, pearl, tintypes, luster, papier-mâché, and gutta-percha, the buttons that relate to children and were undoubtedly produced with children in mind are the Victorian children's story buttons. These were made of brass or other metal, pearl, and glass. They reached their peak of popularity in the 1880's and 1890's and were made in Europe and America. Although these buttons are made of cheap materials and, for the most part, with sentimental design and crude workmanship, they are interesting and make a delightful collection. There are pictures of cats, dogs, and other animals, scenes from operas, and scenes from children's books such as nursery rhymes, *Robinson Crusoe*, *Aesop's Fables*, and *Little Lord Fauntleroy*. There are also buttons with groups of children playing with toys. The group with toys and games includes a child with a jumping jack, two children playing with a toy boat, hoop rolling, children on a toboggan, "Ride a Cock Horse," a boy with a butterfly net, a boy in a swing, a child riding a dragonfly, and children wading at the seashore. Other quaint scenes include a child and a dog in a dog house, a girl with an umbrella, hooking a snail, robbing a bird's nest, playing house, "You Dirty Boy," and a boy and a girl at the pump.

Nursery rhymes illustrated on children's buttons include "Hey, Diddle Diddle"; "Old King Cole"; "See Saw"; "Three Little Kittens"; "Pussy Cat, Pussy Cat"; "Puss in Boots"; "Little Jack Horner"; "Little Boy Blue"; "Jack and Jill"; "Little Bopeep"; "Mary and Her Lamb." "Jack and the Bean Stalk" and "Red Riding Hood" were also popular buttons designs. "Little Red Riding Hood" buttons were made by several different companies in various sizes and designs. This button was also made in various materials including pewter, brass, and ceramic. Although the makers of the majority of these buttons cannot be identified, the "Red Riding Hood" with the inner leaf border was made by Lane Manufacturing Company, Waterbury, Connecticut.

One of the most interesting and popular groups of children's buttons were those taken from the Kate Greenaway books which were published in England in the 1880's. *Under the Window* and *Kate Greenaway's Birthday Book* furnished most of the illustrations on the buttons. The majority of these buttons were made in England. They were made in relief metal and in black glass with an

Metal story buttons: Top and bottom left: *"Jack and the Beanstalk."* Top right: *Puss-in-Boots and the farmer.* Bottom center: *Pease Porridge.* Bottom right: *Georgie Porgie.* Collection of Sally Luscomb, author of *The Collector's Encyclopedia of Buttons.*

Metal story button: "*Red Riding Hood.*" Collection of Sally Luscomb, author of *The Collector's Encyclopedia of Buttons.*

Metal story button: "Mary and Her Little Lamb." Collection of Sally Luscomb, author of The Collector's Encyclopedia of Buttons.

Metal story button: "Red Riding Hood." Lane Manufacturing Company, Waterbury, Connecticut. Collection of Sally Luscomb, author of The Collector's Encyclopedia of Buttons.

Metal button with pressed wood center: "Ride a Cock Horse." Collection of Sally Luscomb, author of The Collector's Encyclopedia of Buttons.

Metal button: child with toys. Collection of Sally Luscomb, author of The Collector's Encyclopedia of Buttons.

Kate Greenaway, Ring-a-ring from "Marigold Garden."

Kate Greenaway, Summertime.

Kate Greenaway, Hand in Hand
from "Birthday Book for Children."

a

(a) Kate Greenaway, See-Saw Jack from
"Mother Goose." (b) Page from book.

See-Saw-Jack in the hedge,
Which is the way to London Bridge?

b

iridescent background of gold, rose, or blue. Sometimes the entire illustration was used, and sometimes only a detail. There were many buttons that imitated the designs, but buttons are only known as Kate Greenaways when they are identified with an illustration. The old English Kate Greenaway button dies were used later in the twentieth century, and molded jasperware Kate Greenaways were made in the United States by Marie La Barre Bennett. "Hand in Hand," a button in metal relief of two children holding hands, was taken from the cover of *Kate Greenaway's Birthday Book*. Miss Patty, and Miss Patty and Master Paul were taken from *Under the Window*, as were the "Johnny" buttons which were made in several sizes and designs. "Ring-a-Ring" is from *Marigold Garden*, and "See-Saw Jack" from *Mother Goose*.

The subject matter used for the decoration of buttons mirrors every facet of the life of the era in which the button was made from classic designs of the eighteenth century to Art Nouveau of the late nineteenth and early twentieth centuries. However, except for the Kate Greenaways and the nursery rhyme subjects, it is difficult to say that the button was made for use on a child's costume. Subjects with dogs, cats, and other animals appeal equally to animal lovers as well as to children. However, the late realistics with fruit, vegetables, and objects such as ships and cars do not seem to have been made with the grown-ups in mind. Also, the plastic buttons with rabbits, ducks, teddy bears, and gingerbread men can hardly have been for use on an adult costume. These plastic buttons were made as late as the 1950's and 1960's, but since they were easily destroyed by laundering they are already scarce and thus of interest to collectors.

No one seems to have collected data on the buttons that were used on children's clothes, but a fascinating collection would include both the old clothes and the buttons—not only the kind of buttons used, but how many, and where used, and how they were grouped.

4

Schoolbooks and Schooling

Hornbooks and Primers

I n colonial America as in England the child's first schoolbook was the hornbook. In our sense of the word the hornbook was really no book at all. It was a leaf of paper printed on one side and pasted on a thin oak board with a stubby handle shaped like a battle-dore. The paper was then covered with a layer of translucent horn and secured by a narrow rim of copper and tacks. The handle was usually pierced with a hole so that the hornbook could be carried by a string or hung around the neck or from the belt. This tiny hornbook was about four or five inches long and two inches wide. The printed page of the hornbook began with a cross which was always in the upper left hand corner of the first or "crisscross row." This cross indicated to the child that he must cross himself before starting the lesson, which included the alphabet in small letters and capitals, combinations of consonants and vowels, the Exorcism, and the Lord's Prayer. The back of the English hornbook of this type had a portrait of Charles II on horseback coarsely stamped in red. German hornbooks were stamped with double eagles, and a Mexican hornbook has a painting of the Holy Child on its back. Hornbooks of this general type have been found in America but, although they were frequently advertised in Boston, Philadelphia, and even

76

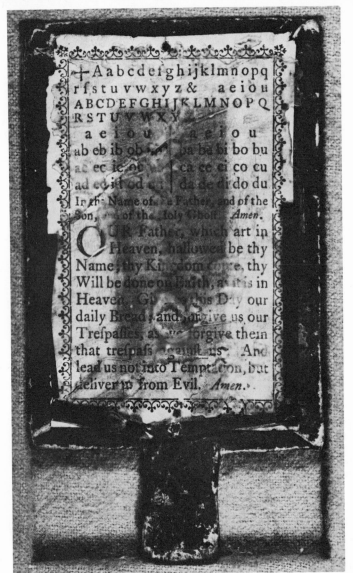

Hornbook, American, eighteenth century. Rare Book Division, The New York Public Library, Astor, Lenox and Tilden Foundations.

Charleston, South Carolina, newspapers from 1727 to 1760, they were all probably imported from Holland or England. The account book of Old South Church, Boston, contains the following item in 1708: £1 10s. for "Hornes for Catechizing." "Gilt and plain hornbooks" were advertised in Philadelphia and New York newspapers in the 1750's and 1760's.

Hornbooks were often bound in brass, leather, ivory, or silver. Some are made completely of ivory or silver with the letters hand-painted on the ivory or engraved on the silver. Still other hornbooks are framed in silver filigree. Hornbooks of carved English oak have not only hand-carved letters but also typical geometric carving similar to that on Elizabethan furniture. A German hornbook has letters printed in gold. Hornbooks were also stamped on tin, worked in needlework, and stamped with wooden molds from which gingerbread hornbooks were made to be sold at English fairs. A hornbook has been found with the wires and beads of an abacus fastened to its

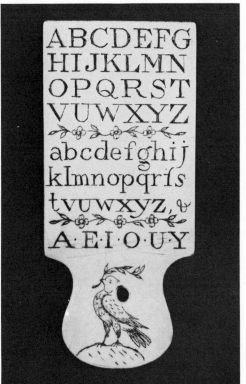

Ivory hornbook, with crest of the Tallow Chandlers' Company. English, eighteenth century. Rare Book Department, The Free Library of Philadelphia.

Bone rattle with horn "windows" and bone letters. German, nineteenth century (?). Rare Book Department, The Free Library of Philadelphia.

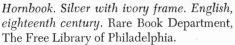

Hornbook. Silver with ivory frame. English, eighteenth century. Rare Book Department, The Free Library of Philadelphia.

back; another hornbook has the head of a wooden doll at the top of the frame, and an American hornbook with a printed lesson and illustration from a Philadelphia primer of 1821 is framed in wood with a short turned-wood handle. A unique jumping-jack hornbook was made in Germany in the nineteenth century.

Few hornbooks used by American children have survived, so the collector interested in owning a hornbook must be satisfied with one found in England or on the Continent. He must also be prepared to pay a big price. A group of hornbooks were on the market recently, and were bought by the Free Library of Philadelphia to add to their extensive collection.

The printed cardboard battledore was the successor of the hornbook. It was made up of two or three pages of stiff cardboard on which were printed or impressed letters, numerals, and the Lord's Prayer. Battledores were issued in great numbers by many different publishers. J. Newbery of London printed many battledores down to 1840. The best known was The Royal Battledore which was adorned with cuts of objects illustrating the alphabet including "a Apple,"

Jumping jack hornbook of wood. German, nineteenth century. Rare Book Department, The Free Library of Philadelphia.

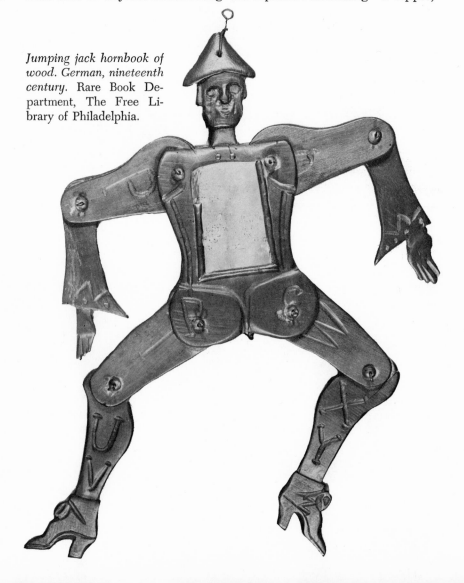

The following table and illustrations appear in the primer image:

Words of four Syllables.	
Ac·com pa·ny	Accompany
Be·ne vo·lence	Benevolence
Ce·re·mo·ny	Ceremony
Dif·con·tent·ed	Difcontented
E·ver·laft·ing	Everlafting
Fi·de·li·ty	Fidelity
Glo·ri·fy·ing	Glorifying
Hu·mi·li·ty	Humility
In·fir·mi·ty	Infirmity.

Words of five Syllables.	
Ad mi·ra·ti·on	Admiration
Be·ne·fi·ci al	Beneficial
Con·fo·la·ti·on	Confolation
De·cla·ra·ti·on	Declaration
Ex·hor·ta·ti·on	Exhortation
For·ni·ca·ti·on	Fornication
Ge·ne·ra·ti·on	Generation
Ha·bi·ta·ti·on	Habitation
In·vi·ta·ti·on	Invitation

A — In *Adam's* Fall We Sinned all.

B — Thy Life to Mend This *Book* Attend.

C — The *Cat* doth play And after flay.

D — A *Dog* will bite A Thief at night.

E — An *Eagles* flight Is out of fight.

F — The Idle *Fool* Is whipt at School.

The New England Primer, 1727. Rare Book Division, The New York Public Library, Astor, Lenox and Tilden Foundations.

"c Cat," "o Owl," "t Top," and "z Zany," a figure of Punch or a jester. Other battledores were illustrated with cuts of nursery rhymes. There are battledores by various publishers that are available for the collector.

The lineage of American schoolbooks, like other children's books in the Colonies, goes back to Europe, mainly England. The few books published in America followed English models, and were permeated with religion, duty, and rules of civility. They included catechisms, primers, spellers, and Latin grammars. Even the arithmetics were filled with morbid pietism and the duty of an early conversion as a prelude to an untimely death. There was a scarcity of books in the colonial era, and the Bible, Addison, and Goldsmith substituted for textbooks in many colonial schools. Boston was the leading printing center before the Revolution, Philadelphia became the center after 1815, and from 1815 New York became the center.

The first book that succeeded the hornbook in general use in the schools of the colonies was the New England Primer. The first New England Primers were printed between 1686 and 1690, and for a century and a half thereafter more than three million copies were printed. The earliest surviving copy was printed in 1727 by S. Kneeland and T. Green of Boston. It was a poorly printed little book about five inches long and three inches wide and had about eighty pages. In addition to the alphabet it contained a syllabarium with words up to six syllables, a morning and evening prayer, and a grace to be said before meals. It also included religious catechisms,

and each letter of the alphabet is illustrated with little blurred pictures mostly representing biblical scenes beginning with "In Adam's fall / We sinned all" and including the dreary "Xerxes did die / And so must I." At first "K" had a rhyme of the British king, but in Revolutionary days the verse was changed. Later patriotic verses sang the praises of George Washington. There was also a page of proper names designed to teach children how to spell their own names. The majority of these names were from the Bible. Every New England Primer also contained this somber couplet: "I leave you here a little booke / for you to look upon / That you may see your father's face / When I am dead and gone." Verses of the Bible were used for the alphabet, after which came the Lord's Prayer and Apostles' Creed. There were also pictures; the largest and most interesting was that of the burning of John Rogers. The little prayer, "Now I lay me down to sleep" is usually found in New England Primers dating after 1737, and sometimes John Cotton's catechism called "Spiritual Milk for Boston Babes" is included. After the middle of the eighteenth century a few short stories such as the "History of Master Tommy Fido" were added. New material was also added to the New England Primer at the beginning of the nineteenth century, but the use of the book tapered off in the first quarter of the century.

There were many other primers in the nineteenth century. The New England Primer, The Royal Primer, published by Newbery in London, and the New York Primer contained almost identical material. Other primers printed in nineteenth-century America included the Columbia Primer, the Franklin Primer, 1802–1831, and the Child's Primer, printed in Philadelphia in 1800. The latter was the first primer to include nursery rhymes. A Southern Primer was printed in Charleston, South Carolina, in 1841, and a Confederate Primer was issued in Nashville, Tennessee, in 1861. A Peter Parley Primer was published by Samuel Goodrich. All primers are rare and hard to find, and the New England Primers, even the late editions, are very rare and expensive. However, anyone desirous of learning about colonial American children should acquaint himself with the stern lessons and puritan mood as portrayed in the New England Primer.

When the child advanced beyond the hornbook and the primer he was ready for grammar. Throughout the colonial period there was a demand for instruction in Latin and Greek. Both were necessary for boys who were going to college. Lilly's grammar was taught by Ezekiel Cheever, who later wrote *The Accidence* which was used at Andover and other schools. The first English grammar used in the Boston public schools was a tiny book with a long title, *The Young Lady's Accidence, or a Short and Easy Introduction to English Grammar, design'd principally for the use of Young Learners, more especially for those of the Fair Sex, though Proper for Either.*

The *Grammar of the English Tongue* was written in verse, and
Marmaduke Multiplys Merry Method of Making Minor Mathematicians, published in 1817, set the multiplication table in rhyme.
Rhymes had also been used in Cocker's *Arithmetic,* an edition of
which was published in Philadelphia in 1779. This fashion of
rhyming textbooks goes back to the sixteenth and seventeenth centuries, but the custom continued into the nineteenth century. Cotton
Mather in his diary (March 1705–1706) comments on the use of
verse as an aid to memory. "About this time sending my little son to
school, where the child was learning to read, I did use every
morning for diverse Months to write in a plain Hand for the child,
and send thither by him, a Lesson in Verse to be not only Read, but
also gott by Heart." These verses, which were lessons in "Goodness," were printed by T. Green in 1706 under the title of *Good
Lessons for Children; or Instructions provided for a little Son to
learn at School, When learning to read.* At this time there was also a
Poetical History of the Bible.

Early spelling books used in American schools included Thomas
Dilworth's *The Child's New Spelling Book.* However, the teaching
of spelling in many schools was conducted without a book, and it
was not until the time of Noah Webster and his *American Spelling
Book,* first published in 1783, that there was any uniformity in the
teaching of spelling. From this time on Noah Webster's blue-backed
spelling book and Bingham's spelling and reading books took over
the field.

Arithmetic in the eighteenth century was taught by methods in
Hodder and Cocker, both English books. However, there were arithmetic books printed in America in the eighteenth century. Isaac
Greenwood, a graduate of Harvard who taught mathematics at
"Mrs. Belnap's House in Queen Street, Boston," in 1727, wrote
Arithemetic, Vulgar and Decimal, which was published in 1729. In
1730 a Dutch algebra, *Arithemetica or Cypher,* by Koust, was
published in New York by Peter Zenger. After the Revolution many
textbooks by American authors were published, and the *New and
Complete System of Arithematic* by Nicholas Pike published in
Newburyport, Massachusetts, in 1788, and *An Introduction to
Arithmetic* by Erastus Root, 1796, replaced the English arithmetics
of Cocker and Hodder. From 1800 on, there were many American
arithmetic books. The two most used were Frederick Emerson's
North American Arithmetic and *The Little Arithmetic* by Joseph
Ray, both published in 1834. Ray's book continued to be used into
the 1860's.

Although there may be few collectors of American schoolbooks in
general, and the spellers or arithmetic books may interest only those
connected with instruction in these fields, "readers" are in a different category. Readers are fascinating little books. From the first
American reader by Noah Webster down to McGuffey's Readers,

these books contained attractive cuts, quotes from well-known people, and poems.

Webster's *Grammatical Institute of the English Language* was published in three parts. The first part, Spelling, was published in 1783, Grammar followed in 1784, and Reading in 1785. This last volume contained material on United States history, including the story of the Boston Massacre. In 1790 Webster's *Little Reader's Assistant* contained the story of Columbus. There were also stories with moral lessons such as the Christian Indian getting the better of the heathen Indian, and there were dialogues giving rules of behavior. The Franklin Primer (1802–1831) had lessons in verse such as Watts's poems. Caleb Bingham's readers, *Child's Companion, Columbian Orator,* and *The American Preceptor,* which contained speeches of Pitt and material about Jefferson and Franklin, were equally popular. But the most popular American readers until the time of McGuffey were *English Reader* (1799) and *Sequel to English Reader* (1801) by Linley Murray. These contained material from *Rasselas,* poems by Thomson, Pope, and Cowper, and selected readings with religious and moral messages.

The McGuffey Reader was to the nineteenth-century child what the New England Primer was to the eighteenth-century child. It reflected the moral spirit of the age. It taught promptness, goodness, kindness, honesty, truthfulness, reverence, and piety. Each reader had eighty-five lessons in reading and spelling and sixteen pictures on its sixty-six pages. At first the readers contained little new material, but there were new stories and poems in each successive edition. Such titles as "The Lame Dog," "The Story Teller," "The Cruel Boy," "The Broken Window," "The Cool Shade," and "The Little Dog" reflect the sentiment and homely virtues of the Victorian era. The well-known "Twinkle, Twinkle, Little Star" first appeared in Jane Taylor's *Rhymes for the Nursery* in 1809, but it was McGuffey who made its popularity nationwide. He performed a like service for "Mary Had a Little Lamb" when it began to appear in his readers in 1848. McGuffey Readers were printed for the first through the sixth grades. Between 1836 and 1895 there were many editions. The first and second readers appeared in 1836, the third and fourth in 1837. In all, there were more than 120 million copies of the various editions. The McGuffey Museum at Miami University in Oxford, Ohio, owns 140 McGuffey Readers, and no two are alike. There is also a large collection in the Henry Ford Museum, and Henry Ford published reprints of McGuffey Readers. The American Book Company printed revised McGuffey Readers in their printing of 1920. While only the early editions have value to the serious book collector, any McGuffey Reader is interesting because of the social and historical material and fascinating pictures.

There were many other nineteenth-century American readers published before the Civil War, of which the best known were *Goodrich School Readers* published by Peter Parley; the readers of

McGUFFEY'S

NEW

SECOND ECLECTIC READER:

FOR YOUNG LEARNERS.

By WM. H. McGUFFEY, LL. D.

VAN ANTWERP, BRAGG & CO.,

137 WALNUT STREET,   28 BOND STREET,

CINCINNATI.   NEW YORK.

McGuffey's Second Eclectic Reader. Title page, Remodeled Series 1885. Collection of John Mackay Shaw.

George F. Holmes; the six readers of George S. Hillard; the Worcester Readers; and Lyman Cobb's *New Juvenile Readers*. Charles W. Sanders published five readers between 1838 and 1860. Sanders readers were the first to include the well-known story of the boy who saved the dykes of Holland, "The Little Match Girl," and the poem including "The Breaking Waves Dashed High," the first line of the well-known "Landing of the Pilgrims" by Felicia Hemans.

Writing and Penmanship

Writing had much more importance in colonial days than today. Children's instruction in writing began at an early age, and one of the chief requisites of a colonial schoolteacher was that he should be qualified in penmanship. The writing of the Pilgrim and Puritan fathers, including that of Governor John Winthrop, was not very good, but from the beginning writing was stressed in the private schools of such cities as Boston. The writing schools, which were generally kept by men, were considered on a higher level than the girls' or Dame Schools. Writing schools usually taught arithmetic in addition to writing. Although writing was taught in private schools, there was also a public writing school in Boston in 1684 known as the Writing School in Queen Street. This school admitted only boys at least seven years of age who had already learned to read. Instructors at this school who later became well-known writing masters were Samuel and Abiah Holbrook and John Proctor. In 1700 the North Writing School was established and John Proctor and Abiah Holbrook became instructors there, and in 1719, when the South Writing School was opened, Abiah and Samuel Holbrook taught there. Anna Green Winslow was a pupil of Samuel Holbrook in 1771. The writing schools of Boston continued to thrive until interrupted by the war in 1775, but the North and South Writing Schools reopened and continued until 1789. One of the first times a private school in America was mentioned was in 1667 when "Mr. Will Howard" was given "liberty to keep a wrighting schoole to teach children to writte and to keep accounts." In *The Letter-Book of Samuel Sewall* we learn that John Sanford, a writing-school master in the 1660's was the teacher of Hannah Hull. Hannah, who was four or five years old at this time, was later the wife of Samuel Sewall. Sewall also mentions the names of several other writing teachers, but the most important sources of information are the newspapers. In 1709 Owen Harris taught writing and "Arithmetick in all its parts." John Green was one of the early teachers of writing. He also taught geometry and trigonometry. A few years later Samuel Grainger taught "Writing after a free and easy manner in all hands usually practised." John Proctor was master of the North Writing School in 1830. Abiah Holbrook, the best-known writing master because of the preservation of his manuscript in the Harvard College Library, served an apprenticeship at North Writ-

CTIONS FOR HOLDING THE PEN & SIT-
IN A PROPER ATTITUDE FOR WRITING

body must be bent but a very lit-
forward. the breast must not
h the dask. the elbows almost
to the sides, & the right arm
nove easily with the fingers.
nen to point to the right front
is to be held in the fingers
tly as represented in the en-
ved sketch.

EASY SYSTEM OF SHORT HAND
word has but one syllable. write
first & last letter for the word. if

-more than one syllable. write the first letter of each syllable & the last letter of the
word: proper names to be written in full.
Example. "We shall conduct you to
the hill side, laborious indeed, at
the first ascent, but else, so green,
so smooth, so full of goodly pros-
pects and melodious sounds on every side, that the harp of Orpheus
was not more charming." Milton.
—— The same abreviated ——
We sl cdt yu to te hl se, lbros idd, at
te ft act, bt ee, so gn, so sh, so fl of gb
pps & mldos ss on evy se, tt te hp of Orpheus
w.s nl me cmg. Milton. ——

any other system of Short Hand seldom or never repays the labour of learning.

Directions for holding the pen and sitting from "Three New and Elegant Sets of
Alphabetical Copy Lines . . .," New Haven, 1807. Rare Book Division, The
New York Public Library, Astor, Lenox and Tilden Foundations.

ing School and became Master of the South Writing School in 17
He also conducted a private writing class after hours. John Tiles
was also a well-known writing master. He was connected with the
North Writing School, of which he became Master in 1761.

The first writing masters were from England and they taught
"divers sorts of Writing viz. English and German Texts; The Court
Roman Secretary and Italian Hands." However, round hand tech-
nique of writing with rounded connecting letters was the most
accepted in the eighteenth century. Pens were cut from a goose quill
with the feathers left on the handle. The schoolmaster made the
pens but each student brought his own homemade ink. Quill pens
were usually imported, according to the following newspaper item.
However, directions for making them are also given. "Goose Quills.
Mr. Gaine: The following Method of Manufacturing our own Country Goose Quills has been found to make them equal to any English
or Holland Quills imported; And as it may be of Use to the Public,
you will be pleased to insert it in your paper. First scrape gently the
Outside of the Quill, make a Vent or cut off a small End of the Pith;
then tye them up in a Bundle, and sink them down into a kettle of
Water, so that the Water may come just above the Pith and boil
them for about three Hours, or 'til they boil clear; then drain out
the Water, and Bake them in an Oven at Pleasure." (The New-York
Mercury, February 2, 1765.) Later writing books gave instructions
on how to make a pen, how to hold the pen, and the proper sitting

THE

JUVENILE PENMAN,

OR

PRACTICAL WRITING-BOOK,

BEING A NEW PLAN OF COPIES,

ENGRAVED ON BRASS,

DESIGNED FOR THE USE OF SCHOOLS.

BOOK, NO. 1.

'Before any thing is effected, we think it impossible ; but, when it is done, we stare—and wonder—why it was not done before. The mind then receives it with a degree of affinity, as if we had known it before.'
BACON.

☞ ADVERTISEMENT. ☜

Notwithstanding the superabundance of publications on the art of writing, yet instructors in general have not been much relieved from their toils, nor learners very materially benefitted. Simplicity of design, and the fundamental principles of the art, analytically and methodically arranged, and rendered familiar by practical examples, ensure a greater degree of improvement to the learner, than theoretical definitions or arbitrary rules. The saving of the teacher's time and labour, and the improvement of the pupil, is the primary design of this plan. The ruling of books and the writing of copies, is certainly one of the most severe and irksome tasks of an instructor, and occupies that portion of his time, which ought to be devoted to the inculcation of other branches. Under these impressions the author submits the 'PRACTICAL WRITING-BOOK' to those engaged in the instruction of youth, and hopes that on a fair trial it will be found to answer the end in view. *Manhattan School, New-York, Jan. 1817.*

DISTRICT OF NEW-YORK, ss.

BE IT REMEMBERED, That on the eighth day of March, in the thirty-seventh year of the Independence of the United States of America, A. PICKET, of the said district, hath deposited in this office, the title of a Book, the right whereof he claims as proprietor in the words following, to wit, 'The Juvenile Penman, or Practical Writing-Book, being a new plan of copies, engraved on brass, designed for the use of schools. In four Books. By A. PICKET, Author of the 'Juvenile Expositor,' &c. 'Before any thing is effected, we think it impossible ; but, when it is done, we stare—and wonder—why it was not done before. The mind then receives it with a degree of affinity, as if we had known it before.' BACON.

In conformity to the act of the Congress of the United States, entitled 'An act, for the encouragement of learning, by securing the copies of Maps, Charts, and Books, to the authors and proprietors of such copies during the time therein mentioned' And also, to an act, entitled 'An act, supplementary to an act, entitled 'An act for the encouragement of learning, by securing the copies of Maps, Charts, and Books, to the authors and proprietors of such copies, during the times therein mentioned, and extending the benefits thereof to the arts of designing, engraving, and etching historical and other prints'
THERON RUDD, *Clerk of the District of New-York.*

New-York :—Published by Smith & Forman,

AT THE FRANKLIN JUVENILE BOOKSTORES,
190 and 195 Greenwich-Street.

1817.

The Juvenile Penman or Practical Writing Book, *A. Picket. New York, Smith & Forman, 1817.* Rare Book Division, The New York Public Library, Astor, Lenox and Tilden Foundations.

position. Much attention was centered on good letter writing. In 1774 John Druitt instructed Young Ladies in ". . . Epistolary-writing."

Flourishing or ornamental pen drawing originated in the method of handwriting known as "English Round Hand," and many calligraphic copybooks printed in England contained examples of this system. In addition to alphabets and ornamental initials, the books contained pages of flourished designs of animals, fish, and human figures. Many of these books reached America, where they were reprinted by such well-known printers as Christopher Sower in Philadelphia and Isaiah Thomas in Worcester, Massachusetts. The English copybook that had the most influence was probably *The Universal Penman* (1733–1741) by George Bickham. This book was an important source for American writing masters, even though there were being published American copybooks such as Benjamin

Franklin's *The American Instructor or Young Man's Best Com-*
panion, which appeared in 1784. This book was patterned after the
English and was the first printing of handwriting in America. *The*
Writing Scholar's Assistant, published by Isaiah Thomas in 1785,
was the first American copybook. The second American copybook,
New Set of Round Hand Writing Copies, was published by Miles
Beach and Isaac Sanford, Hartford, Connecticut, in 1786. In 1791
The Art of Writing by John Jenkins was published, and in 1817 the
Juvenile Penman or Practical Writing-Book by A. Picket was published in New York and subsequently used in Manhattan School in
New York. Joseph Perkins in the *Practical Penmanship* published
in 1830 gave instructions on how to make a pen. From this time on
there were numerous copybooks on penmanship printed in America,
as the nineteenth century showed an increased interest in handwriting. There were also roaming instructors who traveled throughout the countryside holding penmanship classes in private homes or
in the village school or setting up shop on a street corner to write
flourished calling cards.

From 1848, when his first book and copy cards were published,
the designs and style of Platt Roger Spenser became the important
influence in American handwriting. The Spenserian Method, with
the use of Spenserian steel pens, was taught up to 1900. Although
flourish drawings are often referred to as "Spenserian Work,"
flourishing was in use long before Spenser published his book, and
there were many later books published after the Civil War that
sought to improve upon the system. There were also books on self-
taught penmanship, with illustrated models of flourishings to copy.
These included a lion with heavy dark shaggy mane, a leaping deer,
an eagle with spread wings holding a ribbon in its mouth, and a
galloping horse. There were also completely flourished pictures
consisting of flowers, trees, and ladies on horseback. School diplo-
mas, marriage licenses, and other documents also included flourishing.

Calligraphic drawings ideally used no pen strokes in the creation
of their images. An ordinary outline of a form was considered less
desirable than the suggestion of the form by repetitions of suitable
school exercises; thus outlines are made with repeated scallops
rather than a single unbroken line.

That these pictures, especially the lion, deer, and eagle, were all
copied from the same or similar books, is evident from the sameness
in the length and number of pen strokes. The most popular subjects
and thus those most often found in shops today are the deer, lion,
eagle, and various other birds, and the horse. Human heads,
cherubs, fish, and small animals are less frequently seen. The
majority of the examples found in shops today date from the last
half of the nineteenth century.

Although the collector's interest is usually centered in original
examples of flourishing, the collecting of the handwriting books

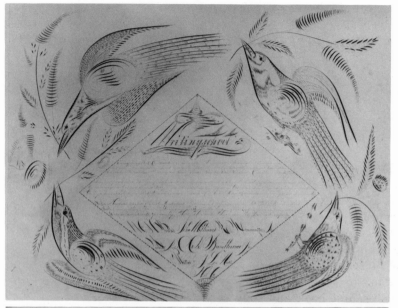

Writing School Certificate with bird flourishes. IBM Art Collection, New York City.

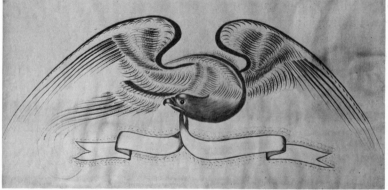

Spenserian flourish, American Eagle, American Heritage Collection. *Artist: C. L. Horton.* Colby College Art Museum.

Pen flourish, lion. American Heritage Collection *Artist: C. L. Horton.* Colby College Art Museum.

themselves should not be overlooked. Those of the eighteenth century are expensive and hard to find since they were not published in great quantities. However, from 1830 to 1900 there were dozens of penmanship books published in America, and because they were printed in large editions there are many still around. Look in the attic, cover the sidewalk bookstalls and the thrift shops. The regular book dealer already knows their worth.

Art Instruction

Although as early as 1711–1712 Cotton Mather decided that "It may be many Wayes for the Advantage of my Daughters, to have them well-instructed in Shorthand," the usual instruction for American girls included "Reading with Elegance, and Propriety," "English Diction," epistolary writing, and penmanship. However, the stress was on the "polite Accomplishments" which included French, music, dancing, waxwork, Japanning, quilting, needlework, painting upon glass, the "Art of Painting on Gauze and Catgutt," and "Drawing with Pencil and all kinds of Water Painting." There were many opportunities for learning such accomplishments, as is evidenced by the advertisements of private schools for young ladies in the colonial newspapers of Boston. Painting upon glass seems to have been the favorite form of painting in the eighteenth century. There were advertisements in Boston newspapers for teaching painting upon glass as early as 1714, and in 1758 Eleanor McIlvaine taught "painting on glass, shellwork, tent stitch and other Works proper for young Ladies." It was a few years later in 1762 that the first advertisement mentions "Drawing with the Pencil and all Kinds of Water Painting," although interest seemed to be more on needlework, and painting—with the exception of glass painting—is seldom mentioned. In 1761 an advertisement in the *Boston News-Letter* mentions a book by Hudson, *Art of Drawing in Water-Colours and in Miniature*. There were also notices of drawing books and copybooks, but these were probably English. However, in 1787 the following notice appeared in a New York newspaper: "Art of Drawing—By Subscription, price twenty-four Shillings, a useful necessary Method to learn the Art of Drawing without a Master. Compiled from the first Masters in this art, and adorned with 26 copper plates, engraved after the manner of Raphael, Rubens, and Julius Romain, etc., consisting of near 250 pages large quarto. By a Citizen of America who has studied this useful art in Europe" (*Daily Advertiser*, February 21, 1787). At this time painting was mainly taught by copying, and drawings and prints of birds and landscapes were sold for copying at home or in school. As early as 1790, however, painting was taught in Mrs. Brodeau's School in Philadelphia by an Englishman from London.

By 1791, there were several drawing masters in New York, including John Lawrence, who gave private drawing lessons; and

THE YOUTH'S COMPANION is published every week by N. Willis, at No. 11 Cornhill, Boston.—It has been printed upwards of sixteen years, and is the largest juvenile paper published, containing twice as much matter as some that are offered at a lower rate. Price one dollar a year—six copies for five dollars.

The Companion has come.

there were regular classes in drawing and water colors taught by Archibald and Alexander Robertson at their school in New York, the Columbian Academy of Painting. In 1802 Archibald Robertson published the first comprehensive attempt at a book of drawing instruction called *Elements of the Graphic Arts*. It contains plates of head, hand, eye, arm, and leg studies, practice of the use of pen and pencil, tree forms, and architectural perspective. By 1813, when the Russian water colorist Paul Svinin visited America, he noted, "Drawing has recently been admitted into the school curriculum." From this date to the 1820's there were numerous drawing books giving instruction on how to draw the human figure, landscapes and flowers. One of the best known and most desirable from the collector's standpoint is *Lucas' Progressive Drawing Book* by Fielding Lucas, Jr., Baltimore, 1827–1828. It contains plates of American scenery colored by Anna Claypoole Peale. A group of drawing books for the use of amateurs, especially young ladies, were published in the first half of the nineteenth century, including *Thackara's Drawing Book for the Amusement and Instruction of Young Ladies and Gentlemen in the Pleasing and Elegant Art of Drawing*, ca. 1816. *A New Juvenile Drawing Book* was published for the use of Philadelphia schools in 1822. Osborne's Superfine American Water Colors were made in Philadelphia in the 1820's, and in 1835, Rembrandt Peale's *Graphics; A Manual of Drawing and Writing for the use of schools and families* was published in Philadelphia and later endorsed by the controllers of public schools of Philadelphia. This book was later enlarged. Benjamin H. Coe's *Easy Lessons in Landscape Drawing*, 1840, was also designed for the use of schools. It includes directions for using the lead pencil.

From the 1840's the teaching of drawing by the use of drawing cards became the popular method of instruction. Decks of lithographed sheets of drawing cards for copying included cottage or landscape views, animals, flowers, birds, and the human figure. The first of these cards, "Abbott's Cottage Series" and "Abbott's Head Series," were published by Saxon & Miles in New York in 1845. Several other sets of drawing cards were also published in 1845, including "The New York Artist's Class Manual" by Edward Purcell. This set of drawing cards is rich in American views, including views of the Hudson River and Long Island. In 1848, "Initiatory Drawing Cards" by B. F. Nutting were printed. These appeared in four packs with eighteen lithographed cards in each, and similar packs were also published in 1849. There are views of landscape and countryside including toll gates, lighthouses, mills and barns, still life, and everyday articles. The series advances, and Part Four includes perspective. George W. Winchester also published a series of drawing cards similar in pattern and format. In 1855 W. N. Bartholomew issued five sets of drawing cards with twelve cards each, together with instructions, and in 1856 B. F. Nutting published "Pioneer Drawing Cards" which were larger and more advanced than his earlier series. Drawing Cards continued popular for many years. Burgess' "Shaded Drawing Cards" were published by Tyler Bros. in San Francisco, ca. 1860. These drawing cards were not only used in schools, but were also one of the means of amusement when the family gathered around the table of an evening. Today the cards not only give information on early art education in America, but their subject matter gives us views of early America which were the source of much American primitive painting.

However, none of these books seem to be directed toward very young children. The first real attempt to provide drawing lessons for young children was *Drawing for Young Children*. This was published under the supervision of the Society for the Diffusion of Useful Knowledge, in London, ca. 1838. The lessons were also printed in *Peter Parley's Magazine* in 1838 and the book was published by C. S. & J. H. Francis in New York, Boston, and Washington in 1841. The pictures for copying include simple geometrical forms, fruit, flowers, animals, toys, common household articles such as a spoon, cup, teakettle, candlestick, and key, the human figure, and landscape. The first lesson pages begin with line drawings of an object such as a leaf. The lessons next proceed to shading and a group of leaves which become a tree. Finally, composition is introduced in the form of landscape. Fisher & Brother of Philadelphia published *My First Drawing Book*, ca. 1840–1845. There is a frontispiece picture of a mother and five children engaged in painting and drawing, and the twelve leaves of the book contain seventy-four illustrations of objects, scenes, flowers, fruits, animals, human figures, and landscapes, including a covered wagon on a bridge. *The Juvenile Drawing Book* by Thomas Edwards, third edition, 1844, is a small book also designed for the young child. *The Juvenile Drawing Book* by John Rubens Smith, ca. 1844, also has simple studies, architectural details, bridges, trees, leaves, dogs, horses, cattle, common household articles, and human figures. *Child's Drawing Book of Objects* by George Childs, Philadelphia, 1845, has 288 lithographs of objects relating to life in America, all in simple outline suitable for copying. John Rubens Smith also published another *Juvenile Drawing Book* in 1845, and this book includes an interesting catalogue of woodenwares, glassware, and china of the period. Josiah Holbrook's *Child's First Book*, published in Hartford, Connecticut, in 1846, is definitely American in its provenance and designed for the very young child.

In 1846, W. & R. Chambers' *First Book of Drawing* had cuts of everyday objects, scenes, animals, insects, and human figures simply drawn and obviously designed for children and young persons to copy on slate and blackboard. A book, *Slate Pictures for the Useful Self-employment of Young Children*, was printed ca. 1850 in card form. These cards, which were used in the schools of Syracuse, New York, had studies in white on black of familiar objects, toys, animals, and genre scenes. The book was published in six parts,

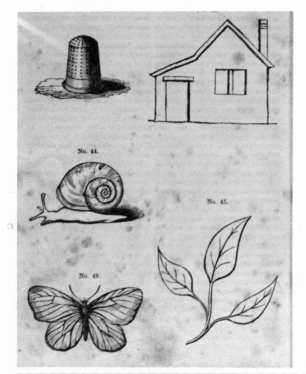

Drawing lessons from Peter Parley's Annual, *1838.* Collection of John Mackay Shaw.

Page of household articles to copy from the Juvenile Drawing Book. John Rubens Smith, ca.1844. The New York Public Library.

with sixteen plates to each part. In 1872, *The Teacher's Companion to the American Drawing Slates* by Walter Smith, was published by Noyes, Holmes & Co. of Boston, Massachusetts. It included line combinations, triangles, ovals, spirals, and curves, and such simple objects as a top, egg cup, wine glass, lamp, candlestick, cup and saucer, vase, pitcher, and chair.

Milton Bradley's "Little Artist" painting books were issued in 1860. McLoughlin Bros. printed slate drawing books, and in their catalogue of 1867 six kinds of slate drawing books are listed:

LITTLE FOLKS COLOR KIT.

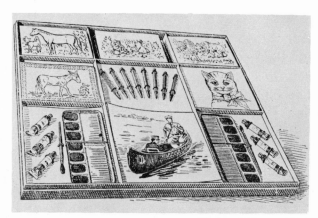

Little Folks Color Kit, Milton Bradley, ca.1905. Similar to "Little Artist" series first published in 1860. Collection of John Mackay Shaw.

"Birds, Animals, Boats, Houses, Figures, and Common Things." *Art in the Nursery, Pictures for Baby to Draw and Laugh At* was published by D. Lothrop in Boston in 1870. A *Little Folks Painting Book* with outline drawings for the child to color was given as a prize in a competition of *Little Folks Magazine* in 1879. The drawings were from Kate Greenaway books and afterward the book was published by Cassell, Petter & Galpin. In 1881, *Little Folks Magazine* advertised the *Little Folks Painting Books* series which included: *Pictures to Paint* with plates by Kate Greenaway and M. E. Edwards; *Little Folks Nature Painting Book; Little Folks Black and White Painting Book;* and *Little Folks Proverb Painting Book.* A *Kate Greenaway Painting Book* was also published by George Routledge & Sons. It was later published by Frederick Warne & Co. and went into many editions. Kate Greenaway also did a *Marigold*

Advertisement announcing "Little Folks Painting Book." Little Folks Magazine, 1879. Collection of John Mackay Shaw.

Prize Competitions. 183

The "Little Folks" Painting Book Competition.

THE "LITTLE FOLKS" PAINTING BOOK, containing a Series of Outline Drawings by KATE GREENAWAY, intended for Water-colour Painting, with amusing letterpress descriptive of the pictures, has been specially prepared for the LITTLE FOLKS Prize Competitions for 1879. The following Prizes and Medals are offered to readers of LITTLE FOLKS who shall send in the best painted pages of this book :—

A Prize of £4 and a Silver Medal of the LITTLE FOLKS Legion of Honour for the best complete book coloured.

Page from Kate Greenaway Painting Book, *1879.*

Nursery Tiles painting book. Wide Awake, *1881.* Collection of John Mackay Shaw.

Painting Book. In 1881, *Nursery Tiles—The Boys and Girls Paint-ing Book,* consisting of twelve tiles, twelve poems, and twelve pictures, was advertised in *Wide Awake Magazine. A New Painting Book for Boys and Girls—The Artists' Autograph Album,* with thirty outline illustrations to color, was published by Winkley, Throp & Dresser of Boston and advertised in *The Youth's Com-panion* in 1883. In 1891 Frederick Warne & Co. published *The Children's Painting Book.* There were many books of this type, in-cluding those by Louis Prang & Co., whose *Little Dots' Painting Book* was advertised in *The Youth's Companion,* October, 1894.

In addition to the numerous drawing books for young children, many children's magazines printed series of drawing lessons for the children. The earliest was the series in *Peter Parley's Annual* in 1838 and 1839. In 1867 Demorest's Young America published a series of lessons in drawing by R. M. Shurtleff. These included simple objects, such as a train of cars, in the first lesson. Lessons Four and Five included the different parts and features of the

Drawing. Peter Parley's Annual, *1838.* Collection of John Mackay Shaw.

Lessons in Drawing. Dem-orest's Young America, *1867.* Collection of John Mackay Shaw.

Slate pictures to copy. St. Nicholas, *vol. 6, December 1878.* Collection of John Mackay Shaw.

human figure, and Lesson Eight included trees. "Slate pencil drawings from Fisher & Brothers' very pretty Drawing-Books" were published in *Godey's Lady's Book* from 1861 through 1863. In 1870 *Our Young Folks* published articles on "How to Draw," and *St. Nicholas,* Vol. 6, published "Pictures to Copy on the Slate."

In the early twentieth century, F. Warne & Co. published three painting books by Beatrix Potter. The pages were taken from illustrations used in her books. *Peter Rabbit's Painting Book* was published in 1911, *Tom Kitten's Painting Book,* ca. 1907, and *Jemima Puddle-Duck's Painting Book* in 1925.

School Accessories

In addition to the many schoolbooks and examples of children's drawings, painting, and writing, other items connected with schools include slates, pencil boxes, and even school desks. Slates were advertised in American newspapers as early as 1737, by James Marshall, English bookseller. "Slates in frames" were advertised in the *Boston Gazette,* May 9, 1749; and "Small and large slates" in the *Boston Gazette,* May 7, 1754. In 1752, John Ten Broeck wrote from school to his father in Albany, New York: "Please send me a slate and some pensals." The *Morning Chronicle* of November 30, 1804, also advertised "Good soft black slates."

The first slates were frameless and had a pierced hole by which they could be hung. Later slates were framed in wood. In *The Youth's Companion*, October, 1879, a Pocket Rolling Slate was advertised.

There are slates available to collectors today, but it is difficult to distinguish old from new since slates were used in schools to the end of the nineteenth century, and continue popular as toys today. The frame is perhaps the best criterion, since old frames were made of better wood and were handmade with fitted dovetail corners, whereas newer slates were framed in rough pine boards held together by nails.

Pencil boxes are mentioned in eighteenth-century newspapers, but the material is not designated. Many nineteenth-century pencil boxes were made of attractive fruit woods. The long slender box usually had a sliding lid, and the lid might be decorated with simple

Group of slates. Top left: *Book slate ca. 1870's.* Right: *Slate with indented letters for instruction of penmanship, 1880's–1890's.* The Henry Ford Museum.

inlay or a painted flower or decoupage under varnish. The old school desk was usually made of hardwood, and many desks had seats with laminated stripes of light and dark wood. The old glass inkwells were sunk in the upper right hand corner of the desk and had flap covers of cast iron. The desks and seats were upheld by brackets of cast-iron scrolls which were riveted to the floor.

Rewards of Merit

The "Reward of Merit" was passed out by the schoolteacher to deserving pupils for excellence in various subjects and also for good behavior.

A Philadelphia boarding school of the eighteenth century gave crowns for rewards of merit. "There were five crowns, two principal for Eminence in Lessons, and Virtue. They were crowned in great style in the Assembly Rooms in the presence of 500 Spectators."

Rewards of merit were also often in the form of circular or oval silver disks, and some of these date from the late eighteenth century and are rare. By the end of the century the usual award of merit was a simple slip of paper. The paper rewards of merit were given in both private and public schools. They were printed in large quantities and many of them exist today. The earliest paper rewards of merit were hand-written and ornamented with pen flourishings, designs of cut paper work, or hand-painted designs of flowers and birds. They were usually about the size of a bank note but some were large elaborate pieces suitable for framing.

The printed rewards of merit made in the nineteenth century were made in much larger quantities, and therefore many more are available to collectors today. That these tiny pieces of paper were treasured shows the importance attached to excellence. Their value in the eyes of children was also due to the fact that nineteenth-century children had fewer possessions than today's children. The earliest printed rewards of merit were tiny bits of thin cheap paper $1\frac{1}{2}''$ x $2''$. They contained a verse from the Bible such as "Humble yourselfes under the Mighty hand of God that he may exalt you in due time" (I Peter 5:6). The verse was enclosed in a narrow geometric border. These tiny bits may have been for Sunday-school attendance since some were printed by the Baptist Society. Many of these date from the first years of the nineteenth century. In a few years the reward of merit increased in size, and some rewards given by Mrs. Baker's Seminary in Washington, Pennsylvania, in 1810 were an inch or two larger. These were labeled "Reward of Merit" together with the name of the school, but except for a narrow geometric border they have no other decoration. The reward of

Rewards of Merit, American, late nineteenth century. Rare Book Division, The New York Public Library, Astor, Lenox and Tilden Foundations. ▶

REWARD OF MERIT.

THIS CERTIFIES.

That *Mr Emery King*
for diligence and attention to studies, and good conduct in school, merits my approbation and esteem.

Reuben Comins Instructor.

THE INFANT HERO.

REWARD OF MERIT.

THIS CERTIFIES.

That *Master C. H. King*
for diligence and attention to studies, and good conduct in school, merits my approbation and esteem.

H. McIntyre Instructress.

I'M POOR AND ALONE.

REWARD OF MERIT.

Granted to *Mr C. H. King*

for diligence and attention to study, and good behavior in school. *Reuben Comins Inst.*

RESOLUTION.

Amidst the various ills that lie,
In ev'ry path my feet would try,
Thee, Father, I would still revere,
Determine well, and persevere.

With firm resolve, and equal mind,
Lord, make me to thy will inclined:
Help me thy favor to pursue,
And keep thee always in my view.

Then peace, sweet peace, I shall enjoy;
A peace that man can ne'er destroy!
A peace to virtue only giv'n;
A peace that leads to joy, and heav'n.

Sold by F. Dunbar, Taunton, Mass.

REWARD OF MERIT.

THIS CERTIFIES,

That *Mr Edward H. King*
for diligence and attention to studies, and good conduct in school, merits my approbation and esteem.

Reuben Comins Instructor.

Presented to *Phebe Goble* *Hoboken New Jersey*
By *1859* *E Havens Instructor*

Presented to *Phebe Goble* *Hoboken New Jersey*
By *E Havens Instructor*

merit gradually became larger, and in addition to the narrow border there were pictorial designs. The pictures were taken from cuts of newspapers and from the illustrations in contemporary children's books. There were pictures of animals, birds, and toys such as the rocking horse. There were also scenes of the schoolroom and of children reading and going to church. The instructive value of the latter scene was increased by a verse titled "Early Piety." Many rewards had scenes of children such as "good" and "bad" boys, or children's games including marbles, ball, or kite flying. Scenes providing moral lessons of virtue and diligence were particularly popular. There were also scenes of the Crucifixion and the tomb. Other rewards were printed with portraits of George Washington, while still others had pictures of eagles, or oval scenes of the four seasons, the blessings of peace, or the horrors of war.

The reward of merit in the form and size of a bank-note certificate with values marked in the end panels was thought to have been invented by John W. Barber, who was a pioneer bank-note engraver. This type was also made by other Connecticut engravers, including Abner Reed. In Barber's scrapbook of samples of his work there are rewards of merit illustrating the four seasons, a schoolroom scene with schoolmaster and pupils seated at their desks, a scene of boys playing ball, a night scene, and a winter scene of skating and sledding. There are also rewards of merit pasted in the scrapbook that are stamped with the names of other engravers including R. Rawdon, A. Willard, and W. Mason. Between 1810 and 1825 rewards of merit were printed by Abel Bowen, Henry Bowen, Lincoln & Edmands, and James Loring, all working in New England. In the collection of rewards of merit in the print department of the Metropolitan Museum of Art, there are rewards stamped by printers and booksellers of many New England cities and towns including Henry Bowen of Boston; N. S. Simpkins, Boston; Charles Whipple, Newburyport; G. & C. Merriam, Springfield, Massachusetts; S. A. Howland, Worcester, Massachusetts; David Watson, Woodstock, Vermont; John F. Brown, Concord, New Hampshire; H. & E. Phinney, Cooperstown, New York; F. Dunbar, Taunton, Massachusetts; and George P. Daniels, Providence, Rhode Island. Other rewards are also marked "Robert Foster, Portsmouth, New Hampshire," and some, with cuts of animals, are marked "John Cheney." These, like most rewards, were printed eight or more to a sheet and were sold to the school master who cut them as needed for distribution.

The illustrations on rewards of merit were not the property of any one printer but were used by all according to their tastes or the availability of the cut. Some few illustrated awards were probably especially designed for the purpose, such as the one with the school-teacher and the verse: "How lovely, how charming the sight, / When children their teachers obey! / The angels look down with delight / This beautiful scene to survey." Other designs, including

one with a glass decanter and other pieces of tableware, were taken
from newspaper cuts familiar to all researchers in old newspapers.

After 1850 lithography and color lithography were used for rewards of merit produced by such well-known lithographers as J. W. Orr, C. Magnus, Joseph Laing & Co., and T. W. Strong. There were also rewards of merit made by Louis Prang & Co. of Boston. These lithographs were decorated with bold and splashily colored flowers, birds, butterflies, and landscape scenes enclosed in flower wreaths. Many cards were embossed. The lithographic cards are heavy and have a glossy surface.

Finally, there were special books produced to be given as rewards of merit. McLoughlin's catalogue, 1867, states: "We have in hand a large assortment of Little Books for SCHOOL REWARDS, which we hope to make very acceptable and so cheap, that they will have a large sale."

I do not know how many collectors there are of rewards of merit, but there are quantities of cards available. The designs are interesting and give a picture of American printing of the nineteenth century, and many are marked with the printer's name. Prices are reasonable for the printed rewards of merit; however, if you aspire to the handmade or early engraved award, be prepared to pay higher prices. The handmade or hand-colored awards are rare. One awarded to Noah Webster by the School Committee, Boston, July 3, 1790, was engraved by Samuel Richardson and is rare both because of the name of Webster and as an example of the work of an early engraver.

5

Books for Amusement

*Story and Poetry Books**

uilding a collection of children's books demands a fondness for children, a love of books, the acquisitive nature that is the birthright of every collector, and a budget, large or small.

Book-collecting is not necessarily an expensive hobby. Like every other field of collecting, it is no more expensive than the collector wants to make it. A very respectable collection can be built by spending less than the amateur photographer spends on camera equipment and film, or the hunter-fisherman on guns, rods, and boats; and the average annual cost of membership in a golf club would furnish many a book collector with all the funds he needs.

A widely held fallacy is that the source of supply is drying up. This is a favorite topic when dealers, librarians, and collectors get together. The argument runs that more and more of the desirable books have been flowing into institutional libraries and are thus removed from the market forever. The beginning collector of children's books will find this to be true only if his heart is set on such rarities as a Bay Psalm book, an 1865 "Alice," a pristine copy of the

---

* This section, on Story and Poetry Books, was written by John Mackay Shaw.

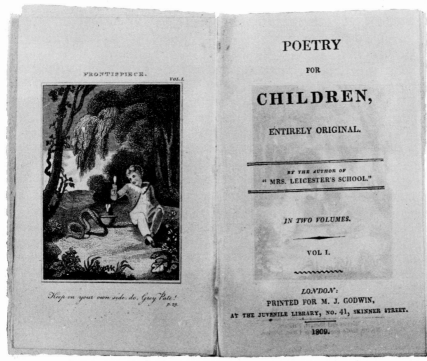

FRONTISPIECE.   VOL. I.

Keep on your own side. do, Grey Pate!
p. 29

POETRY

FOR

CHILDREN,

ENTIRELY ORIGINAL.

BY THE AUTHOR OF
" MRS. LEICESTER'S SCHOOL."

IN TWO VOLUMES.

VOL I.

LONDON:
PRINTED FOR M. J. GODWIN,
AT THE JUVENILE LIBRARY, NO. 41, SKINNER STREET.

1809.

Poetry for Children. *London, 1809. The book of which Charles Lamb himself could not find a copy.* Collection of John Mackay Shaw.

Later Editions. Collection of John Mackay Shaw.

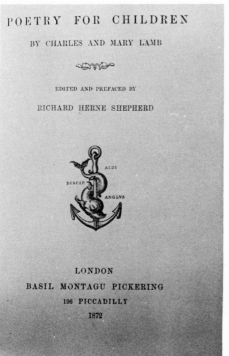

POETRY FOR CHILDREN

BY CHARLES AND MARY LAMB

EDITED AND PREFACED BY

RICHARD HERNE SHEPHERD

ALDI
DISCIP
ANGLVS

LONDON
BASIL MONTAGU PICKERING
196 PICCADILLY
1872

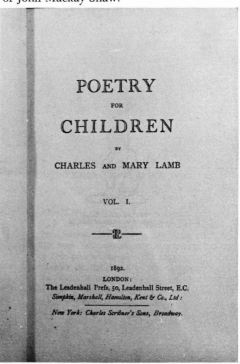

POETRY

FOR

CHILDREN

BY

CHARLES AND MARY LAMB

VOL. I.

1892.
LONDON:
The Leadenhall Prefs, 50, Leadenhall Street, E.C.
Simpkin, Marshall, Hamilton, Kent & Co., Ltd:

New York: Charles Scribner's Sons, Broadway.

first printing of Lear's "Book of Nonsense," or the Lamb 1809 "Poetry for Children," of which Lamb himself could not find a copy.

Even should these treasures make their appearance, the aspiring collector will find them beyond his reach. Yet books that are well within his reach keep welling up from a never-failing fountain, and for every ancient treasure removed from the market, a hundred new books appear on the scene, any one of which may, with the passage of time, become as much sought after as any of those that disappear into the recesses of the Morgan, Huntington, or Harvard collections. The fiction that the supply of collectible books is drying up was recently ascribed by an eminent scholar-dealer to "lazy librarians, unimaginative dealers, and silly collectors." Rest assured, aspiring collector, that there will be more books available than you will ever have the time to acquire and enjoy, though you be rich as Croesus.

Why collect children's books? If you have to ask the question, you shouldn't even begin! The only sensible reason is personal enjoyment—in other words, to have fun. The fun lies chiefly in the joy of searching for and finding something that seems desirable, and secondly in the pleasure of possessing it.

It is better not to look on your collection as an investment. Though some book collections have appreciated in value after a number of years, more often an accumulation of books is disposed of at less than its cost. If the collection is a good one and well selected, it may some day go, by sale or gift, to an established library, so that the collector has the satisfaction of preserving for posterity some artifacts that might otherwise be lost. But it is doubtful that any collector ever started out with this avowed purpose.

A patient collector can have a lot of fun ransacking the cellars and attics of friends whose children have outgrown the juvenile library. This is as good a way as any to begin. The huge expanse of collectible material will quickly become apparent. And study of the books thus acquired will enable the novice collector to select the area that is likely to afford him most pleasure.

Bookshop browsing is one of the pleasures of collecting. Every city of size, and many small towns, have at least one secondhand bookshop, presided over by a booklover like yourself. If you do not enjoy browsing, give up now, for the true collector is never so happy as when searching through a likely lot of old books in hopes of finding the one on which his heart is set. Feel no compunction about browsing, for the dealer knows this is part of the game. The price of the book will be lightly marked in pencil on the inside cover. Some collectors, it is said, take this to be a bargaining figure, and accept something less, and perhaps some booksellers agree with this procedure, and may even enjoy matching wits with the careful buyer.

Such periodicals as *The New York Times Book Review, The Saturday Review,* and *The London Times Literary Supplement* list the names and addresses of people who sell books by mail and who issue priced catalogues. Some deal in books in all fields, and some are specialists. Quite a few, on both sides of the Atlantic, deal exclusively in children's books. Often they have begun as collectors themselves, and almost always they have a scholar's interest in the books they are selling. It would be well for the novice collector to write for one or more of these catalogues. As you become more knowledgeable and more sophisticated in your chosen field, these will become your favorite reading, and you will find the best of them taking their place on your shelves with other indispensable reference tools.

The scarcer and more valuable books are frequently acquired by collectors through auction houses, of which the better known are the Parke-Bernet Galleries and the Swann Auction Galleries in New York, and Sotheby's and Christie's in London. Their catalogues are available far in advance of the sales and usually at a small charge. The books are placed on exhibition a week or so before the sale in order that prospective buyers may examine them for condition and for those small points of type of binding that so often affect the value of the book. Bids are usually acceptable by mail, and estimates of the probable prices are given on request. The private collector is well advised not to bid in person at these sales, but to have an experienced dealer bid for him, a service the dealer will provide for a percentage of the buying price. The book-auction room is no arena for the amateur. The more important sales are recorded in "American Book Prices Current," the back files of which are the main reliance of the collector or librarian in determining the value of rare items.

Enjoyment of the collection, and the process of acquiring it, will be in direct proportion to the knowledge of the collector about his books, their format, and their content. Many good reference books are available. Some of these are out of print, but copies can often be found in the public libraries. Descriptions of the books will be found in bibliographies of the more important authors, and more general information will be found in books listed in the Bibliography.

Besides these permanent sources, the collector will do well to keep abreast of the publication of new books in his field of interest, by subscribing to one or two of the magazines and journals that carry current news, reviews, and articles by authors, critics, and collectors. Particularly good are *The Horn Book Magazine,* 585 Boylston Street, Boston, Massachusetts, 02166, a monthly magazine "about children's books and reading"; *Top of the News,* a quarterly published by the Children's Division of the American Library Association, 50 East Huron Street, Chicago, Illinois 60611; and *Antiquarian Bookman,* published weekly in the interest of the old book trade (but considered "must" reading by many collectors as well). There are also frequent articles in the standard literary magazines and newspaper book sections that make reference to children's books.

The beginning book collector will soon find it to his advantage to narrow his collecting interest to one period, one subject, even to one author or illustrator. Some of the most exciting collections are, in fact, those that contain all that the collector has been able to lay his hands on by and about one writer of his choice. Others choose to confine their collecting activities to books by various authors in such subject categories as biography, history, science, adventure, poetry, mystery, fairy tales, nursery rhymes, or textbooks, all of which and many more have been the favorite hunting grounds of writers for children. The list of possibilities seems endless, and within the compass of one short chapter it is possible to mention only a few by way of suggestion.

Nursery rhymes are an important category. Mother Goose is the most prolific of all authors. Her rhymes are of infinite variety and her characters have been pictured by a countless host of artists over a period of two centuries. Who she was is a matter of controversy. Of one thing we can be sure. She has been aided by the largest staff of editors and revisers in the history of English literature.

Fairy tales offer another field of collectors' interest. The collector who wishes to "list the mystic lore sublime, of fairy lore of ancient time," as James Hogg put it, should familiarize himself with the work of Andrew Lang (1844–1912) and Arthur Edward Waite (1857–1912).

Andrew Lang was an indefatigable gatherer of fairy tales from the folklore of many nations. He published the results in a series of colorful collections illustrated by H. J. Ford, beginning with the *Blue Fairy Book* in 1891 and continuing with the Green, Pink, Yellow, Crimson, and so on. These have been often reprinted and are readily available, although a complete set of the first editions could be brought together today only by assiduous search and at considerable cost. A familiarity with Lang should prove a good starting point for the collector of fairy tales.

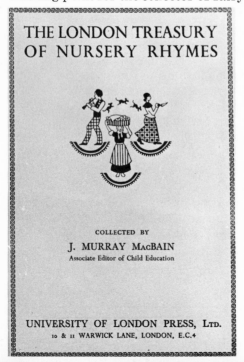

THE LONDON TREASURY
OF NURSERY RHYMES

COLLECTED BY
J. MURRAY MacBAIN
Associate Editor of Child Education

UNIVERSITY OF LONDON PRESS, Ltd.
10 & 11 WARWICK LANE, LONDON, E.C.4

Nursery rhymes present an endless challenge to the scholar and the collector. Collection of John Mackay Shaw.

Arthur Edward Waite performed a similar service for those who may be especially interested in the poetry of fairyland. His anthology of English fairy poetry, *Elfin Music*, was the first of several collections. He published it in London and New York in 1888.

Although England has her elves and sprites, Ireland her leprechauns, Scotland her brownies and bogles, and America is the inheritor of them all, it is to the Danish Hans Christian Andersen and the German Grimm Brothers that we must look for the most frequently published and most widely read books of fairy lore in the English language. Putting together a reasonably complete library of the English editions of either of these writers would test the skill and patience of any collector.

Closely allied with the lore of faery are the tales of the fabulists, deeply rooted in Aesopus of ancient Greece, translated by Croxall and L'Estrange, and imitated by John Gay, William Roscoe, Joel Chandler Harris, and a host of modern writers for children, in prose and verse. John Marchant in 1751 urged upon his fellow teachers to give over the folly of teaching "children truth and morality by direct falsehood, or the highest improbabilities." Lucy Aikin, fifty years later, stated blithely that all such improbabilities had "vanished from our nurseries before the wand of reason." But the children themselves have always preferred the wand of the magician to the wand of reason, and have gone on just as blithely listening to and themselves embroidering these age-old improbabilities. If the collector seeks a field that will not disappear with the passage of time, the fantasy of the fairy tale and the fable is for him.

Before publishers and authors were aware of such a thing as a juvenile market, children had already appropriated to themselves a number of works of fiction intended for their fathers and mothers. Notable among these were *The Pilgrim's Progress, Robinson Crusoe,* and *Gulliver's Travels.* The collector will find the first editions of these early works not only elusive, but unprocurable. But, as successive generations of childhood made heroes of Christian, Crusoe, and Gulliver, new edition followed new edition, and illustrator vied with illustrator to catch the fancy of the boys and girls. There is thus no dearth of collector material in these three titles alone. By the time the nineteenth century had arrived, the world was ready for the golden age of children's literature, which has continued to the present time. The problem confronting the collector is now one of selection. Among the thousands of stories written especially for children, there are many oft-printed classics that include the fantasies of Carroll, Baum, and Grahame, and the tales of Henty and Ballantyne in Britain, and the Little Women Series of Louisa May Alcott and Mary Mapes Dodge's *Hans Brinker and the Silver Skates* in America. As this is written comes the announcement of yet another printing of *Little Women,* still popular after a century.

THE

CASKET;

A

LITERARY PRESENT

FOR

YOUTH.

LONDON:

W. MARSHALL, 1, HOLBORN BARS.

1834.

"The Casket," *gift book, 1834.* Collection of John Mackay Shaw.

Alphabet books are another field of children's book collecting. As discussed in Chapter IV, one of the earliest books in America was the New England Primer, first published in the middle years of the seventeenth century. Charles F. Heartman identified no less than 362 issues before the spring ran dry in the nineteenth century. His bibliographical checklist, *The New England Primer,* issued prior to 1830 with preface, introduction, and index, was published in 1922.

"In Adam's fall, we sinned all. / This life to mend, this Book attend." So began the rhymed alphabet of the Puritans, and their successors have used this device in infinite variety to the present day. Every year the publishers of children's books issue new alphabet books, richly embellished with the work of the best illustrators. The collector who is not afraid of being inundated can have a lot of fun digging in this mine.

Children's reading books are enhanced by alluring illustrations. Indeed the art of illustration has, in the past century, been applied far more to books written for children than to those written for their fathers and mothers, and many collectors concentrate on illustration.

The chapbooks of the eighteenth century, sold from door to door by itinerant pedlars, were adorned with crude woodcuts to charm the eye of the small beholder. Toward the end of the century, Thomas Bewick (1753–1828) overcame the crudity of the medium and transformed the woodcut into high art. He had many pupils and

FRONTISPIECE.

This man has got dainty fine cakes,
Which he will give away:
To those who learn to read and write,
And mind their Prayers to say.

THE

ENTERTAINING STORY

OF

LITTLE

RED RIDING HOOD.

TO WHICH IS ADDED,

TOM THUMB'S TOY.

ADORNED WITH CUTS.

YORK:
Printed and Sold J. KENDREW, Colliergate.

THE
COMIC ADVENTURES
OF
MOTHER HUBBARD, &c.

Mother Hubbard's old dog Tray,
If this account be true,
Had not an equal I dare say,
Come tell me " what think you?"

AND HER DOG. 3

Old Mother Hubbard,
Went to her cupboard,
To give the poor dog a bone,
When she came there
The cupboard was bare,
And so the poor dog had none.

TOM TUCKER.

Little Tom Tucker,
Sing for your supper,
What shall I sing for?
White bread and butter,
How shall I cut it,
Without a knife;
And how shall I marry
Without ever a wife?

Small Chapbooks. J. Kendrew, York, England, ca. 1825. Collection of John Mackay Shaw.

imitators, notably Alexander Anderson (1775–1870), the American engraver. The collector Sinclair Hamilton has given us an invaluable reference tool in his *Early American Book Illustrators and Wood-engravers, 1670–1870,* published in 1958. His collection is now in Princeton University Library.

The children's books of the early nineteenth century were small (about 5″ x 3″) paperbound volumes of 16, 32, or 64 pages. The child had his choice of black-and-white or color, the color being achieved by passing the printed sheets along an assembly line of little girls, one of whom applied the blue watercolor, one the green,

"The Infant's Library" Collection of small books in bookcase. John Marshall. London, ca. 1800. Museum of the City of New York.

one the red, all according to a prearranged pattern. Each of these copies is thus unique and distinct from all the others, and the fortunate collector who manages to get hold of them 150 years later will be struck by the true tone of the color.

As the century advanced, the invention of lithography brought color printing into vogue, and by the 1880's we find Edmund Evans (1826–1905), the engraving and printing genius, encouraging the work of Walter Crane (1845–1915), Kate Greenaway (1846–1901), and Randolph Caldecott (1846–1886). The work of these contemporaries set the stage for the twentieth century, the golden age of children's book illustration. The life and work of Evans, Crane, Greenaway, and Caldecott are available in a number of biographies

THE

PEACOCK " *AT HOME:*"

A SEQUEL

TO THE

BUTTERFLY'S BALL.

———

WRITTEN

BY A LADY.

THE TWENTY-NINTH EDITION, WITH NOTES.

———

LONDON:
PRINTED FOR J. HARRIS, AND SON,
CORNER OF ST. PAUL'S CHURCH YARD.

1819.

The Peacock "at Home" *was an early children's favorite.* Collection of John Mackay Shaw.

LITTLE

PRATTLE

OVER

A BOOK OF PRINTS.

WITH

EASY TALES

FOR CHILDREN.

LONDON:

Publifhed by Wᵐ Darton and Joʰ Harvey.
according to Act of Parliament. Septʳ 29. 1804.

Price 6 pence.

Little Prattle over a Book of Prints with Easy Tales for Children, *published in 1804 by Darton and Harvey.* Collection of John Mackay Shaw.

Little Folks, *A Magazine for the Young.* Collection of John Mackay Shaw.

LITTLE FOLKS:

A Magazine for the Young.

———

NEW AND ENLARGED SERIES.

CASSELL, PETTER, GALPIN & CO.:

LONDON, PARIS & NEW YORK.

and autobiographies, and excellent historical works have been published in recent years which collectors in the field of children's book illustration will find invaluable.

Children's periodicals and annuals offer another field of collecting. From 1825 to 1860, gift books and annuals were the chief literary fare of children as well as adults. The second half of the nineteenth century saw a number of phenomenally successful children's periodicals. The monthly numbers of *St. Nicholas, Wide Awake, The Youth's Companion,* and many others were eagerly awaited, and the annual volumes, consisting of the bound-up monthly numbers, November to October, were on every mantelpiece alongside the Christmas stockings. So popular were they that the printings were large, and though the accumulation of a complete run of most of them requires both time and patience, individual copies frequently appear and are not beyond the range of the impecunious collector.

The *St. Nicholas* magazine first appeared in 1873 under the able editorship of Mary Mapes Dodge, and her successors continued it after her death in 1905 until the late 1920's, after which it declined despite several abortive efforts to revive it. Mrs. Dodge introduced American children to the stories and poems of Laura E. Richards, Frances Hodgson Burnett, Kipling, and many others, and to the illustrations of Palmer Cox, Reginald Birch, and Arthur Rackham.

For the collector who wants to settle on collecting a few authors, or only one, the problem becomes one of selection. Some may prefer to collect well-established present-day writers such as Elizabeth Coatsworth or Doctor Seuss, who have not yet achieved the status of a formal bibliography. Explorations in the writings of these contemporaries of our own have the excitement of uncharted regions that will appeal to the more daring. Others may prefer to collect the books of those who charmed an earlier generation of children. Some

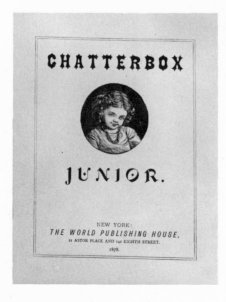

Chatterbox Junior, *a children's periodical of 1878.* Collection of John Mackay Shaw.

Chatterbox, *1919, a children's periodical founded by J. Erskine Clark.* Collection of John Mackay Shaw.

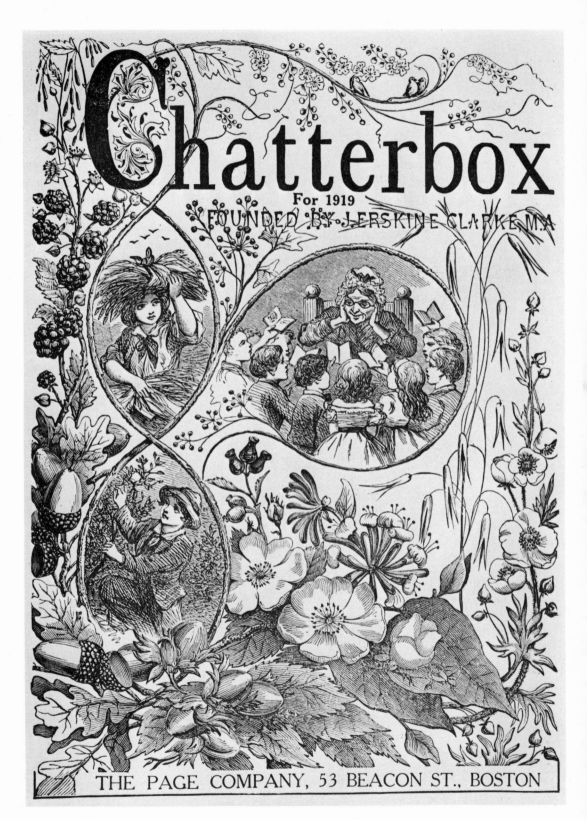

Chatterbox

For 1919

FOUNDED BY J. ERSKINE CLARKE, M.A.

THE PAGE COMPANY, 53 BEACON ST., BOSTON

of these books have become classics and are frequently reprinted. This is in some ways an easier field to cultivate, for their work has been thoroughly documented and extensive bibliographies are available to guide the collector every step of the way. The collector of Robert Louis Stevenson has George Mackay's six-volume catalogue of the Beineke collection to lean on, and no Riley collector can get lost who has before him a copy of the catalogue prepared by the Russos for the Indiana Historical Society. Another author who is a favorite with collectors is Rudyard Kipling. It was Mary Mapes Dodge of *St. Nicholas* who first prevailed on the uncrowned laureate of the British Empire to write for children, and "The Jungle Books" were the immediate result. The stories first appeared in that magazine in the early nineties, and were published by The Century Company in two volumes in 1894 and 1895. *Kim* came along in 1901, *The Just So Stories* in 1902, and *Puck of Pook's Hill* in 1906.

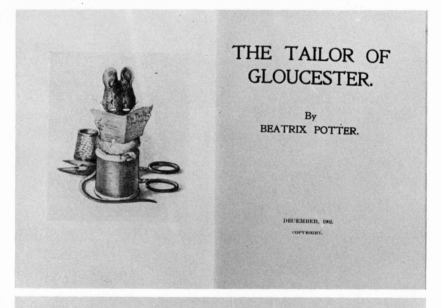

Top: *The privately printed first edition of Beatrix Potter's* The Tailor of Gloucester. *Collection of John Mackay Shaw. Bottom:* The first trade edition. *Collection of John Mackay Shaw.*

The work of Kate Greenaway, the English artist-author, is much admired and much collected. Her neatly dressed, rosy-cheeked girls and boys appeared in a series of books published by Routledge eighty years ago, and are still being published by Warne. Her drawings greatly influenced the trend of children's fashion on both sides of the ocean, and she had many imitators. Her first book, *Under the Window*, appeared in 1878 and was followed by *A Day in a Child's Life* in 1881 and *Marigold Garden* in 1885. Her almanacs, alphabets, and birthday books are much in vogue. An excellent account of her life and work, profusely illustrated, will be found in *Kate Greenaway* by M. H. Spielmann and G. S. Layard, published in 1905 and recently reprinted. Collections can also be made of such authors as Beatrix Potter, Kenneth Grahame, George Macdonald, Charles Kingsley, Walter de la Mare, Lewis Carroll, and Edward Lear.

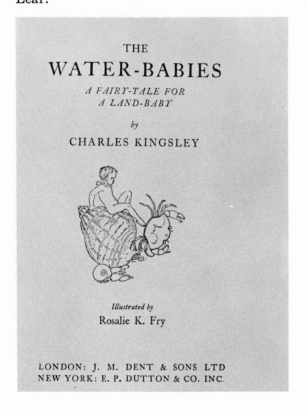

One of the numerous illustrated editions of a children's classic. Collection of John Mackay Shaw.

Riddle Books

The riddle as a means of imparting knowledge originated in the hieroglyphics of Egypt, and all books were first published in hieroglyphics. This rebus method was later used for Bibles and was popular for about eighty years. In the mid-eighteenth century *The Hieroglyphick Bible with Emblematick Figures* was published in England by T. Hobson, with illustrations by Thomas Bewick. *A Curious Hiergloptick Bible for the Amusement of Youth* was published by Isaiah Thomas in Worcester, Massachusetts, in 1788, and

CHARADE.

The puzzle page of Our Young Folks. Collection of John Mackay Shaw.

A New Hieroglyptical Bible for the Amusement and Instruction of Children, with cuts by Alexander Anderson, was published in New York by the Bookseller (John Reid) in 1796. The only copy of this very rare book is in the American Antiquarian Society in Worcester, Massachusetts. A similar hieroglyptical Bible was published by Harper in 1837 with illustrations by John Adams, and such little Bibles continued popular for many years. Riddles as an aid to education were especially favored in the eighteenth century. The Riddle or Guess Book was thought proper reading for children. There were guesses in *Mother Gooses Melodies* in 1760. Hugh Gaine, New York publisher, put out *Food for the Mind, a New Riddle Book*, in 1762. This book was also printed by Isaiah Thomas in 1794. It is a tiny little book, 2½ inches by 3⅞ inches. *The Puzzling Cap, a Collection of Riddles,* was listed among the little books for the "Instruction and Amusement of all Good Boys and Girls" by Boston booksellers in 1772. Anna Green Winslow also speaks of it in her diary. This little book, 2 inches by 4 inches, is printed on rough paper and has a faded-blue paper cover. It includes twenty-five woodcuts with accompanying riddle verses. In 1818 an edition was published by H. & E. Hosford of Albany, New York. A copy of this edition, once owned by Hannah Morse, aged eight in 1823, is now in the New-York Historical Society. Other guess books of the eighteenth century included *Merry Tales of the Wise Men of Gotham, The Sphinx or Allegorical Lozenges,* and *Guess Again.* Newbery of London published many of these riddle books. In 1781 a little book titled *Thomas Thumb. A bag of nuts ready cracked or Instructive*

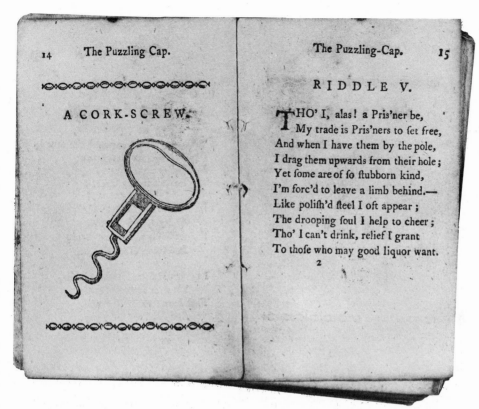

A CORK-SCREW.

RIDDLE V.

THO' I, alas! a Pris'ner be,
My trade is Pris'ners to fet free,
And when I have them by the pole,
I drag them upwards from their hole;
Yet fome are of fo ftubborn kind,
I'm forc'd to leave a limb behind.—
Like polifh'd fteel I oft appear;
The drooping foul I help to cheer;
Tho' I can't drink, relief I grant
To thofe who may good liquor want.

2

The Puzzling Cap, *London, 1795.* Rare Book Department of the Free Public Library of Philadelphia.

Fables, Ingenuous Riddles and Merry Conundrums, was published by Newbery. In 1787 Isaiah Thomas reprinted this book and another riddle book, *The Big Puzzling Cap.* There was a little chapbook called *Birds and Riddles* by Miss Polly and Master Tommy, published by J. Kendrew of York, England. These little chapbooks that were reprints of volumes sold by pedlars began to deluge America in the eighteenth century. They were also reprinted by Isaiah Thomas. In 1805 *A Pretty Riddle Book for Little Children,* by Christopher Conundrum, was published in Newburyport, Massachusetts. It contained thirteen riddles in rhyme and was illustrated with woodcuts. *The Whim Wham,* a collection of riddles, charades, questions, and transpositions, was published by Johnson & Warner in Philadelphia in 1811. The book has a decorative frontispiece of a mother, with a book, and three children sitting on a rustic bench. The prolegomenon in verse is as follows: "Life's a medley all agree, / This Book's a medley, you will see, / Sometimes serious, often gay, / Showing like an April day, / Sunshine for the Youthful mind, / And serious thoughts for those inclin'd: / Words transpos'd, Enigmas rare / Charades compos'd with puzzling care; Riddles, for those who like them best, / And questions to amuse the rest."

Title page and frontispiece of The Whim Wham: or, Evening Amusement, *Philadelphia, 1811.* Rare Book Department of the Free Public Library of Philadelphia, Rosenbach Collection of Early American Children's Books.

Miss Polly & Master Tommy's Collection of Birds and Riddles. *J. Kendrew, York, ca.1825.* Collection of John Mackay Shaw.

This man cries Muffins, eve and morn
And you'll of them partake;
But if to learn your book you scorn,
You don't deserve a cake.

POLLY and CANARY BIRD.

Polly be quiet, let the Canary sing,
It can't hurt you poor innocent thing,
Nature has form'd us to unite in love
Go you to school and don't it move.

THE RIDDLE BOX.

REBUS.

VENT F

V

OGETHER

CHARADE.

My first comes from the Emerald Isle,
  Or else is given in play;
My second is a useful grain,
  Or else a crooked way.

My last is silver, paper, shell.
  Sometimes 't is ruddy gold;
Or else it is a Scottish word—
  At least, so we are told.

My whole, though hoarded by the sire,
  Is wasted by the son.
With all the hints that I now give,
  My meaning must be won.

SYNCOPATION.

My name, as you will plainly see,
Denotes a flower, but not a tree;
Syncopate, then give me hay,
And you can ride me far away.

NUMERICAL ENIGMA.

AM composed of 20 letters:

. My 12, 13, 15, 7, 8, 20.   Hark! how merrily they
g on this crisp Christmas morn.

. My 16, 17, 1, 5.   A twinkling little light, that led
Eastern seekers to our Lord.

. My 18, 15, 16, 17, 13.   Dear St. Nick to the hearts
his patrons brings this!

. My 2, 3.   Little reader, it 's only I!

. My 9, 19, 11.   Light in this form was the key to a
nd discovery.

. My 12, 13, 8, 14, 4, 6.   A tree or its fruit.

My whole, dear friend, sincerely I wish you.

CROSS WORD.

My first is in bugle, but not in horn.
My second in meal, but not in corn.
My third is in oyster, but not in clam.
My fourth is in sheep, but not in lamb.
My fifth is in cut, but not in shave.
My sixth is in good, but not in brave.
My seventh is in dance, but not in jig.
My eighth is in sloop, but not in brig.
My ninth is in prune, but not in fig.
The letters placed rightly, all clear and distinct.
Will show you a quadruped long since extinct.

A page of puzzles from "The Riddle Box" in St. Nicholas of January, 1874, and the answers in the February issue. Collection of John Mackay Shaw.

120

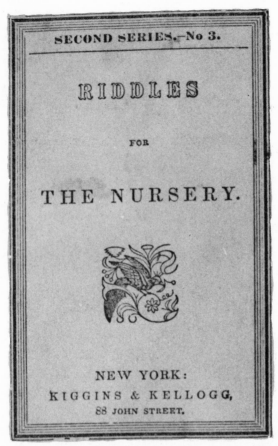

SECOND SERIES.—No 3.

RIDDLES

FOR

THE NURSERY.

NEW YORK:
KIGGINS & KELLOGG,
88 JOHN STREET.

Riddles for the Nursery. *Kiggens & Kellogg.* Collection of John Mackay Shaw.

In 1824 Sidney's Press, New Haven, Connecticut, published *The Riddle Book—for the Entertainment of Boys and Girls.* It has a frontispiece by Alexander Anderson. Anderson also did the illustrations in the *Juvenile Riddle Book*, a tiny book of riddles in verse with cuts illustrating the bees, a squirrel, a cannon, fox-chase, fire, a sword and a drum, and other subjects. *The Columbian Riddler* or *Entertaining Puzzle Book* was published by S. King in New York in the 1820's. There are enigmatical engravings of a cat, mouse, kite, and other objects of interest to children. This was probably an English reprint. *The Picture Riddler*, illustrated by Ann Anderson Maverick, was also published in New York in the first half of the nineteenth century. In the scrapbook of Ann Anderson Maverick there is a clipping of the frontispiece which she engraved for *The Picture Riddler*. A book of riddles and charades was published in Cooperstown, New York, in 1829, and in 1832 Mahlon Day of New York published *Riddles for the Nursery for All the Good Boys and Girls in the United States.*

The interest in riddles and puzzle books increased in the nineteenth century. *The Sphinx or Allegorical Lozenges* was reprinted. *Merry's Book of Puzzles* was put out by the editors of Merry's

Museum (1841–1862), and *The Child's Token,* by Samuel Colman, New York, 1841, contained six riddles in verse together with steel engravings and woodcuts. *Riddles for the Nursery* was published by Kiggins & Kellogg in the 1850's. In 1878, the *Home Book of Puzzles* was published by Smith and Porter in Boston. Lewis Carroll, the creator of *Alice in Wonderland,* wrote several books of mathematical puzzles, but these were not for children. For the collector there were many riddle and puzzle books published in America at the end of the century which are worthy of a collection today. These include *Guess,* 1901; *Guess Again,* 1901; *Jest Nuts,* 1903.

In the first quarter of the nineteenth century children's magazines began to print pages of riddles. *The Juvenile Miscellany* published by Putnam & Hunt in Massachusetts (1826–1832) contained pages of charades and conundrums. The columns of puzzles in *The Youth's Companion* called "Nuts to Crack" included enigmas, charades, rebus, double acrostics, geographical puzzles and conundrums. Peter Parley's Magazine, 1837, has an illustration entitled "Little Girls Guessing Riddles," together with a short article explaining different kinds of riddles—an enigma, "This sort of riddles have been inserted in this magazine"; a charade, a rebus, and a conundrum. "Merry's Museum," 1841, also included puzzle pages.

By the middle of the nineteenth century, when the juvenile magazine came into its own, practically every one of the magazines in-

Little Girls Guessing Riddles. Peter Parley's Annual, *1837.* Collection of John Mackay Shaw.

LITTLE GIRLS GUESSING RIDDLES.

cluded a page or a column of riddles. Those in *Beeton's Boys Annual* were in verse accompanied by unique cuts set within the framework of a cat's head, a heart, or some other interesting form. The column in *Demorest's Young America* was titled "Evening Amusement," and the mast cut shows a family sitting around a table. The puzzles included geographical enigmas, charades, rebus, anagrams, and enigmas. The puzzle pages of *Children's Friend,* published in England in the 1860's, included lessons in English history and geography. "The Riddle Box" in *St. Nicholas* included charades, rebus, double crostics, anagrams, decapitations, and hidden words. Some were in verse. There were also puzzles in diamonds and squares, and a chess puzzle. The puzzle page of *Our Young Folks* was called "Round the Evening Lamp," and that in *Wide Awake* was "Guess Work." There were also puzzles and riddles in *Chatterbox, Little Folks,* and other children's magazines.

The majority of the little riddle books are rare, and, considering their frail makeup, it is remarkable that any have survived the wear and tear of use. Almost every library or private collection of children's books includes a few of the little riddle books. The tiny crude cuts and amateur verses were too fascinating to resist. Riddle books also give a record of early American printers of children's books. A few years ago such books were cheap. Today, most of them are still comparatively inexpensive.

Puzzle title page, Demorest's Young America, *1873.* Collection of John Mackay Shaw.

The county of [rose emblem] and [horn] -ED cattle, but especially for a breed of

is famous for its large black [horse] [sheep] which produce fine lon, [comb] -ING wool.

The chief town Leicester has some large manu- [mill] connected with the woollen trade, and [boy reading] F- for the sale of cattle, sheep, and [cheese on plate]

It is an ancient place, and still has some very [timbered house] Near the town are the ruins of [ruins] where the noted [portrait] died. The town of

[tree] -EY-DE-LA ZOUCHE is famous for its mineral [springs/vessels] A large quantity of hemp is G- [tree and boat] -N in the neighbourhood of [castle tower] -DONNINGTON.

Hinckley has a large and ancient [church] The other towns of note are Market Bosworth, Melton- [man mowing] -BRAY, on the River [eye] Loughborough, and Market Harborough.

LEICESTERSHIRE

Riddle page from The Children's Friend, *January, 1872.* Collection of John Mackay Shaw.

Autograph albums of the John Vogler children (1831–1833). Hand-painted floral decorations and messages in German script and English. John Vogler House, Old Salem, Winston-Salem, North Carolina.

The history of the humble autograph album begins with the German *Stammbuch* or *Album Amicorum*. The first of these books with hand-painted coats of arms, autographs, and inscriptions in Latin or German date back to the sixteenth and seventeenth centuries and are related to the old tourney books in which the participant of a tournament registered his credentials. The *Album Amicorum* was a heraldic autograph album. Later it was used by students in German universities or while traveling in their *Wanderjahr*. Thus sketches of scenes and places gradually took the place of coats of arms. The *Stammbuch* was also popular among the bankers and merchants of Augsburg and Nuremberg in the seventeenth and eighteenth centuries. Some eighteenth-century *Album Amicorums* are filled with sketches of amusements, feastings, drinking, and obscenities, but there were also interesting hunting and hawking scenes, love ballads, music, rhyming, and acrostics. In addition to the hand-painted scenes, many of these books are written on old colored marbled papers.

In the eighteenth century Lord Chesterfield, in his famous letters to his son, advises him to "keep a blank paper book which the Germans call an album," but, instead of scribble, collect worthwhile material. Thus, although the album idea started in Germany, it spread to England and the continent. At the end of the eighteenth century albums were illustrated with silhouettes. There are several Album Amicorums in the print department of the Metropolitan Museum of Art that date from the late eighteenth century. The album of Gedenkboek Myner Golde Vrinde (1785–1824) is decorated with silhouettes, sketches, and verses mostly in German script, but when the owner of the album travels to India there are many salutations written by English friends. Another Liber Amicorum (1785–1859) has silhouettes and hand-colored drawings. The verses are written in English, French, German, and Spanish. These rare hand-decorated albums with their original sketches, careful penmanship, fine old marbled and watermarked papers, and leather bindings were gradually replaced by more ordinary volumes. However, up through the 1830's, albums contain much handwork and such embellishments as hand-painted flowers or figures, bits of needlework, or hairwork. The hand-cut or painted silhouette was also a popular means of ornamentation. Silhouettes and locks of hair are found in many of the late-eighteenth century and early-nineteenth-century albums. Some autograph albums were made up entirely of silhouettes and there were also hair autograph books. Many of these books were handmade of sheets of rough paper and had covers of cardboard or wallpaper.

A handmade silhouette album in the print department of the Metropolitan Museum of Art contains profile silhouettes together with autographs of all the members of the 1823 graduating class of Bowdoin College. Such an album is a rare collector's piece for, though each member of the graduating class may have owned one, the class in 1823 was undoubtedly small.

The hair album was equally rare and interesting. In the late eighteenth century, hairwork became the rage in Europe, and as early as 1763 Charles Oliver Bruff, New York silversmith and jeweler, was advertising hairwork. Other well-known silversmiths and miniature painters advertised hairwork from this time on through the first quarter of the nineteenth century. Particularly valued was the lock of hair of the departed one which was encased in rings and lockets and often dissolved and painted into a memorial picture. The Victorians became addicted to hair jewelry and not only was it made by experts, but amateurs took up plating and weaving of hair, and numerous books of instruction were printed. Thus, it is not strange to find that locks of hair were gathered for the autograph book. Many books contain a few locks fastened to the page together with a verse. There were also rare books of hair autographs that might form a class in themselves if enough of them were found.

The hair autograph book of Miss Chloe P. Thayer, dated 1838, is now in the Henry Ford Museum. It is a homemade book with a wallpaper outer covering. The book contains pages of samples of hair of her various relatives and friends, together with their autographs. The hair of the girls or women is braided and fastened in circles or chains by a sealing wax on which is stuck a small cut-out piece of heart-shaped colored or printed paper. The hair of the men is arranged in a simple loop, but it too is usually fastened with a heart. Some pages contain a verse, and one page has a rough sketch of a child entitled "Rossalina with her lap full of roses." On another page the hair is arranged to imitate a penmanship flourish. This decorates a four-line verse. The salutation to "Miss C. P. Rutland, Vt." indicates that the album may have come from that locality.

As the nineteenth century advanced and sentimentality became rampant, the album increased in popularity, and many companies in England and America were printing autograph albums. Some albums included plates of steel-engraved landscapes and sentimental pictures. The covers were usually of imitation leather embossed and ornamented with gilt decorations. An album with autographs dated New York and Brooklyn between 1835 and 1859 has pages of embossed hand-colored flowers including the moss rose, heart's ease, the passion flower, the convolvulus, and the amaranth, together with appropriate verses. There are also pages of short verses from well-known Victorian poets that extolled virtue, contentment, maternal love, and other homely virtues. The other pages are divided into spaces in the form of rectangles and ovals with embossed borders, and in these spaces the autograph and verse or other salutation is written. This particular book in the Metropolitan Museum of Art is embellished with original drawings and water-colors, and steel engravings are also cut and pasted on the pages so that the book becomes a sort of scrapbook. By the mid-nineteenth century the autograph album became the rage. The book had started as a sentimental record of friendship among adults, then of younger ladies and gentlemen. It was initiated as a gracious ceremony among adults, many of them talented, so that early albums contain not only sketches but often original poems. But later in Victorian days the autograph album became the hobby of schoolgirls, many as young as ten years old, and its contents no longer had any artistic value.

The autograph albums afforded a popular pastime which lasted throughout the Victorian era, but has now passed out of style. Since it records history and a mode of life of another era, the old autograph album now becomes a collector's item. The covers of early albums were often of fine tooled and gilt leathers with the owner's name impressed in gilt letters. Others were found in black papier-mâché adorned with flowers of mother-of-pearl and arabesques. The title pages were a lacework of gilt or embossed scrolls.

A book of poems by Mary Elliott, *The Sun Flower or Poetical Truths* published in London in 1822, contains a long narrative poem "The Albums" on the content of two girls' albums.

Harriet's Album

"Come shew me your Album," cries Harriet to Jane. . . .

"I have verses and riddles, and all sorts of news." . . .

Contents of Jane's Album:

Jane had not pretty verses sought
Or asked from ev'ry friend a thought. . . .
But she selected, with much care,
Accounts of things, saying when and where.

The pages of early-nineteenth-century albums are also sprinkled with contemporary verses and rhapsodic testimonies to the charm, wit, and beauty of the owner of the album. The content of the verses reflects the sentiment and homely virtues of the Victorian age, and the belief in God and Heaven, and the sentimental interest in death. The writers approached their pages with dignity, and evidently deemed it an honor to be asked to fill a page.

Although the authorship of many of the verses is original, others cannot be traced; but there are album verses by such well-known poets as William Wordsworth, who wrote the following verse in an album in 1835:

Small service is true service while it lasts;
Of friends, however humble, scorn not one;
The daisy by the shadow that it casts
Protects the lingering dewdrop from the sun.

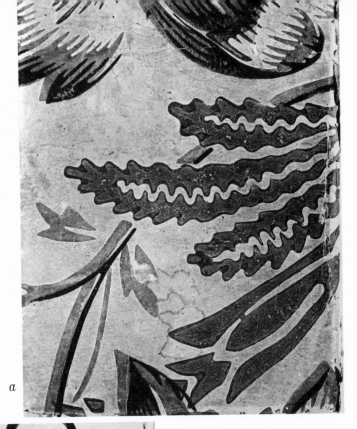

a

Hair album of Chloe P. Thayer, 1838. (a) Wallpaper cover. (b) Frontispiece water color. (c) Page with hair designs. (d) Page with poem and hair flourishes. (e) Page from album. The Henry Ford Museum.

b

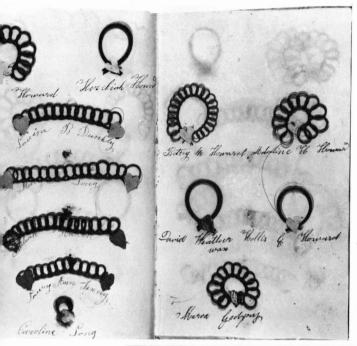

c

d

'Tis sweet to meet affections smiles
Beaming from those we dearly love
Artless and free from every guile
To meet them thus is sweet to roam

Miss C. P. T.
Rutland

e

Miss Chloe P. W. Thayer ;

Book   1858

I'll never forget the friends
Whose locks adorn these pages
The distance far from them;
I am; the different collows
They possess; the different
Virtues to; and this for each
I'll Cherrish Cherrish
A fond Rememberance

There are also album verses by the Irish poet Thomas Moore, and the following verse shows his impatience with the custom of album-writing, which had become a nuisance:

"To Lady J——y, on being asked to write in her album: O albums, albums, how I dread / Your everlasting scrap and scrawl, / How often wish that from the dead / Old Omar would pop forth his head / And make a bonfire of you all!"

Francis Scott Key wrote the following album verses:

My Sister's Album 1857—To My Sister:
"I think of thee, of those bright hours
Rich in life's first and fairest flowers.
When childhood gay delights were ours,
My sister."

He also wrote this verse in Miss Triplet's album:

"You ask, fair maiden, for one line, but I must give you three,
For a couplet at the least, for the rhyme's sake there must be,
And a Triplet for your name's sake therefore take from
F. S. Key."

An album of Octavia Walton, who was the daughter of the first civilian governor of the territory of Florida, is dated from 1827 to 1832, and contains a nine-line poem attributed to Edgar Allen Poe. The album was recently acquired at a nominal price by Columbia University. Albums containing autographs of composers, Civil War heroes, and other famous people, including the "400" of New York, are in the manuscript department of the New York Public Library.

However, the heyday of the album was the late Victorian era which began in the 1850's and lasted into the 1860's and 1870's. The introduction of colored lithography made the album cheap and within the reach of all. The format also included groupings of pastel blue, green, and pink machine-made papers. Now small inexpensive albums were available, and every little girl possessed one. In the majority of these later albums we no longer find verses but only couplets, and their cheap sentiment is repeated in doggerel that suggests a pony was available which contained "verses suitable for albums." Indeed, albums were so popular that manuals of etiquette of the 1870's included pages of "Selections for the Autograph Album" and here we find the traditional affectionate and sentimental quips which have now become album literature. The "Sunbeam" album, 1857–1862, gives a representative sampling of the scribblings:

"Little things / On little wings / Bear little souls to heaven."

"Way over here / Clear out of sight / These four lines / I quickly write." June 24, 1863.

"I loved thee on earth / May I meet thee in Heaven."

"When far away in distant lands, / And stranger forms you see / Forget not him who penned these lines / To wake thy memory."

There were now also pages with a network of card outlines on which each person wrote his name and inserted pressed flowers or a lock of hair.

In an album of 1878, which has a blue plush cover, the following verses spell the deterioration of popular album autographs:

"As the ripple follows the ship at sea / So may happiness follow thee."

"May your joys be as deep as the ocean / And your sorrows as light as the foam."

And finally, in my mother's tiny album of 1879, which is ornamented with penmanship flourishes and small floral decals with such mottos as "Friendship" and "Thine Forever," the following verses are typical writings of the day:

"May your life Leila Perry / Never be sad, but always be merry, / And righteousness your thoughts attend / Is the wish of your teacher and friend. J. W. Thompson."

"To Leila. On this blank page / I claim one spot / to write these words / Forget-me-not. Minnie Nason."

"Leila—I wish you a husband gallant and true, Proud of himself, but prouder of you; / Handsome and witty, cheerful and gay, / One you may love, honor and obey. Nellie Vile."

"To Leila. May you live happy / and have good times / And marry a man / Supplied with dimes. Your friend Walter." San Felipe, Jan. 5, 1881.

Autograph albums were printed in New York as early as the 1820's. J. C. Riker, New York publisher and bookbinder, was the best-known printer of albums at this time. In addition to a fancy gilt or colored frontispiece, many albums had pages of landscapes and sentimental engravings. An album printed by Riker in 1835 has the following layout: A colored frontispiece, "The Mothers Joy," and black and white steel engravings of popular subjects of the era: "Body Guard of Shriek of Boron"; "Ischia Y. Procida"; "The Pet Lamb," by W. Collins; "The Father's Pride," and "Capture of Andre." "The Token Album" is illustrated with engraved pictures with such subjects as Judas, The Sentinel, and a boy with his dog.

Another album published by Riker in 1835 is illustrated with engravings of A. B. Durand, including Catskill Mountains, Falls of Sawkill, Fort Putnam from a painting by Robert Weir, Delaware Water Gap, and Weehawken. Because of these engravings, this album is a valuable collector's item. In 1855 Riker brought out the "Jenny Lind Album" which contained engravings by John Sartain of Philadelphia, including "Forest Worship" and "The Summer Stream." Other engravings found in albums published by Riker include "The Rose," "A Dream," "Friendship," "A Refusal," "A

Album of Leila Perry, 1879–1881. Cover and Spenserian frontispiece. Collection of Catharine Ashley.

Frontispiece of Jenny Lind Album, 1855–1856. Manuscript Division, New York Public Library.

Wish," "The Attraction of Love," "The Slighted," and "Inovocation." As early as 1826, Durrie & Peck of New Haven, Connecticut, published an album called "Leaves of Affection," and one called "The Token Album." The popularity of these lasted through the 1860's when albums with similar titles were published by Leavitt & Allen of New York. The "Leaves of Affection" was illustrated by pages of steel engravings including the following titles: "The Gift," "Visit of Charity," "The Maiden," and "The Orphan's Guard."

From 1879 through the 1880's the craze for albums is evidenced by those given as premiums and advertised in the pages of *The Youth's Companion*. The Companion Autograph Album given for the name of one new subscriber had embossed gilt covers and gilt edges and facsimile autographs of famous personages on the cover; the inner pages not only included autographs of distinguished poets, historians, statesmen, and journalists, but stanzas of poems in a facsimile of the handwriting of the poets, including Longfellow, Whittier, Bryant, John Howard Payne, S. F. Smith, and Emerson.

Autograph Albums for every Reader of the Companion.

School boys and girls delight in obtaining the autographs and sentiments of classmates and friends. We want our readers to have just such an album as will please them. We have selected from a large variety of styles the choicest. We know you will find the album you want.

Autograph Album No. 374. Autograph Album, Ivory, No. 554. Each given for one new name.

These two albums are alike inside. Each album contains one hundred and eighteen pages of plain tinted paper—and seven full-page elegant floral and landscape designs in natural colors. The covers are the same in design. The humming-birds with their beautiful plumage, the calla lily, the yellow and red roses and the green foliage, all embossed or raised on the cover in natural colors, make it more beautiful than we can show in our cut. No. 554 is embossed on imitation of ivory, and is truly elegant. Either one of these two books given for one new name. Price

of each book, $1.00. **Postage and packing of each, 10 cts.,** when sent as a premium or purchased.

Tennyson's Complete Poems and Companion Autograph Album. Both given for one new name, and 15 cts. additional.

This edition of Tennyson is very popular. It includes his late poems, such as "Queen Mary," "Harold," and the "Ballad of the Fleet." It contains 553 pages, many full-page cuts, and clear type. Size of book, 5x6 inches. Usual price, $1.00. Cloth bound.

The Companion Autograph Album. This Album has embossed gilt covers, round corners, and gilt edges. It contains fac-simile autographs of distinguished poets, historians, statesmen, and journalists. *In addition* we have reproduced in the handwriting of the authors, stanzas from many famous poems. These we photographed directly from the original manuscript.

The album contains the usual number of blank pages for collecting the names of your friends. This edition of Tennyson and Companion Autograph given for one new name and 15 cts. additional. Price of both, when ordered at one time, $1.25. **Postage and packing, 15 cts.** Price separately, 90 cts. each. **Postage and packing on each, 10 cts.**

Golden Floral Autograph Album, No. 94. For one new name.

This Autograph Album is made of Leatherette, and is a perfect imitation of Red Russia Leather. The floral decoration of the cover is in gold, green, purple, and two shades of red. The Album contains one hundred and twelve pages of fine paper in four different tints and six full-page beautiful colored floral chromos. The corners are round.

Given for one new name. Price, $1.00. **Postage and packing, 10 cts.,** when sent as a premium or purchased.

Autograph Album, No. 534, Bric-a-brac Pattern. Given for one new name, and 15 cts. additional.

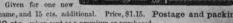
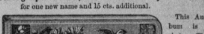

This Album takes its name from the style of embossing on its cover. The variety of articles shown on cover is certainly legion. The colors are old gold, gold and silver. The paper is tinted. The cover is Imitation Russia Leather.

Given for one new name, and 15 cts. additional. Price, $1.15. **Postage and packing, 10 cts.,** when sent as a premium or purchased.

Autograph Album, No. 474. Given for one new name.

This Album is rich in plainness compared with some of the other patterns we offer to our subscribers. It contains 112 pages of tinted paper. The cover is imitation of Red Russia, with an embossed decoration in centre of back cover and a gilt border and lettering on front cover.

Given for one new name. Price, $1.00. **Postage and packing, 10 cts.,** when sent as a premium or purchased.

Autograph Album, No. 644 (Butterfly Illustrations). Given for one new name and 15 cts. additional.

This Autograph Album is exceedingly choice. The cut shows the ornamented cover. The birds and foliage are embossed in natural colors. The Album contains 112 pages of delicately-tinted paper and seven full-page cuts of brilliantly-painted butterflies and foliage.

Given for one new name, and 15 cts. additional. Price, $1.15. **Postage and packing, 10 cts.,** when sent as a premium or purchased.

Albums given as premiums. The Youth's Companion, *1879.* Collection of John Mackay Shaw.

There were also quotations from Lincoln, Holmes, Sam Woodworth, Cozzens, President Hayes, James T. Fields, John G. Saxe, Louisa Alcott, Dickens, Wilkie Collins, Queen Victoria, Victor Hugo, Thackeray, Irving, and Bayard Taylor.

The covers of these albums were sometimes red, gold, silver, or blue leatherette with floral decorations in gold, green, purple, and red. Some covers of late autograph albums were embossed with patterns of flowers and birds or a bric-a-brac pattern or imitation ivory; some were covered with blue or garnet plush often with nickel-plated letters. There are inner pages of colored chromos of elegant flowers and landscapes, birds, or brilliant butterflies.

The value of an old autograph album from the collector's standpoint lies first of all in the realm of nostalgia. As with all objects relating to children, we associate them with our own childhood. Thus any old album can take on interest and associational value. The monetary value increases if the album contains the autograph of a well-known person or celebrity, and, if it should contain a verse or bar of music in the poet's or composer's hand, the value is tripled. An album with watercolor sketches, silhouettes, or hair autographs is rare and valuable. There are many old albums in attics, trunks, at the Good Will and Salvation Army stores, and even in antique shops. The collector should get there ahead of the crowd, and there is always the chance that he may find an album with a valuable autograph hidden in its yellowed pages.

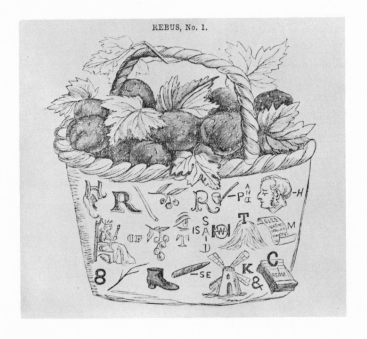

REBUS, No. 1.

6

Children's Furniture

hildren's furniture has been neglected by collectors for many years partly for lack of interest, but also because there is a scarcity of the earlier pieces and, until recently, the available nineteenth-century pieces were not considered worth collecting. As time goes on, however, collectors are becoming more and more interested in children's furniture.

Children's cradles, chairs, and standing stools were used in Europe from early ages and are illustrated in books as early as the fifteenth and sixteenth centuries. However, furniture was comparatively scarce in America in colonial days. It consisted of chests, tables, and stools of carved oak, high-backed closed chairs, and settles. There were also Brewster ladder-back chairs, and a rare Carver-type armchair with three horizontal spindles in the back and a rush seat. Furniture of these types was probably made to order for children, as few such pieces have been preserved. However, a Carver-type child's chair is in the Wadsworth Atheneum. A high chair of Brewster type with rush seat, belonging to Cotton Mather, is preserved in the Worcester Antiquarian Society, and there is also one in the Chicago Art Institute. Needless to say, these are very rare. There were also Pilgrim slat-back chairs made for children. Children's chairs in Dutch New York in the early eighteenth century were made with serpentine slat backs or reeded bannister

American cradle, paneled oak, seven-teenth century. Other furniture of the same period. Left: Chair-table. Center: Carved chest. Right: Carver armchair. The Metropolitan Museum of Art.

Wicker cradle with hood. Delaware, ca. 1830. Index of American Design.

backs, and some wing chairs were also in use. Wing-back rocking potty-chairs were used in eighteenth-century England and were also made and used in colonial America.

There are also cradles dating from colonial days that are in museum collections. The Mayflower cradle owned by the Pilgrim William White is made of wicker; its date is 1620 and it is in Pilgrim Hall, Plymouth, Massachusetts. It is of Dutch origin. A similar wicker cradle is in the Essex Institute, Salem, Massachusetts, as is a heavy wooden cradle that once belonged to the Townes family of Topsfield, Massachusetts. Samuel Sewall records a swinging wicker cradle in his diary of the seventeenth century. A paneled

Baby in wicker basket. Joseph W. Stock, ca.1840–1850. Collection of Edgar William and Bernice Chrysler Garbisch.

oak cradle made for the children of Dr. Samuel Fuller, one of the "Mayflower" passengers, is now in the Wadsworth Atheneum, Hartford, Connecticut. It is of chest form with projecting turned foot posts, a hood which served to keep out draughts, and a gallery of spindles which allowed the mother to keep watch on the child. A galleried oak cradle is in the Rhode Island School of Design, and a paneled cradle with closed hood is in the Metropolitan Museum of Art. In the Museum of Fine Arts, Boston, a room from West Boxford, Massachusetts (1675–1704), contains an oak-paneled cradle with wooden canopied top. This type of cradle continued to be made

Cradle on frame, painted, early nineteenth century. Shelburne Museum.

Room from West Boxford, Massachusetts. Portrait of Robert Gibbs and child's paneled and hooded cradle. Museum of Fine Arts, Boston.

Doll's hooded cradle, early nineteenth century. Shelburne Museum.

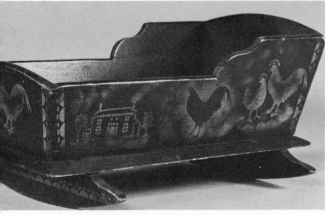

Doll's cradle, painted black with stenciled decoration in gilt. Old Sturbridge Village.

in the eighteenth century. The later cradles were often made of mahogany, pine, or maple. Similar cradles were also made for dolls both in the eighteenth and nineteenth centuries, and are illustrated in many children's books. Many of these cradles were homemade, but some were made by cabinetmakers. *The Impartial Gazetteer,* New York, August 9, 1788, describes a federal procession in which cabinetmakers and their apprentices, working on a stage drawn by horses, completed a cradle and a table during the march. One cabinetmaker's name was Robert Carter; he was later in business with Thomas Burling, well-known furniture and cabinetmaker of New York City. In the mid-eighteenth century there were cradles of Windsor-chair design. A Windsor cradle with rockers on legs and a turned-spindle hood was made by Saver & Frost, Boston. This type is extremely rare. There were also Windsor cradles with head and foot similar to chair backs; others were of oval bassinet type. In Pennsylvania Dutch country the cradles were scrolled and decorated with painted or stenciled hex signs or floral patterns and often had heart-shaped hand holes. An eighteenth-century cradle in the Essex Institute swings on turned posts. It is made of maple. Another is barrel-shaped. Cradles continued to be made matching the various furniture styles in vogue down through the eighteenth and nineteenth centuries.

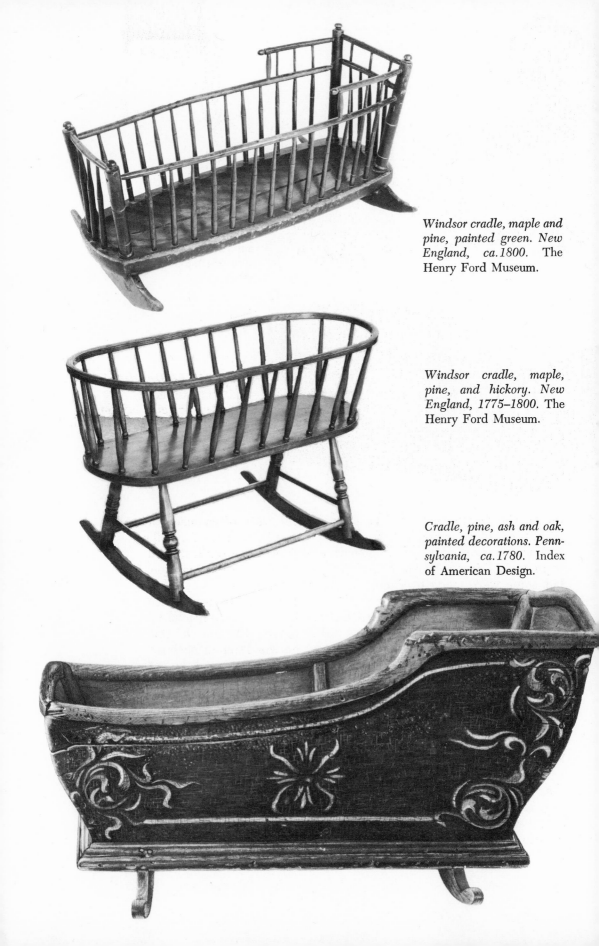

Windsor cradle, maple and pine, painted green. New England, ca.1800. The Henry Ford Museum.

Windsor cradle, maple, pine, and hickory. New England, 1775–1800. The Henry Ford Museum.

Cradle, pine, ash and oak, painted decorations. Pennsylvania, ca.1780. Index of American Design.

Pine cradle painted in flame pattern of red, green and yellow. Red interior, green rockers. Ohio, ca. 1850. The Henry Ford Museum.

Barrel cradle, painted green with holly decoration, nineteenth century. Old Sturbridge Village.

The baby's walking cage, or standing stool, was designed to teach a child to walk. Early standing stools or go-carts are to be seen in European prints and paintings and date as far back as the fifteenth century. An early example in America dating from about 1700 was made of turned maple. The frame sits on a square base with a wheel at each corner. Two spindle supports go up from three sides and connect with a small square frame support above, which holds the child's body. One section of the top frame swings out to admit the child's body, and a bar across the front carries wooden rings which can be slid back and forth. A simpler go-cart of the same type is shown in the child's book, *Little Prattle Over a Book of Prints*, which was published in 1801. Crude homemade standing stools were made of panels of wood. These had no wheels or casters and were only made for standing. A small shelf in front held the child's toys. In the nineteenth century these were known as baby tenders, and baby jumpers, and some were made with springs to allow the child to jump up and down to exercise his legs. Several companies in Boston and New York, including G. Halsted and George Tuttle, advertised baby jumpers in the 1850's. The firm of Richardson,

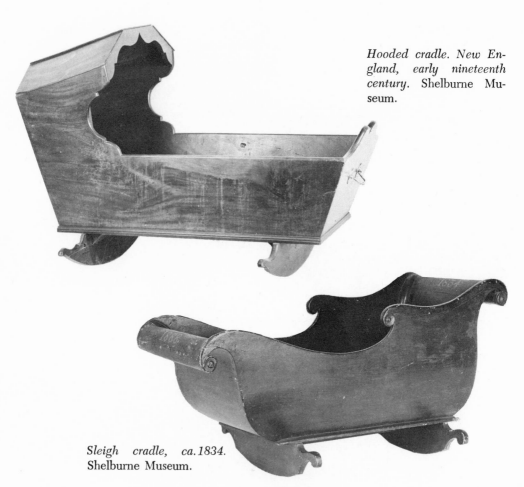

Hooded cradle. New England, early nineteenth century. Shelburne Museum.

Sleigh cradle, ca. 1834. Shelburne Museum.

Cradle with spindles and posts, ca. 1850. Made by Jasper Longe. Index of American Design.

Baby's walking cage, maple, turned posts, ca. 1700. Ginsburg & Levy, Inc., New York.

Child's wicker walking cage, early nineteenth century. Collection of John Mackay Shaw.

TODDLEKINS.

Who's coming?
  Can you ask it?
Toddlekins,
  In his basket.

"Rattle, rattle,"
  See him walking;
"Coo, coo,"
  Hear him talking.

Hear, hear:
  Now he's saying,
We can work
  While he's playing.

Hark! hark!
  Is he crying?
Here, there,
  See us flying.

Walking cage fastened to ceiling, late nineteenth century. Collection of John Mackay Shaw.

THE CHAIR BABY JUMPER SONG.

"Oh Mother, I see, Willie weighs 30 pounds."

Respectfully dedicated to all

MOTHERS

BY

Lith by J.H.Bufford

RICHARDSON, EMMONS & CO.

Proprietors of this celebrated Chair

BOSTON

Published by **OLIVER DITSON** 115 Washington St.

C.C. Clapp & Co. Boston.   S.T. Gordon, N. York.   Beck & Lawton, Philad?   H.D. Hewitt, N. Orleans.   D.A. Truax Cinn.

Entered according to act of Congress in the year 1856 by O.Ditson in the Clerks office of the district Court of Mass.

ALL PURCHASERS OF THE "CHAIR BABY JUMPER" ARE ENTITLED TO A COPY OF THIS MUSIC.

[1856]

Emmons & Co. gave away copies of a song, "The Chair Baby Jumper Song," with each purchase of a chair. The chair, as illustrated on the title page of the sheet music, was a high chair set on a sturdy frame and equipped with springs which let the chair go up and down. The song was published by Oliver Ditson of Boston in 1856, and the lithograph of the chair was by J. H. Bufford. Throughout the nineteenth century, baby jumpers and baby tenders were advertised in Chicago, Muncie, Indiana, and other cities. A low chair on wheels was advertised as a Child's Chariot Chair by the Hale, Kilburn Mfg. Co. of Philadelphia in 1879.

By the mid-eighteenth century there were several cabinetmakers who made children's furniture, as evidenced by the advertisements of the time—*New York Gazette or Weekly Post Boy*, April 18, 1765: "Andrew Gautier. Windsor chairs, children's dining and low chairs"; *South Carolina Gazette*, June 23, 1766: "Windsor chairs imported from Philadelphia. A large and neat assortment of Windsor chairs made in the best and neatest manner and well painted, high back'd, low back'd, sack back'd children's dining and low chairs" (In the eighteenth century the child's bow-back, knuckle-arm Windsor chair was referred to as a "sack-back" chair.) ; "To be sold by Jonathan Hampton. Windsor chairs, Children's dining and low chairs."—*New York Journal or General Advertiser*, May 19, 1768.

A child's high chair, Windsor bow-back type, made ca. 1750, is in the Brooklyn Museum. It is of oak stained brown. A bow-back Windsor high chair of interesting country workmanship is in the Shelburne Museum, and children's bow-back Windsor armchairs of the late eighteenth century are to be seen at Old Sturbridge Village. These are made of hickory, maple, or pine, and are painted red or green. There were also small Windsor rockers painted to imitate wood graining, and rare Windsor love seats in children's sizes. Firehouse Windsors and captains' chairs were also made in children's sizes. Windsor high chairs and low chairs were arch-back, loop-back, or spindle-back with a horizontal comb, or rod-back with vertical spindles and a horizontal slat at the top. Windsor chairs are made of several kinds of wood. The spindles are usually of hickory, the seats of pine, and the turned legs of maple or birch. The eighteenth-century children's Windsor chairs are rare and expensive, although many were made. Windsor high chairs are rarer than arm or side chairs.

◄ *"The Chair Baby Jumper Song,"* 1856. The New-York Historical Society.

Bow-back Windsor high chair, eighteenth century. Shelburne Museum.

Windsor high chair, oak, ca. 1750. Index of American Design.

Child's Windsor armchair, 1780–1790. Old Sturbridge Village.

Seven-spindle comb-back Windsor high chair, early nineteenth century. Henry Francis du Pont Winterthur Museum.

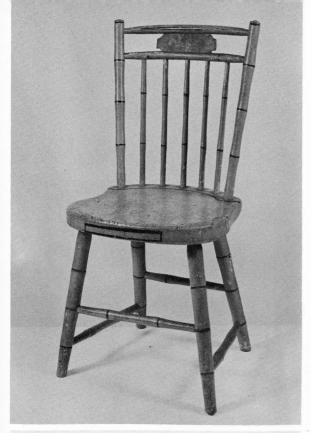

Painted chair with bamboo spindles, early nineteenth century. Henry Francis du Pont Winterthur Museum.

Windsor side chair for child, 1765–1810. Henry Francis du Pont Winterthur Museum.

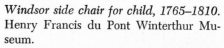

Hitchcock-type high chair, pine, maple, hickory, and poplar, painted yellow, 1820–1840. The Henry Ford Museum.

Painted high chair, ca.1830. The Henry Ford Museum.

Child sitting in painted Hitchcock-type chair, ca.1840–1850. Artist unknown. Collection of Mrs. Helen Slosberg.

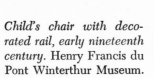

Child's chair with decorated rail, early nineteenth century. Henry Francis du Pont Winterthur Museum.

In the early nineteenth century, children's Windsor and fancy

chairs were made by many chair makers. William Buttre advertised
children's chairs in the *Albany Advertiser* in 1815; in the *Albany
Gazette,* January 10, 1819, John Bussey advertised as follows: "Has
constantly for sale a large assortment of elegant, well-made and
highly finished fancy chairs, settees, conversation, elbow, rocking,
windsor, and children's chairs of every description." George G.
Jewett also advertised children's chairs. "A choice assortment of
Grecian, curled maple, rosewood, fancy, bamboo, cottage windsor,
and common chairs, rocking, sewing and children's do. Also settees
of all descriptions" (*Albany Gazette,* December 24, 1819). The cuts
accompanying these advertisements are of elaborately styled chairs
which were certainly not made for children, but children's portraits
of a later date show Sheraton bamboo-style chairs and painted
chairs with rush seats and painted decoration. Some had painted top
rails with colorful fruit and leaves similar to Hitchcock-type chairs.
Children's chairs were also made at the Hitchcock factory. Other
fancy chairs had turned legs and stretchers and a turned rail at the
top of the back. These were painted brown or green lined with
yellow and had cane seats. A Windsor child's rocker had painted
decoration of red apples and green leaves and yellow, green, and
gold stripes, and a Windsor cradle settee in the Monmouth Historical Society, New Jersey, has vertical bamboo spindles and a top
panel decorated with a gold stencil of oak leaves. Many ladder-back,
rush-seated armchairs were made for children in the nineteenth
century. These are usually painted black or dark brown, and the
splats are crudely decorated with painted leaves and flowers. There
were also crudely made country children's armchairs, high chairs,
settees, and benches. These were usually made of pine or hickory,
and the seats were of hickory splints, woven raw hide, or cow hide.
The posts had crude turnings and the slat backs were without
decoration. In the southern states the chairs were often made by
colored slaves, and those in the West were made by ranchers or
cowhands. Many of these date as early as 1830; others were made
late in the century, but the style and construction are similar.

Children's chairs also followed the furniture styles. In addition to
early slat-back and Windsor styles, there were rare Queen Anne,
William and Mary, Chippendale, Adam, Sheraton, and Hepplewhite
chairs for children. These were all made to special order and thus
were never in quantity. Perhaps the majority of those found today
are of English make. However, such children's chairs were made in
America, although mention of them is seldom made in advertisements or recorded in inventories of household goods. Children's
chairs, tables, and chests of drawers made in the more sophisticated
styles such as Sheraton, Hepplewhite, and Chippendale are to be
seen in museum collections. In design, materials, and workmanship
they often compare favorably with larger pieces of the same period.
There were also later carved poster beds made in children's sizes.

In the 1840's John Hall of Philadelphia and Joseph Meeks & Sons

Child's table with circular tapered legs and disk feet, 1735–1790. Henry Francis du Pont Winterthur Museum.

Victorian child's chair, stained maple with gilt scroll and line trim and floral stencil, 1860–1875. The Henry Ford Museum.

Child's rush-seated ladder-back armchair, nineteenth century. Painted dark brown with white bands and floral decoration on back splats. Old Sturbridge Village.

Tom Thumb rocking chair, 1860–1870. Shelburne Museum.

Child's circular pedestal table, nineteenth century. Henry Francis du Pont Winterthur Museum.

"Little Miss San Francisco." Charles Nahl, ca. 1853. Maxwell Galleries, San Francisco.

of New York were making mahogany furniture in children's sizes with scroll arms, legs, and feet. There are small children's rocking chairs made of mahogany or walnut with upholstered seats and backs that are duplicates of larger ones. Victorian pedestal tables were also made in children's sizes. An 1852 portrait in the Shelburne Museum shows two little girls seated on a small Victorian sofa which seems to be a child's piece of furniture. An 1872 catalogue of "Cane Seat Chairs" put out by Philander Derby of Gardner, Massachusetts, includes children's straight chairs and rockers of walnut with cane seats. Boston and Lincoln rockers as well were made in children's sizes. P. T. Barnum ordered a set of walnut furniture made for Tom Thumb. It consisted of a sofa, two armchairs, two side chairs, and a rocking chair. Duplicates of the set were available, and one of these is now in the Shelburne Museum.

In the Lion House, Salt Lake City, a set of three chairs that once belonged to Brigham Young includes a child's armchair. The chairs are walnut, lined with color, and have a panel of spindles in their backs. They were made in 1850 but they are of a type that continued to be made for several decades.

Child's Eastlake-type rocking chair, maple, 1875–1890. The Henry Ford Museum.

A child's portrait painted by Charles Nahl of San Francisco in 1852 shows a unique child's chair of ebony or papier-mâché with inlays of mother-of-pearl. This chair may have been imported from China or France, or may have been made to order in San Francisco. Late in the nineteenth century, 1880–1900, when the folding chairs with carpeting upholstery were in style, these were also made in children's sizes, as were Eastlake rockers, and, in the early twentieth century, Morris Chairs.

Babies' high chairs were made in wicker and bentwood as well as in the Windsor style. Children's cribs and cradles of Windsor spindle type were advertised by Jordan & Moriarity of New York in 1886. "Folding spool cribs, $3.00, Spindle cradles, Windsor cradles $1.00 up." There were also wire bassinets. In the 1880's Thoesen & Uhle, New York, advertised walnut cribs, cradles, and high chairs, and Eastlake ash folding cribs. Rattan cribs, cradles, and chairs were also made at this time. Children's chests were advertised by J. Watrous of Andover, Connecticut, in the 1870's. Potty-chairs were made with Windsor spindles and also in wicker and rattan. There were chairs for children with cut-out side supports in the shape of cats, dogs, horses, and other animals similar to those seen on old carrousel seats. These were painted with crude representations of the animals. All these various types of chairs are available for collectors today.

It is not certain when baby carriages were first made, but from the middle of the nineteenth century, many companies throughout the East and Middle West manufactured them. The first baby carriage manufactured in America was reportedly made by Benjamin Potter Crandall, who set up shop in Westerly, Rhode Island, in 1840. The carriage was similar to today's baby strollers. It had only two wheels with a wooden arm in front to draw it by and a metal support that balanced it when stationary. It was made of basswood, with an upholstered seat and a folding canopy. Later, there were two wheels at the front of carriages and a bar at the back for pushing. Benjamin Crandall had four sons, all of whom were in the business in Connecticut, New York, or Pennsylvania, and the Crandalls were the best-known manufacturers of children's carriages, rocking horses, velocipedes, and sleds in America in the nineteenth century. Through the years the Crandalls took out many patents for the improvement of their carriages, which developed into elegant four-wheeled affairs with springs and a fringed top. In 1870 a patent was taken out for a combination carriage and sleigh. The Crandalls also made doll carriages. When English-style carriages with solid bodies went out of style, they made reed and rattan carriages. Adolph Meinecke of Milwaukee operated a factory in the 1860's, after the Civil War, specializing in carriages made of willow. He grew his own willow trees and employed several hundred workmen in his factory. In addition to children's carriages, Meinecke made hobbyhorses, shooflies, wagons, croquet sets, and

Baby carriage, ca. 1850–1860. Index of American Design.

Baby carriage. Ludlow Toy & Mfg. Co., Vermont, ca. 1874. Index of American Design.

willow baskets. After 1873 a silver-plated brand name was attached
to every hobbyhorse and sleigh made by Meinecke. Colby Brothers
of Waterbury, Vermont, also made willow children's and dolls'
carriages and baskets. The Holman Baby Carriage Company of
Chicago made wicker carriages, cradles, and carriages on runners
which sold for from $8 to $30. In 1888, Luburg Manufacturing
Company of Philadelphia advertised: "Baby Coaches, 100 different
designs." In 1889 W. B. Nutting Company of Boston advertised in
The Youth's Companion: "Carriages of bleached reed with wheel
guards, 'satine' upholstery, a plush roll and a 'satine' parasol with
scalloped edge." They sold for $15 each. At this time also, Dann's
patent reclining go-cart was made of rattan at a works in New
Haven, Connecticut. There were also wicker doll carriages with
parasols and flowered upholstery. The third annual catalogue of the
Vermont Novelty Works, dated 1866, shows forty different kinds of
carriages and perambulators of the two- or three-wheeled variety.
They ranged in price from $2.50 to $11.75. Other nineteenth-century
makers of children's carriages were Brown & Eggleston of New
York; C. W. F. Dare of New York; A. Christian of New York;
Bradford Kingman of Boston; Simeon Clark of Amherst, Massachusetts; and Cole and Ballard of Newark, New Jersey. All these
companies also made hobbyhorses and wagons or sleds, in addition
to carriages.

7

Hobbyhorses, Shooflies, and
Velocipedes

obbyhorses were known to Greek children in the time of Socrates and Horace, and were illustrated in a French Book of Hours of the fifteenth century. Other medieval French, German, and English books and prints showing children's games also illustrate the hobbyhorse. These early horses were sticks with the carved figure of a horse or horse's head to which a leather strap or rein was attached. These were made with and without wheels.

This type of hobbyhorse was also the first kind used in America. However, in the eighteenth century, the advertisement of William Long, cabinetmaker from London, in the *Pennsylvania Packet*, September 10, 1785, states that "he makes Rocking-Horses in the neatest and best manner, to teach children to ride and give them a wholesome and pleasing exercise." The accompanying cut shows a horse with saddle and bridle set on double rockers with a small platform for mounting. Similar horses were illustrated in the advertisements of Brown & Eggleston of New York and Bradford Kingman of Boston in the 1850's.

Gideon Cox of Philadelphia was making hobbyhorses in 1825. There were also many homemade hobbyhorses. These were usually made from a plank of wood with carved-out rockers and were low-set without feet. A seat support and a carved horse's head were made separately and attached. Rocking horses of this type of Penn-

The Hobby Horse. Artist unknown, ca. 1850. National Gallery of Art, gift of Edgar William and Bernice Chrysler Garbisch.

Rocking horse, white with black spots. Index of American Design.

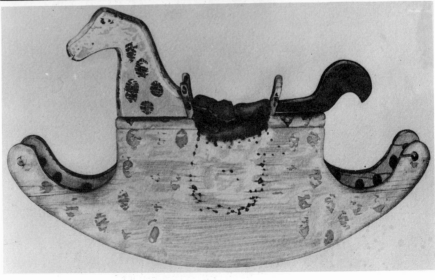

Rocking horse, early nineteenth century. Index of American Design.

The Country Hobbyhorse. St. Nicholas, 1870's, vol. 1, page 2. Collection of John Mackay Shaw.

THE COUNTRY HOBBY HORSE

Rocking horse. Benjamin P. Crandall, 1853–1856. Index of American Design.

Child's rocking chair, mid-nineteenth century. Index of American Design.

sylvania German craftsmanship are now in Bucks County Historical Society, in Doylestown, Pennsylvania, in the Philadelphia Museum of Art, and in the Henry Ford Museum. They date from the
early nineteenth century and are crudely carved and painted. Many
local carpenters and carvers made hobbyhorses. In the 1840's the
well-known ship carver Woodbury Gerrish of Portsmouth, New
Hampshire, made a horse of painted wood with upholstered saddle
and leather ears. The horse's head was set in the rocker, and there
were no legs or body.

Benjamin Potter Crandall made his first hobbyhorse in the
1840's. It had a crude head and cut-out legs set on rockers, it was
called the "Cricket," and was an improvement on one imported from
Germany. The Crandalls also experimented with stuffed horses but
found the wooden horses more practical. The bodies of these horses
were painted tan, red, gray, or dappled with swirls to suggest hair.
They had leather ears, real horsehair tails and forelocks, leather and
metal trappings, and a carpet seat. The feet were set on the ellipse

160

Child's rocking chair, mid-nineteenth-century. The Henry Ford Museum.

Rocking horse, mid-nineteenth century.

The Rocking Horse. Youthful Recreations. *J. Johnson, Philadelphia.* Collection of John Mackay Shaw.

Mary Emma Woodward and brother Harry with large rocking horse and horse-headed cane. George Morrison, 1820–1893. Shelburne Museum.

"Whoa! Who'll have a ride with me?" St. Nicholas, *vol. 1, part 2, 1874.* Collection of John Mackay Shaw.

Rocking chair with cat cut-out sides. Shelburne Museum.

of the rockers. These large rocking horses were made in several pieces—legs, head and neck, and body, which were later assembled. They were dipped or sprayed with paint, and the eyes and noses were finished by hand. Some expensive horses were covered with real hide and had manes and tails of horsehair, while cheaper ones had cows' manes and tails. Crandall also made a seat set between two cut-out horses on rockers, and this became the popular "shoofly." Another company manufactured a contraption consisting of an upholstered carriage seat set on a rocking platform to which were attached two horses' heads so that two children could "drive the horses" at once.

In the 1860's the Crandall horse was put on springs affixed to a platform and advertised in *Harper's Weekly* as "J. A. Crandall's Patent Spring Rocking Horse." These were large horses, and their hind legs fastened to a platform by a strong metal spring gave considerable movement. In 1865 W. A. Marqua of Cincinnati, Ohio, took out a patent for a similar horse which could be obtained with a sidesaddle for girls. Marqua became one of the most important manufacturers of hobbyhorses. Morton E. Converse of Rindge, New Hampshire, also made large hobbyhorses.

"OH NO, I'M A BUILDER NOW."

"Please, Hugh, let me be driver;
I'll keep right here by the side."
So, whip on his shoulder, he marches
With more than a soldier's pride.

Now back, calling, "Mamma, mamma,
Here's a 'tunnin' hop-stool for you;
'Twas growing close up by the fountain,—
Oh dear! *now* what shall I do?

"WHOA! WHO'LL HAVE A RIDE WITH ME?"

What, you, my brave young farmer?
"Oh no, I'm a builder now.
I build big barns and houses;
Come out and I'll show you how."

Soon, starting, he hears the oxen
Dragging the big hay-cart;
And, houses and barns forgotten,
Away he flees like a dart.

Why, there is my fast, wild Rollo,—
Whoa! who'll have a ride with me?
This small one's my work-horse, 'Daisy;
He's steady and old, you see."

So, hour after hour, through the daytime,
He works and plays with a will;
The brown little hands always busy,
The quick little feet never still,

"SO, WHIP ON HIS SHOULDER, HE MARCHES."

In the 1860's, after the Civil War, moving vehicles of all sorts were popular toys, and there were many companies in Boston, New York, Philadelphia, and midwestern cities supplying the demand not only for hobbyhorses but for velocipedes. A velocipede was a cart set on wheels with a horse's head attached to a small front wheel. It was propelled by sticks which were connected with the back wheels. The same style vehicle was later propelled by foot pedals. There was also a three-wheeled velocipede.

The first American velocipede was made by Benjamin Potter Crandall in the 1840's. One velocipede was made with a horse's head of wood and a sulky seat, and patented as the "American Trotter." Many different types were made, including a "Cantering Tricycle" that rocked up and down in a horselike motion as it moved forward, and some vehicles had four wheels instead of three. In the 1860's "Cantering Horses" were set on three wheels, and, as the rider rocked the horse, the wheels turned and the tricycle moved forward. In 1877 the first Montgomery Ward catalogue to advertise toys included an illustration of a three-wheeled tricycle with metal seat and pedals and guiding handle attached to the larger front wheel. These were made in four sizes and sold for from $3.15 to $5.85. The catalogue also illustrated several kinds of rocking horses, carriages, wagons, and sleds. The Fairy Tricycle made in Elyria, Ohio, had an upholstered seat with fringe. It was set between two tall wheels and had a steering stick attached to a small front wheel, and was propelled by pedals. "The Boys Companion Tricycle" and Kohler's adjustable tricycle were made in Canton, Ohio, in 1889.

Tricycle. W. J. Bowen & Co. Wide Awake Advertiser, 1881. Collection of John Mackay Shaw.

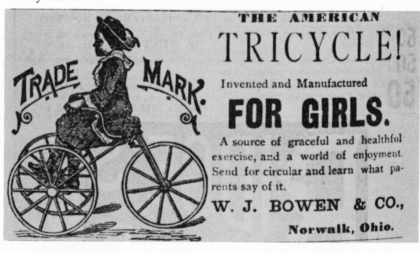

Scene on the Common. Boy on tricycle. Dolls in doll carriages. The Nursery, *vol. 15, no. 4, 1874.* Collection of John Mackay Shaw.

Bicycle, ca. 1840. Index of American Design.

8

Children's Dishes

Pottery and Porcelain, Britannia

mall dishes of several sizes have been made by European potteries since the sixteenth century. Tea sets and dinner sets for children were made in potteries in Germany, Holland, and England in the eighteenth century. At first the children's sets were not made in wholesale quantities, but only for the wealthy who could afford such things. However, at a later date, such sets of dishes became quite common. Children's sets were made in several sizes depending upon their purpose; however, the most complete and interesting sets were those made for the child herself to use. The average-size set usually had teacups measuring about two inches, plates from one and one-half inches to two and one-half inches, and platters or meat dishes and covered tureens about six inches in size. Of course the exact sizes vary with each set.

In general, children's dishes copied adult dishes in form and style of decoration, although, beginning with the nineteenth century, the decoration related more to the child's interests, such as Mother and child scenes, animals, and games. The early small dishes were also usually executed with care and the hand-painted design was of good workmanship. Early majolica and hand-painted Nuremberg pottery as well as stoneware, rare Lambeth delft, salt glaze, Whieldon, and

A LITTLE girl,
  Quite well and hearty,
Thought she'd like
  To give a party.

But as her friends
  Were shy and wary,
Nobody came
  But her own canary.

Little girl's tea party. St. Nicholas, *vol. 1, part 2, October, 1874.* Collection of John Mackay Shaw.

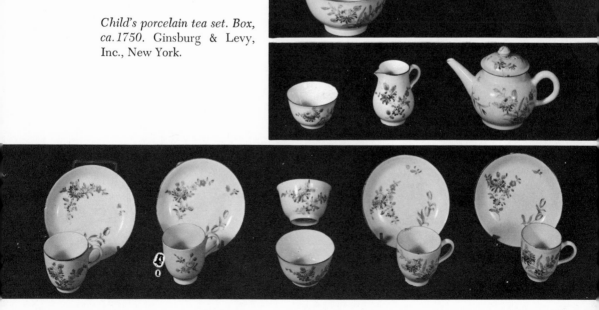

Child's porcelain tea set. Box, ca.1750. Ginsburg & Levy, Inc., New York.

Dolls' tea set, tea leaf pattern, late nineteenth century. The New-York Historical Society.

pierced Leeds ware were also made in children's sizes and in miniature. These tiny miniature dishes are to be seen in English and Dutch dolls' houses of the seventeenth and eighteenth centuries.

One of the earliest children's sets that I have seen is a tea set made by Whieldon. It is of the brown mottled pottery known as tortoiseshell ware and consists of six handleless cups and saucers, not more than two inches in size, a teapot, a hot water pot or coffee pot, a creamer, and a covered sugar basin. The handles and spouts are simple and the covers of the teapot, coffee pot, and sugar basin have plain rounded finials ending in a blunt point. An interesting feature of this set is that metal chains attach the covers to the handles of the teapot and the coffee pot. Tortoiseshell ware such as this was first made by Whieldon in about 1740, and this set was probably made between 1740 and 1760.

Miniature tea and coffee service: Leeds creamware, King's Rose pattern, ca. 1830. Shelburne Museum.

Miniature tea and coffee set. Black transfer on white, scenes with children, dogs and horses, ca. 1830. Shelburne Museum.

Another child's tea set which dates from the eighteenth century was made at Caughley. It is creamware hand-decorated with a black rope pattern of loops and tassels and tiny scattered leaves. The set consists of a teapot, a coffee pot, a creamer, a covered sugar basin, slop bowl, and cups and saucers both with and without handles. Leeds Pottery also made children's dishes in creamware with a raised feather edge, hand-painted borders, willow pattern, and pierced decoration. A blue and white transfer pattern with an oriental scene was also probably made at Leeds or Worcester. Worcester tea sets in blue and gold and in canary yellow and gold have also been found with the crescent mark. A Spode child's dinner set with an oriental design in blue transfer is complete with soup and sauce ladles, salad bowls, and cheese plates. Marked Wedgwood child's dishes include blue Willow pattern dinner sets, and tea sets printed in transfer with one color such as the one made in pink transfer for Queen Victoria. This is similar to another one in pink transfer with scenes of a mother and child sitting in a Regency chair, and of a child riding a hobbyhorse. The edges of the pieces are outlined in blue and the set dates about 1820. Wedgwood also made a child's tea set with exotic birds printed mostly in apple green and edged in black.

Small sets of creamware dishes were made at Leeds and Wedgwood potteries in the eighteenth century. Children's tea sets of Wedgwood creamware were decorated with hand-painted roses.

Child's tea set. Wedgwood Creamware, eighteenth century. Ginsburg & Levy, Inc., New York.

Child's China Trade porcelain tea and coffee service with pink and blue flowers, touches of gold, 1790–1800. The Henry Ford Museum.

Wedgwood also made a small set with a transfer pattern of exotic birds, and a Leeds set was decorated with yellow butterflies. Small tea sets of Bow porcelain had sprays of roses and other flowers. There were also small tea sets of Derby and Worcester porcelain and of Chinese export procelain. In her book, *Chinese Export Procelain*, Jean McClure Mudge quotes from the memo book of Captain Benjamin Shreve, 1819: "D. L. Pickman wishes me to get a small dining set of ware for his children to cost 3 or 4 Dolls. Small number of pieces—if it cannot be had for that then buy a few pieces small ware. They have a tea set." In 1788 Samuel Fleming of New

York wrote Captain Ranall of the "Jay" in Canton: "Purchase also a child's tea set, for my daughter." These small tea sets usually had decorative crests with space for an initial or monogram. One tea set had a design of hearts flaming upon an altar in black and gold. Another set made in 1810 had transfer scenes from the engraving "Playing at Marbles," by Bartolozzi. Many of these sets had tea caddies and cups both with and without handles, and some sets had as many as twenty-four pieces. A small tea set with landscape transfers and gold borders was made by Lowestoft in the early nineteenth century and used by Queen Victoria as a child. Victoria also had a tea set of Leeds pottery.

Some of the loveliest and rarest children's tea sets are made in silver-resist luster on a canary or blue ground. The design is of leaves and conventional flowers, and the cups are handleless. The shapes of the cups, teapot, and sugar and creamer indicate a date about 1820.

After 1830 Davenport made many children's tea sets and dinner sets. One dinner set with a pheasant and fruit is in brown transfer and is complete with plates of several sizes, platters, covered and uncovered vegetable dishes, soup tureens, and a gravy boat. The same set has been found in light blue transfer. Flowing blue and flowing brown children's dinner sets were also made by Davenport, and plain white ironstone and tea leaf ironstone tea and dinner sets were made in the late nineteenth century. Interesting tea sets were made in the Meissen onion pattern and also in spatterware, mochaware, spring, and moss rose patterns. These are much sought after today, but their value is inflated far beyond their real worth.

Miniature Chinese Export porcelain tea set with scenes of game of marbles. Otto M. Wasserman, New York.

Miniature Lowestoft tea set with blue chinoiseries, mid-nineteenth century. Shelburne Museum.

Miniature tea set. Spatterware, peafowl pattern, G. Adams & Son, mid-nineteenth century. Otto M. Wasserman, New York.

Miniature tea and coffee set with blue transfer pattern of pastimes of childhood, early nineteenth century. Shelburne Museum.

Various later Staffordshire potteries, including Spode and Daven-port, made children's dishes in transfer patterns of landscape scenes, a milkmaid and cows, fruit and flowers, and animals. There were also sets with luster bands and sets of pink Sunderland luster. By the end of the nineteenth century almost all children's sets were of cheap Staffordshire floral patterns, or French china, with blue and pink flowers and gilt borders. These sets came in cardboard boxes and were sold in toy shops. They were also given as premiums by *The Youth's Companion* in the 1880's and 1890's. Late-nine-teenth-century sets included transfer illustrations of Jack and Jill and other nursery rhymes, the Palmer Cox Brownies, Kate Green-away children made by Wedgwood and Minton, and the Sunbonnet Babies and Overall Boys.

Children's dishes are shown in several portraits of American children. In the portrait of a child by an unknown mid-nineteenth-century-painter, a little girl is shown with a Britannia tea set on the table beside her. A tea set of similar design was advertised by James W. Tufts of Boston in *The Youth's Companion*, December 23, 1875. Britannia tea sets, table sets, knife, fork, and spoon sets, plates, and candlesticks are also in the list of Britannia toys made by the Stevens & Brown Manufacturing Company of Cromwell, Connecti-cut, and advertised in their catalogue of 1870. The catalogue also illustrates tin A B C plates, toy waiters, cannisters, coffee pots, cups, pails, sprinklers, and knives, forks, and spoons. Some of these articles were painted and decorated with stencils.

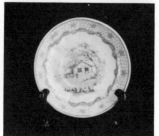

Miniature tea set, John Ridgeway, blue and white transfer, Log Cabin Series, mid-nine-teenth century. Shelburne Museum.

Portrait of little girl in blue dress with toy Britannia tea set. Collection of Edgar and Bernice Chrysler Garbisch.

Child's Britannia tea set, 1850–1860. The Henry Ford Museum.

Child's Britannia tea set. The Children's Museum of Hartford, Connecticut.

Advertisement of James W. Tufts, Boston silversmith, showing child's Britannia tea set. The Youth's Companion, December 23, 1875. Collection of John Mackay Shaw.

Beautiful Christmas Gift!

A Children's Tea Service.

Best of Britannia, formed by hand. Very substantial, and elegantly finished.— **Heavily silver-plated and lined with gold**; handsomely boxed. A most beautiful present for a little girl. Size of Box, 12 in. long, 5 in. high, 7½ in. broad. Price, with Box complete, **$6.00.** Circulars free. JAMES W. TUFTS, 33 to 39 Bowker Street, Boston.

Nineteenth-century children's mugs and plates have long attracted collectors. They are available in a wide variety of patterns and types of pottery from the lusterware and early creamware mugs of Leeds, Bristol, and Liverpool, to the late transfer-printed ironstone. The subject matter that decorates these mugs ranges from early scenes to those of the Kate Greenaway type in the 1880's. One can form a large collection with hardly a duplicate, and prices are comparatively reasonable. Most all children's mugs were made in England and exported to America. Among the earliest mugs, made in the first third of the nineteenth century, are those of creamware decorated with bands of blue, brown, tan, or olive green, together with a name and inscription and sometimes a wreath of hand-painted leaves. These mugs were made in both cream color and canary yellow. The transfer decoration is usually in black, although there are other colors such as vermillion on yellow. One of the mugs of this type has the inscription, "A Trifle from Yarmouth" and these mugs are known as Yarmouth-type mugs. Other inscriptions on Yarmouth-type mugs read: "A Grandmother's Gift," "A Present for Hannah," "A Trifle for William," "For My Sweet Girl," and "A Gift for Jinny." Sometimes a star encloses an initial. Another group of early creamware mugs has the names of children such as Sarah, Martha, Emma, Eliza, Kate, Anne, George, William, Charles, John, James, or Philip painted in black together with a hand-painted band. An early floral-decorated mug has bunches of roses and yellow flowers and is marked "Bristol." A creamware mug with a transfer of a bird's nest and children was made at Liverpool. Sometimes there are pictures in addition to inscriptions. There are scenes of a mother and child, a boy and a house, and a quaint scene of a cow grazing. These have the inscription, "For a Good Child." One group of early transfers on canary ground carries such inscriptions as "A Pony for Edward," 'A Carriage for Ann," "A New Doll for Margaret," "A Harp for Elizabeth," "A Squirrel for Mary," or "A Nightingale for Eliza," together with pictures of the object mentioned. There is also an early black transfer on canary ground with an alphabet border and the inscription, "Come dear child and let me see how you can do ABC."

Another early and rare group of mugs has black transfers of Washington, Lafayette, Adams, or Jefferson on cream or yellow grounds. Many have luster decoration, and there are mugs with copper luster and bands of cream, blue, tan, or floral bands, or transfer patterns and inscriptions. There were also mugs of pink Sunderland luster, and one of these has the incription, "Forget and Forgive" in a wreath. A mug with a scene of a mother and child is

Yarmouth-type painted mugs, ca. 1800–1815.
Society for the Preservation of New England Antiquities.

decorated with pink luster bands, and the well-known pink luster house pattern is one another. Rare mugs are those with silver-resist luster decoration. These have allover geometric patterns or borders of leaves, bands, or scrolls in silver resist on grounds of blue or canary yellow, and sometimes there is an inscription or a scene of a mother and child. A transfer scene of "The Gleaners" with pink luster bands is marked "Davenport." Copper luster decoration is used on Gaudy Welch ironstone mugs made in 1840–1850.

A creamware mug marked "Phillips & Co., Sunderland Pottery" has a scene of a ship and the following verse in black transfer:

> Here's to the wind that blows
> And the ship that goes
> And the boy that fears no danger
> A ship in full sail
> And a fine pleasant gale
> And a girl that loves a sailor.

There were also mugs made in the various patterns of mochaware including checkered, cat's eye, and rope designs.

The Victorians were interested in teaching and instilling in their children the virtues of religion and the righteousness of living, and this is expressed in the series of mugs, "Flowers That Never Fade." These mugs are inscribed with the words "Industry," "Usefulness," "Generosity," "Charity," "Kindness," "Good Humour," and "Liberty." Moral maxims form another group, and such inscriptions as "Idleness is the Parent of Want and of Misery," "Want of Punctuality is Lying," and "Industry is Fortune's Handmaid" appear. There were also religious verses such as "Praise to God," "Evening Song," "Morning Song," and "Early Piety" enclosed in wreaths of flowers. Many late mugs have rhymes, and scenes from children's poems, including the verses of Jane and Ann Taylor and "Dr. Watts' Poems for Children." The mugs with Franklin's maxims from *Poor Richard's Almanack* are among those most sought after by collectors. There were usually two maxims on each mug, but sometimes there were four. One of the most available is "Keep thy Shop and thy Shop will keep Thee." Other maxims include "Industry is Fortune's Handmaid," and "Never Speak to Deceive nor Listen to Betray."

The Reward of Merit series includes "A Present for Serving Well," "A Present for Writing Well," "A Present for Knitting Well," "A Present for Going to School," and "For Attention to Learning." However, the most fascinating mugs are those that definitely relate to the child's daily life, like the series with children's poems and games. The mugs with illustrations of games

Franklin's maxims and other transfers. Society for the Preservation of New England Antiquities.

taken from *The Boy's Treasury of Sports and Pastimes* include
several series made by different potteries. The earliest series includes the following games: ring taw, a marble game; whip top;
shuttlecock; northern spell; French and English; pyramid; and
walk my lady, walk. Other series show playing hoops, skipping rope,
leap frog, and fishing, and blind man's buff. These are printed in
black, brown, red, or blue with crude splashes of red, green, and
yellow. Scenes were also taken from the books *The Peacock at Home*
and *The Butterfly Ball*.

Another attractive series is that of the months of the year. Each
mug has a verse of four lines. A later series of months is marked
"The Seasons."

The series of mugs with pictures of children and animals is
another very popular one with collectors. Included are a child and
dog inscribed "Little Playfellow," and a dog begging for food and
inscribed "Beggars Petition." There is also "Puss' Breakfast,"
"Billy Button" (horse), and "Bird Catchers." A later animal series
includes elephants, tigers, zebra, goats, dogs, and birds. Davenport
made one animal series, and another is marked "Field Sports E.M.
& Co."

There is a variety of alphabet mugs. Some mugs are covered with
allover alphabet patterns and others have a verse for each letter.
Still another series has deaf and dumb symbols. There are mugs
with the stories of Tam O'Shanter, John Gilpin, and Jolly Sailor.

Late mugs were made at almost all Staffordshire potteries and
include blue and white, green, pink, and brown transfers. Clews,
Meakin, Thomas Godwin Adams, and Davenport were among the
makers. Wedgwood also made children's mugs.

A collection of mugs with late transfer scenes can be assembled
with comparatively small expenditure, but the early transfers, hand-
painted, and silver-resist patterns are expensive and scarce.

Plates

Children's plates were not made in as many different patterns as
mugs, although many were made with the same decorations. Some
few plates were made in the late eighteenth century, but most of

*Alphabet plate: chil-
dren's games, raised
ABC border.* Collec-
tion of Mrs. William
Leibowitz.

them date between 1820 and 1860. The most available and most popular type is the alphabet plate. These white or cream earthenware plates usually had alphabet borders, printed or embossed. Some plates had borders of embossed scrolls, dots, daisies, lily-of-the-valley, or roses, or, in rare cases, a flower and a swan. The center of the plate was decorated with a transfer print which was illuminated with crude daubs of color. The transfers are in black, brown, green, red, or blue and the hand-coloring is usually in bright red, green, yellow, or orange. Many of the early plates were made in a series, a half dozen to a set. One series portrays American sports, another shows famous historical places such as Mount Vernon, Plymouth Rock, and the Capitol at Washington. The series called "Our Early Days" depicts scenes in a child's everyday life such as "The Playground" and "Half Holiday." Famous books inspired scenes from *Don Quixote, Robinson Crusoe,* and the Bible.

Many designs included fables, maxims, and moral precepts such as some from Aesop's fables. The most sought-after series is that showing Dr. Franklin's maxims and one with transfer-printed hymns. Later, the "Dr. Franklin's Maxims" series were made by J. & G. Meakin, Clews, and other Staffordshire potters. One group of maxim plates is printed in dark blue and has a border of embossed flowers, fruits, and shells. The maxims on these plates include: "Many a little makes a mickle," "No gain without pain" and "If you would know the value of money try to borrow some." The different makers used different pictures to illustrate the same maxim. The series called "Flowers That Never Fade," used on mugs, is also found on plates. The series of plates with familiar episodes from *Uncle Tom's Cabin* has embossed daisy borders. This is one of the rarest and most-sought-after series. Other series portray domestic and wild animals. Some of these are marked "Wm. Adams & Co." Still another series illustrates Mother Goose nursery rhymes such as "Little Boy Blue."

Alphabet plates: Robinson Crusoe Series, late nineteenth century. Collection of Mrs. William Leibowitz.

Alphabet plates: transfer scenes from Aesop's Fables and Poor Richard's Maxims, early nineteenth century. Collection of Mrs. William Leibowitz.

Black transfer pattern Uncle Tom's Cabin, raised daisy border, 1860's. Collection of Mrs. William Leibowitz.

Alphabet plates with transfer prints of animals. Raised ABC borders. Collection of Mrs. William Leibowitz.

Alphabet plate: transfer, Franklin maxims. The Metropolitan Museum of Art.

A series of alphabet plates had "A is for apple" and "B is for ball" with large letters of the alphabet and an embossed daisy border. H. Aynsley & Co., Longton, made a plate with a sign-language alphabet. One of the most unusual plates is that with the Braille alphabet. Another unusual plate has a border of clock numerals as well as a border of the alphabet so that the child could also learn to tell time. The center has a transfer scene of a boy riding a dog, and is labeled "A Ride on Carlo." Still other plates illustrate "The Village Blacksmith," "The Peacock at Home," "The Sower," "The Plowman," and "The Cruel Boy," the latter showing a boy tying a can to a cat's tail. This plate has an embossed border of roses. The scene is in pink transfer with hand-coloring in pink, green, and yellow. It was made by the Cambrian Pottery at Swansea between 1831 and 1850. There is a plate with a Punch and Judy scene and a haying scene. Plates with religious scenes include the "History of Joseph," "Grace at Meals," and religious poems of which the following is an example:

> "The child that longs to see my face
> Is sure my love to gain
> And those that early seek my face,
> Shall never seek in vain."

In 1903 William Guerin & Company of Limoges, France, made

sets of six children's plates with scenes from Kipling's Jungle Book. These include "Kaas Hunting"; "Mowgli's Brothers"; "The White Seal"; "Toomai of the Elephants"; "Rikki-tikki-tavi"; and "Tiger, Tiger." They are marked with the name of the maker, and with the name of the designer, Mary Bacon Jones.

The majority of the alphabet plates are unmarked. Naturally, those that are marked are more valuable and the early plates made at Leeds Pottery are the most valuable. However, some collectors are interested in the subject matter of the transfer scenes and the decoration of the plate rather than in the maker of the plates. The series with "Dr. Franklin's Maxims," "Aesop's Fables," "Uncle Tom's Cabin," and "Robinson Crusoe" are the most popular and therefore the highest priced. A few years ago children's plates and mugs were cheap, but the price has more than tripled. Prices, of course, depend on rarity, condition, and quality of the transfer.

9

Children's Needlework

I n colonial America children were instructed in diligence and expected to work with their hands. At an early age they were taught to spin and to weave. They wove braids, garters, belts, hat bands, and sundry other articles on small tape looms. They also knit their own stockings. The continued importance of industry in the life of American children in the eighteenth century is shown in the following letter published in *The New York Mercury*, October 16, 1758:

"Needlework. . . . But my Wife's notion of education differs widely from mine. She is an irreconcilable enemy of Idleness, and considers every State of life as Idleness, in which the hands are not employed or some art acquired, by which she thinks money may be got or saved.

In pursuance of this principle, she calls up her Daughters at a certain hour, and appoints them a task of needlework to be performed before breakfast. . . .

By this continual exercise of their diligence, she has obtained a very considerable number of laborious performances. We have twice as many fire-skreens as chimneys and three flourished quilts for every bed. Half the rooms are adorned with a kind of futile pictures which imitate tapestry. But all

Child with golden hair mending dolls. Eastman Johnson. Shelburne Museum.

their work is not set out to shew; She has boxes filled with knit garters and braided shoes. She has twenty coverns for side-saddles, embroidered with silver flowers, and has curtains wrought with gold in various figures, which she resolves some time or other to hang up. . . .

About a month ago, Tent and Turkey-stitch seemed at a stand; my Wife knew not what New Work to introduce; I ventured to propose that the Girls should now learn to read and write and mentioned the necessity of a little arithmetick; but unhappily, my wife has discovered that linen wears out, and has bought the girls three little wheels, that they may spin hukkaback for the servants' table. I remonstrated that with larger wheels they might dispatch in an hour what must now cost them a day; but she told me, with irresistible authority, that any business is better than Idleness; that when these wheels are set upon a table, with mats under them, they will turn without noise, and keep the Girls upright; that great wheels are not fit for Gentle women; and with these small as they are, she does not doubt but that the three girls if they are kept close, will spin every year as much cloth as would cost five pounds, if one was to buy it."

The most interesting record of children's diligence is the sampler. Every little girl, rich or poor, was expected to make a sampler. The sampler was a sample or pattern of stitches, but it also served to teach the alphabet and was an exercise in neatness and perseverance.

The early samplers followed English patterns. They were made of long narrow strips of handwoven linen. The earliest seventeenth-century samplers were made in scattered patterns, but toward the middle of the century the needlework was displayed in horizontal rows. Besides the alphabet there were motifs of fruit and flowers, and stiff little figures of angels, shepherds, and animals such as are seen in old herbals and bestiaries. Motifs included formal borders of strawberry, acorns, Indian pink, pineapple, and fleur-de-lis. The "Tree of Life" was also a favorite motif. The embroidery was worked in hand-dyed, slightly twisted colored silks. The coloring was done in soft shades of greens, blues, yellow, rose, and browns. There were also some all-white samplers in geometric design. The stitches most often used in the seventeenth-century sampler were the cross stitch and the tent stitch, although satin stitch, French knots, and other stitches are sometimes included.

The earliest existing American-made sampler is that of the daughter of Captain Miles Standish, Loara Standish. It is embroidered in bands of conventional flowers in pinks, greens, blue, and brown. A space at the bottom of the sampler includes the verse:

Loara Standish is my name
Lord guide my heart that I may do Thy will
And fill my hands with such convenient skill
As will conduce to virtue devoid of shame
And I will give Glory to Thy Name.

This sampler is in the Pilgrim Hall, Plymouth, Massachusetts. Another seventeenth-century sampler contains the names of Miles and Abigail Fleetwood. The design includes figures of women and a man in Elizabethan dress, and a British lion. A few other seventeenth-century American samplers are recorded, but there are many more dating from the eighteenth century. These can be seen in the Essex Institute, the Fogg Art Museum of Harvard University, the Metropolitan Museum, and other museums as well as in private collections. Some early samplers still remain in the families of the makers. That the sampler was definitely an exercise in stitches is evidenced by the few mentions of the word "Sampler" in the many newspaper advertisements of private schools teaching needlework. Robert Francis Seybolt, who made a study of the newspaper announcements of the private schools of Boston in the seventeenth and eighteenth centuries, quotes only one advertisement with the word "samplar." "Elizabeth Hinche, living in a House of Mr. Jonathan Clark's in Long Lane, does teach plain Sewing, Irish Stitch, Ten(t) Stitch, Samplar Work, Embroidery and other Sorts of Needle Work . . ." (The *Boston Weekly News-Letter,* July 24, August 21, 1755).

There were similar announcements in the New York newspapers in the 1760's, but, again, few that mention "samplars." Almost all the seventeenth- and eighteenth-century samplers contain verses of a religious nature, and some include the Lord's Prayer, Creed, or Ten Commandments or the verse that begins:

Jesus permit thy gracious name to stand
As the first effort of an infant's hand.

The verse is one of the fascinating factors in sampler collecting. Verses are usually of a moral or religious nature, but there are certain variants, such as this, that were particlarly popular:

Mary Jackson is my name
America my nation.
Boston is my dwelling place,
And Christ is my salvation.

This verse records the concern with youthful industry:

This needlework of mine can tell
When I was young I learned well
And by my parents I was taught
Not to spend my time in nought.

The verse which gives the child's age has an added value. Several samplers in the Metropolitan Museum collection were made by children nine years old. The following verse records a child of ten:

> Elizabeth Briggs is my name, and with my
> Hand I have Wrought the Same in the 10th year
> Of my age, Salem, February 15th, 1805.

Toward the end of the seventeenth century the sampler became wider and shorter, and early in the eighteenth century a floral border began to be used. In the middle of the eighteenth century such subjects as Adam and Eve in the Garden of Eden, landscapes, plants in pots, hunting scenes, and houses were popular. The houses

Sampler: Elizabeth Wood, age 9. American, 1815. The Metropolitan Museum of Art, Rogers Fund, 1913.

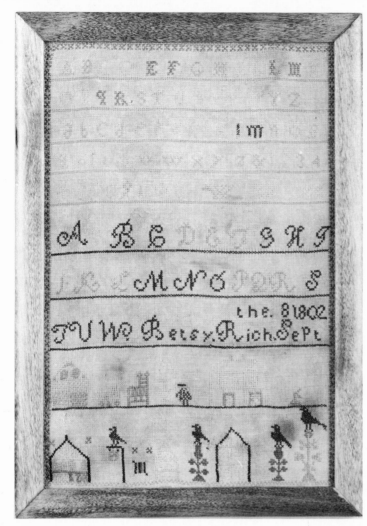

Sampler on coarse linen, Betsy Rich, 1802. Shelburne Museum.

pictured included New England farm houses, brick Georgian mansions, school buildings, and churches. There are samplers with public buildings such as those at Harvard, Yale, and Princeton universities. Buildings of Brown University are on samplers made at Miss Polly Balch's School in Providence, Rhode Island. Many existing samplers were made at this school. But the best-known school samplers of the nineteenth century were those made at the Quaker and Moravian schools in Pennsylvania. These were generally known as Philadelphia-type samplers. Independence Hall, Philadelphia, is pictured on one of these. Eighteenth-century samplers had been made at the Moravian school in Bethlehem, but the most interesting samplers are those made at the Quaker Westtown Boarding School in Chester County. These samplers have a center frame of vines and leaves worked in black, light blue, or tan silk which encloses a moral verse, or samples of the alphabet, together with the name of the school, the name of the girl who made the sampler, and the date. The three-story brick building that housed the school is pictured on some of the samplers. Geometric patterns and stylized flowers, trees, and bird motifs were scattered over the background.

Darning or mending samplers were also made at Westtown School. These consisted of needle weaving in squares, crosses, and diamond shapes worked in colored wools. Flowers were also worked in some darning samplers. These samplers included the name of the child, the date, and the name of the school. Samplers with quilled ribbon borders were made in the Philadelphia area between 1820 and 1840. An attractive sampler of this type has a floral needlework border inside the ribbon border, verses, and flower sprays. At the bottom is a small hillock with a weeping willow tree, sheep, and deer. It was made by Mary Caley in 1837. Silk globes and map samplers which were popular in England in the eighteenth century were also made at Westtown School and at other private schools in New York, New England, and the South; the map is stitched in a black silk outline stitch on a background of white satin. Sometimes there are floral embellishments, and on one rare map sampler there is historical information such as the following: "Population of the State of New York in 1820 was 1,372,812." The majority of these print maps were made in the first quarter of the nineteenth century. This is the period when embroidery on silk and satin was especially popular. Embroidered maps are interesting and valuable because they record old boundaries and names of towns no longer in existence.

There were also many needlework pictures on satin made in the first quarter of the nineteenth century. These included religious subjects such as "Abraham Offering Isaac," "Moses in the Bullrushes," and "Christ and the Woman of Samaria." There were also classical subjects such as "Cupid and Psyche," and sentimental and pastoral scenes including "Paul and Virginia," and "Woman with Harp."

The memorial sampler, probably first made at the Moravian school in Bethlehem to commemorate the death of Washington, is a type of silk sampler very often seen. These mourning samplers pictured a scene with a vase-topped monument, and a group of mourners consisting of several figures but often a whole family. Cypress and weeping willow trees completed the scene. In the earliest of such pictures the monument usually bore the inscription, "Sacred to the Memory of the Illustrious George Washington." Later, family memorial pictures became popular. These pictures combined painting and needlework. The sky is usually tinted, and figures are often painted and appliqued. The letters of the inscriptions are sometimes stitched with the hair of the departed one.

One of the most popular subjects of early-nineteenth-century needlework was the shepherd or shepherdess. There were pastoral scenes with a shepherd and a flock of sheep and individual oval panels of a girl or boy with a shepherd's crook. These were usually

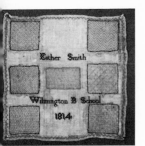

Darning sampler: American, 1814. The Metropolitan Museum of Art. Collection of Mrs. Lathrop Colgate Harper, Bequest, 1957.

Silk embroidery on satin, early nineteenth century. The New-York Historical Society.

Silk-embroidered picture. Deborah Sampson, Warren Academy, 1818. The Metropolitan Museum of Art, gift of Mrs. Paul Moore, 1945.

New York from Weehawken: embroidered and painted on silk, 1830. Ann Stebbins, age ten. Collection of author.

surrounded by a frame of garlands of needlework flowers. Another group of silk-on-satin-embroidered pictures included flower pictures. Sometimes there is a flower arrangement in a vase or basket, or sprays of flowers may be tied with a ribbon after the manner of the French eighteenth century. Another interesting group included architecture or landscape scenes taken from engravings. These were partly painted and partly worked in silk. It is not certain just who did the painting, but the teacher probably assisted. In the *Albany Gazette* in 1810, L. Lemet, the engraver, advertised: "Framing of needlework—He offers to paint the head gratis." The most popular subject for these painted needlework pictures was Mount Vernon, but there were also other scenes including New York from Weehawken. The distant scene is painted, whereas the nearer spaces, such as trees, are worked in silks.

Sewing was also emphasized in the private schools of the nineteenth century. Anna Green Winslow attended Madam Smith's Sewing School where, according to her diary, she learned spinning, plain sewing, and mending. On March 9, 1772, she records: "I sew'd on the bosom of unkle's shirt, mended two pair of gloves, mended for the wash two hankerchiefs (one cambrick) sewed on half a border of a lawn apron of aunts." February 22, 1772: "I have spun 30 knots of linning yearn, and (partly) new footed a pair of stockings."

However, the sampler gradually became a display and a sort of souvenir of the school and a record of attendance. The best-known school samplers of the second quarter of the nineteenth century are the small square samplers with a facsimile of the school building, the alphabet verse, the name and age of the girl, the date, and the name of the school. This type of sampler was made in private schools throughout the eastern states and also in the Middle West. Julia Ann Rule made her sampler at Miss Pequot's School, Union, Missouri, in 1838. It includes a picture of the brick schoolhouse, a tree with a bird, and a cat.

The design of the late-nineteenth-century sampler is more individual. In addition to the church or school building, the child's own house may be pictured. There are also cottage and barnyard scenes. The house with birds and trees is a familiar scene, as is the red brick schoolhouse. The American Eagle bearing the inscription, "E Pluribus Unum" or "Independence" is a characteristic motif. As the century progressed, fewer samplers were made. The materials were no longer handwoven and the stitchery, which was now dominated by the cross-stitch, was often in cottons or colored wools instead of silks. In 1847 *Godey's Lady's Book* printed an alphabet in crochet, and the following reveals the fact that the sampler was now becoming a thing of the past:

Sampler: Silk on linen. Harriet P. Sublett, Lynchburg, Virginia, 1819. Index of American Design.

Sampler: Silk on canvas, American, 1838. The Metropolitan Museum of Art. Collection of Mrs. Lathrop Colgate Harper, Bequest, 1957.

Sampler: cross-stitch in wool on linen. Pennsylvania, 1827. The Metropolitan Museum of Art, gift of Mrs. Robert W. Forest, *1933.*

What lady, whose school days were anterior to the use of indelible ink, but remembers the working of her sampler? The A, B, C's were then the beginning of needlework education— and the accomplishment of the marking stitch was the proud aim of every schoolgirl. And when the alphabet was completed, in letters large and small, the square canvas surrounded with a variegated border in the same stitch, then came the crowning glory, when sweet poesy was married (or marred, as the work too often showed) with silks of all the colors of the rainbow. The choice of this poesy was always an important affair, though for a long time one distich [diptich] had kept its sway in our school, the sampler of every little girl bearing this motto:—

> "The grass is green, the sky is blue,
> This Sampler I have worked for you,
>   My mother."

Nothing could be more to the purpose, and the truth and simplicity of the poetry were in the purest Wordsworth strain.

There was another motto used by some of the older girls, which was thought the perfection of sampler poetry:—

> "The rose is red, the lily's white,
>   And yet they will decay;
>   And youth is sweet, and beauty bright,
>   But both must fade away."

Those were pleasant school days, when the needle and books were alternately in the hands of little girls. Our Book has lessons for those no longer children; but this Alphabet in Crochet carried us back in thought to other times, and though the use of indelible ink has superseded the marking stitch, we are persuaded our fair young friends will find these patterns of much use in ornamental marking.

By the mid-nineteenth century patterns for Berlin work began to appear in *Godey's Lady's Book, Peterson's Magazine, Leslie's Ladies Magazine,* and others. The patterns, together with the canvas and bright wools, came from Germany. The patterns were blocked off in color on squared paper and included flowers, dogs, cats, deer, and parrots, and landscape or other scenes, and were mostly worked in needlepoint or cross-stitch in wools, silk, and chenille. The canvas background was of silk, cotton, or wool. Articles included ottoman and chair seats, carpet bags, hand screens, cigar and glasses cases, and slippers. One of the first patterns for Berlin work was a design for braces printed in Godey's in 1852. Gentlemen's slippers were also very popular articles. In addition to simple geometric and floral patterns, Godey's offered such individual slipper designs as "The Editorial Slipper"; "The National Slipper," 1858; and the "Masonic Slipper," 1859.

Of course, the majority of the larger pieces were made by young ladies, not children, but that samplers and cross-stitch were still considered children's work is evidenced by the Juvenile Department, which included "Samplers for Our Young Friends." The patterns which continued through 1858 and 1859 included cross-stitch letters, numbers, corner designs, and figures of a boat, tree, teapot, engine, horse, or duck, or pear or other fruit.

Perforated-paper work was also popular at this time. A perforated cardboard bookmark was illustrated in Godey's in 1856. Designs of crosses, anchors, flowers, and mottoes were cross-stitched on paper and glued to ribbons. Small needle cases, baskets, slippers, and album covers were also made of perforated cardboard. This was work for all ages and both sexes. The cross-stitch bookmark was the most popular article of children's needlework at this date. They also made cross-stitch table mats, small pictures of children with dogs and cats, religious mottoes with Bible, cross, and anchor, and Easterlily crosses. The framed motto was especially popular. Patterns for these mottoes were offered as premiums by *The Youth's Companion* in October, 1878. The mottoes included: "God Bless Our Home"; "Home Sweet Home"; "Rock of Ages"; "Give Us This Day Our Daily Bread"; "The Lord Is My Shepherd"; "God Is Our Refuge

Liberty Bell: perforated paper and yarn, 1876. Index of American Design.

Motto: perforated paper and yarn, late nineteenth century. The Henry Ford Museum.

and Strength"; "Faith, Hope and Charity"; and "No Cross No Crown." Small square samplers were also cross-stitched in wool on cardboard. However, recognition of the fact that the sampler was a thing of the past is evidenced by the inclusion of the following verse in McGuffey's Fifth Reader, 1879:

The Old Sampler.
Faded the square of canvas,
And dim is the silken thread,
But I think of white hands dimpled,
And a childish sunny head,
For here in cross and tent-stitch,
In a wreath of berry and vine,
She worked it a hundred years ago,
Elizabeth, Aged Nine.

Victorian children's hands were kept busy. Children were taught to sew at four or five years. The pages of *The Youth's Companion, St. Nicholas,* and other children's magazines, as well as of *Godey's Lady's Book,* are filled with suggestions of things for children to make. *The American Girls Book or Occupations for Play Hours,* by Miss Eliza Leslie, was published by Munroe & Francis in 1831. This included many suggestions for needlework. In the section of the book titled "Amusing Work," there were directions for needlebooks,

Amusing work for girls. Parley's Magazine, *1837.* Collection of John Mackay Shaw.

349

AMUSING WORK FOR GIRLS.

ONE of our young female readers says, that she thinks we do not have so many articles in the magazine for girls as we do for boys. Now the truth is, that we intend almost every article we write for the young of both sexes; though sometimes, as in the case of the Letters of Uncle and Aunt Newbury, we have an eye to girls and boys respectively. However, to gratify our young friend and to present something, for once, to amuse very young girls, we will introduce from on the very centre of each side, and with a large needle lay coarse thread or cotton all across down to the middle of the pincushion where the binding is to come. These threads must spread out from the centre in every direction like rays; the space between them widening of course as it descends. Make them very even, and do not allow them to be loose or slack. Then take a needle threaded with sewing silk or fine crewel, and, beginning at the centre from pincushions, and reticules and a jointed linen doll. Needlebooks were in the shape of fireplace bellows and a thistle. There was also a pincushion needlebook and a needlebook workbag. Pincushions were in the shape of hearts, stars, a boot, a guitar, and a swan. There were also pincushion dolls and a reticule doll. These dolls were later illustrated in *Godey's Lady's Book* when Miss Leslie became the editor. Mrs. Pullan, the well-known writer on needlework, gave directions for crochet and tatting in the *Boys' and Girls' Own Annual*, 1861. From the 1860's to the end of the century the most popular articles of children's needlework were bookmarks, watch pockets, pen wipers, needlebooks, and pincushions. The magazines illustrated many different designs, together with directions for making. There were leaf pen wipers, butterfly pen wipers, and pen wipers with tiny birds and chickens of Japanese workmanship standing in their centers. One of the most interesting pen wipers was the Centennial Pen-Wiper, the directions for which were given in *St. Nicholas*, September, 1876. Directions for making the Miss Dinah Pen-Wiper were given in *Godey's Lady's Book*, 1861. "Take a black china baby. . . ." A combination pincushion and needlebook in the shape of a coal scuttle was illustrated in *St. Nicholas*, November, 1877. Children also made such small articles as strawberry or tomato emeries, and patterns for these were printed in *The Youth's Companion, Demorest's Young America*, and other similar publications. But one of the most popular articles was the doll pincushion.

Doll pincushion. Peterson's Magazine, *vol. 47–48, p. 209.* Collection of John Mackay Shaw.

A Centennial Pen-Wiper. St. Nicholas Magazine, *1876.* Collection of John Mackay Shaw.

Pincushion dolls were first made in the eighteenth century. These had painted wooden heads set upon cloth bodies filled with bran. The body was dressed in the style of the times. Although directions for making doll pincushions had been illustrated in *Miss Leslie's Girls' Own Book* in 1831, the earliest doll pincushion to appear in an American magazine was called "A Woman Pincushion." This was illustrated in *Godey's Lady's Book*, January, 1834. The head and arms are of "composition material" (papier-mâché), the body of kid. The directions suggest that the doll be dressed in a velvet or silk skirt with fancy trimming, a sash, puffed sleeves, and a hat with feathers. The pins are stuck in the skirt in clusters of diamonds so that they look like spangles. Directions for "The Lady Pincushion" appeared in *Godey's Lady's Book* in 1861. This was made from a small wooden doll. The directions say: "Dress her according to your taste." The illustration shows the doll in a low-neck crinoline dress with a wreath of flowers on her head. A pincushion doll dressed in Elizabethan style was illustrated in *Godey's Lady's Book*, March, 1868. Although many pincushion dolls were made from wood, there were dolls with china heads at about this date.

Pincushion doll with painted wooden head American, early nineteenth century. The New-York Historical Society.

Sewing dolls were also popular. A sewing doll called the "Work Table Companion" was illustrated in *Peterson's Magazine* in 1860. She is dressed as a Civil War nurse in a red dress with blue bands, and in her pockets are scissors, thread, and other sewing accessories. A sewing pincushion called "The Ladies' Friend" was illustrated, together with directions for making, in *Godey's Lady's Book* in 1864. The doll is dressed in voluminous skirts with pockets that hold a thimble, bodkin, scissors, etc. A spool of thread is fastened to her back and a small basket for buttons is fastened to her head. These dolls are related to the pedlar dolls that displayed their household wares in the eighteenth century (see Chapter 13).

Making doll clothes was another favorite pastime "for idle hands." There were patterns for doll clothes in *Godey's*, 1856—a doll's embroidered collar and a doll's cap—and in 1870, a guide for dressing a Christmas doll. *Demorest's Young America* printed patterns for a doll's trousseau in November, 1869. A doll's trousseau with directions for making, by Mrs. Jane Weaver, was also illustrated in *Peterson's Magazine*, 1874. It included morning dresses, a paletot, a walking costume, a circular cloak, and a chemise.

Pincushion doll, painted wood, six inches tall, early nineteenth century. Shelburne Museum.

Patterns of dolls' clothes were also illustrated in *Young Ladies Journal*, December, 1882, and in *Harper's Bazar* from 1868 to 1892. In the January 11, 1868, issue there are illustrations and patterns

A Woman Pincushion. Godey's Lady's Book, *1834.*

Dinah pen wiper.
Godey's Lady's Book,
1861.

Pincushion doll with china head, ca.
1880's. The Henry Ford Museum.

Pincushion with Queen Elizabeth ruff. Godey's Lady's Book, *March, 1868.*

Pincushion doll with china head, ca.
1870. Dress of brown silk damask and
lace. Red ribbon bands stuck on with
pins. Collection of Catharine Ashley.

The Ladies' Friend. Godey's Lady's Book, *1864.*

Dolls' Fairy Wardrobe. The Youth's Companion, *Oct. 25, 1894. Collection of John Mackay Shaw.*

(a) *The Fashionable Doll.* (b) *The Doll's Trousseau.* Demorest's Young America, *November, 1869.* Collection of John Mackay Shaw.

b

a

for a doll's fancy dress, Breton peasant costumes, a promenade dress, and a walking skirt. There is also a full page illustration of Jenny Wren, the doll's dressmaker, a character in Charles Dickens' *Our Mutual Friend*. In *Harper's Bazar* for January 9, 1869, there are illustrations and patterns for making a doll's visiting dress, a country dress, and a street dress. The descriptions of these clothes suggest the use of such materials as alpaca, foulard, cashmere, and rabbit skin, all popular materials used in children's and adult clothes at this time. *The Doll's Dressmaker*, a magazine, was published in New York from 1891 to 1893. The editor was Jennie Wren.

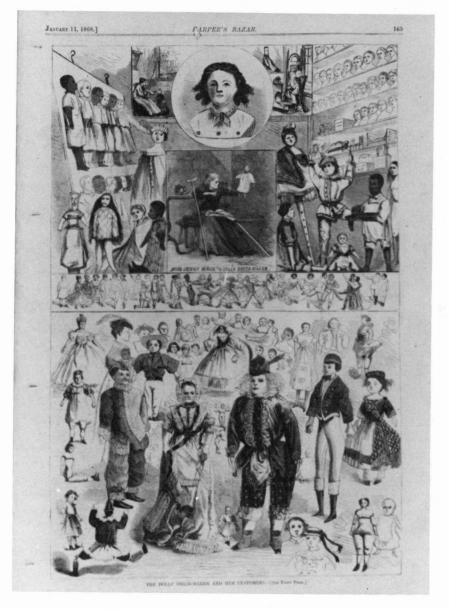

Miss Jenny Wren, the Dolls' Dressmaker and Her Customers. Harper's Bazaar, January 11, 1868.

10

Outdoor Games

Cup and Ball

ne of the earliest games played by American children, and now available to the collector, was "cup and ball." In the mid-eighteenth century Charles Shipman, an ivory and hardwood turner from England, advertised cups and balls (The *New York Journal or General Advertiser*, August 6, 1767). Cups and balls came to England from France where it was known as bilbocquet. It had been a favorite pastime at the court of Henry III, and a late-sixteenth-century French print labeled "La foire franche des Bilbocquets de plus a la mode" shows men, women, and children playing the game. The cup and ball is also shown in Pieter Brueghel's painting of children's games and in a seventeenth-century German print. Cup and ball, which is no longer played, continued popular in Victorian days in England and America. A handbook of 1859 that gave directions for playing the game is quoted by Leslie Daiken in *Children's Toys Throughout the Ages:*

> A ball of ivory or hard wood is attached to a stem of the same substance, having a shallow cup at one end and a point at the other. The player holds the stem in his right hand and having caused the ball to revolve, by twirling it in between finger and

202

CUP AND BALL

Adolphus. The only way to learn to play well is to use it frequently. My professor approves of my playing at it, because it requires some address and an exact eye. The most simple manner is this—to keep the ball upon the point; it is more difficult to hold it at the flat end. When you have tried these two ways, then you will come to what they call the censer; the ball is thrown with more grace, and we receive it upon the point in this manner.—

Amelia. I think I begin to play; I have caught it several times tolerably well.

Adolphus. Good; but that is only the small game; there are other modes of playing, which are more difficult. I throw the ball and the cup alternately—I receive the cup in the ball, or the ball in the cup, sometimes on the point.

DRAUGHTS

Adolphus. I huff you—

Amelia. How?

Adolphus. I gave you that man to take, and you have not taken him; I therefore take up your man, and play again; it is from this that the proverb comes—Huffing is not playing.

Amelia. Oh! but I will remember. Come, put down my man, and I will take you.

Adolphus. That's well, and now I will take three of yours, see—one, two, three!

Amelia. In that case I lose two men; I would rather you should huff me.

Adolphus. Yes, but you have not the choice, and I can force you to take them; here, I again take these two—and crown mine.

Amelia. Oh! if I were to play seriously, this would put me out of all patience.

366

thumb of his left hand, he jerks it up, and catches it, either in the cup or upon the spike to receive by which a hole is made in the ball.

Cups and balls range in size from about three inches long with a tiny bead ball to twelve or fourteen inches in length and a ball the size of a golf ball. The tiny ivory cup and ball was often decorated with carving, while those of wood were painted or lacquered with bands of color and painted with chinoiserie or other scenes. A portrait by James Claypoole, ca.1750's, of Rebecca Doz with cup and ball is at Winterthur Museum. The continuing interest in the game is evidenced by the illustration of a child with cup and ball in a Godey's fashion plate of 1871.

Cup and Ball, Draughts. Juvenile Games for the Four Seasons. Collection of John Mackay Shaw.

Battledore and Shuttlecock

The battledore and shuttlecock were also known to eighteenth-century American children, and many children's portraits show them with the small bat and feathered shuttlecock. Rivington & Miller of Boston advertised imported "Battledores and Shuttlecocks"—(*Boston Gazette*, Dec. 5, 1763). Gilbert Deblois of Boston made and advertised battledores and shuttlecocks in the 1770's. At about this time William Williams painted the portrait of Stephen Crossfield with a battledore and shuttlecock. The portrait of Thomas Aston Coffin painted by John Singleton Copley also includes a battledore and shuttlecock. The popularity of the game was illustrated in "A Rhyme for Shuttlecock and Battledore": "Shuttlecock, shuttlecock tell me true, How many times have I to go through? One, two, three, four, etc." In 1802 a book called *Youthful Recreations,* published by J. Johnson of Philadelphia, has an illustration of two boys playing battledore and shuttlecock, and the text says: "To play with battledore and shuttlecock or with a trap and ball is good exercise." Battledore was advertised in lists of Christmas presents in newspapers in 1833 and 1837, and the game continued popular throughout the nineteenth century. In *The Youth's Companion,* vol. 58, 1885, a battledore with red leather handle and sheepskin racket was given as a premium for obtaining subscriptions to the magazine. Flying a kite, "trundling a hoop," and "skipping along rope" are also illustrated as games to give children exercise.

Hoops

Hoops were shown in "Kinderspiel," a painting by Pieter Breughel, but the hoop really came into its own in Victorian times. Early hoops were of metal; later, handmade wooden hoops were popular. Each hoop was given a name and, in the early republic, patriotic hoops were marked with thirteen notches. John Marshall published

Marbles.

Battledoor & Shuttlecock.

Trap Ball.

a small Infants Library ca. 1800 and it included the hoop among games with morals. Hoop play was also used as an exercise of grace for young ladies in France. These hoops were imported for use in America as early as 1833, according to an advertisement in the *Daily Advertiser* of Newark, New Jersey: "Jumping ropes and Graces." An advertisement in the *Philadelphia Public Ledger*, December 23, 1837, calls them "Jaun de Graces." The game of "Graces" was described in the *American Girl's Book*, Munroe & Francis, ca. 1831. Played by two girls, the game was to fling the hoop off the stick toward the other player who at the same time whirled her hoop to you. The object was to catch the opponent's hoop. The hoops were small and light, bound in tinsel and colored ribbons, and they came with a pair of light hoop sticks. In 1881, Selchow & Richter advertised "Grace Hoops bound in leather and velvet." Graces remained popular throughout the nineteenth century. Premiums given for subscriptions to *The Youth's Companion* in the 1880's included Graces, and a child with a pair of Graces is shown in *Chatterbox Junior*, 1878. Grace hoops were also the subject of a painting by Winslow Homer.

Products of woodenware factories of New England making toys during the nineteenth century included hoops, graces, stilts, wooden handles for jump ropes, ten pins, baseball bats, and tops. The Vermont Novelty Works made boys' stilts and hoops in the 1860's. Wooden hoops were made in twelve different sizes. They were packed for sale in lots of six or twelve hoops. Hoops were also made

Trundling a Hoop.

Skipping along rope.

Marbles, Battledore and Shuttlecock, Trap Ball, Trundling a Hoop, Have a Ride in My Chair, Blindman's Buff, Skipping Rope. Youthful Recreations. J. Johnson, Philadelphia. Collection of John Mackay Shaw.

Winslow Homer, "Snap the Whip," 1880. The Butler Institute of American Art, Youngstown, Ohio.

by Snow and Kingman of Boston in 1855 and by many other companies after this date.

Marbles

Marbles and tops were other game toys that reached the height of their popularity in Victorian times. Both were age-old toys for children. Marbles date back to Roman times, and wooden and stone tops were known to the Egyptians centuries before Christ. It is not known if marbles or tops were among the English and Dutch toys advertised in the *Boston Gazette* in 1725, but mention of them was included in American children's books of the eighteenth century.

In *The Pretty Little Pocket Book*, a Newbery book which was reprinted by Isaiah Thomas in 1787, the following verse was included:

Marbles

Knuckle down to your taw
Aim well, shoot away,
Keep out of the Ring,
You'll soon learn to play.

A MERRY CHRISTMAS.

Child with grace hoops and doll. Chatterbox Junior, *1878.* Collection of John Mackay Shaw.

Homemade wooden rattle, top, and clay marbles. Old Sturbridge Village.

In *The Boys' Own Book* published by Charles S. Francis, New York, 1829, the rating of different kinds of marbles was listed. The cheapest were the Dutch marbles of glazed clay. The next best were those of yellow stone with spots of black or brown, and the best were taws of pink marble with red veins. Old marble games included Ring Taw, Pyramid, Conqueror, Three Holes, Lag Out, Increase Pound, and Snops and Spans, but the only game that seems to be remembered today is Ring Taw. Marbles continued to be imported from Europe until the middle of the nineteenth century.

When the manufacture of marbles began in America, it was centered in Ohio. One of the first companies was that of Samuel C. Dyke of South Akron, who made clay marbles in the 1880's. There were several other makers in the 1890's. Onyx marbles were made by the National Onyx Marble Company and the Navarre Glass Marble Company of Navarre, Ohio, and M. B. Mishler (later Albright & Lightcap) of Ravenna made marbles into the twentieth century.

The game of marbles has a language all its own. Marbles were given names, and the same names are used today. The "agate" was a veined real stone. Marbles were also made of onyx, carnelian, jade, cobalt, and jasper. "Alleys" were made of white marble. When the marble was striped with red it was called a "blood alley." "Taws" or "stonies" were made of brown marble. Dutch marbles were made of glazed clay painted yellow and green, and had dark stripes. Marbles of English clay were called "commoneys." Many American clay marbles of brown or blue glazed clay were made at Bennington, Vermont, and in Ohio, Indiana, and Pennsylvania potteries. Montgomery Ward sold American agate marbles in the 1890's. Different classification names for marbles are given in the advertisement of the American News Company:

Marbles

Jaspies, Crockery	Painted China	Glass
	Glazed, unglazed	Brandies
	Colored eyes	Opal
	Jaspies glazed	Blood Agate
	Crockery { brown blue	Imitation agate

Red & Flint Agate genuine, stone marbles, common gray, common polished, Bowlers, gray, bowlers polished.

Marbles of various kinds are available to collectors today. These include the expensive and rare sulphides of clear glass with encased frosted white figures of animals, birds, flowers, or faces. Glass marbles of Venetian swirl type called "glassies" have ribbons of

Marbles. Sulphides encased with figures of animals. Venetian swirl "glassies" and spotted clay marble. The Henry Ford Museum.

colored glass in a clear glass marble. These were also made at American glass factories and are similar to paperweights. There are also homemade clay marbles and, later, "steelies."

Tops

Tops were made and used all over the world. Many made in different countries and of various materials can be seen in museums. However, the kinds of tops of special interest to the collector today are tops of wood, iron, and tin which were made in Europe and America in the nineteenth century. Wooden tops were made of lignum vitae and boxwood. Many wooden tops made of boxwood were polished, striped, and gilded; others were painted. The cheaper ones had lines of color and the more expensive ones had flowers and other decorations; still more expensive tops had wooden handles or grips. Little iron tops were made often in the shape of a cup with a tin section that snapped on. The top was screwed into motion and the bottom released to spin. This was called a whistling top. This type of top was made in tin by J. & E. Stevens & Co. of Cromwell, Connecticut, ca. 1860, and shown in their catalogue of 1870. They also made a "patent brass spring top." There were three types

Top with painted figure of man, ca.1830. Museum of the City of New York.

The Whipping Top. Moral Songs for the Instruction and Amusement of Children. *John Oakman and Others, London, 1802.* Collection of John Mackay Shaw.

Top and grip: wooden, carved, and painted. Museum of the City of New York.

32. *The Whipping Top.*

1 SEE the tops on the pavement, they
      twirl and they bound,
  And swift is the circuit they take on the
      ground;
  The lads all pursuing, each doubles his
      blow,
  And the faster they scourge them, the
      better they go.

x 3

of tops; peg tops, whip tops, and humming tops. From the many

early illustrations showing boys with whip tops, these seem to
have been the early favorites. Whipping tops are of mushroom or
turnip shape. The whip-lash had a thong of leather or eel skin.
The whip-lash was wound in the grooves of the top, then quickly
torn away as the top was thrown to the ground. The peg top is
shaped like a pear and has a sharp iron peg at the end. Spanish
peg tops have a wooden knob at the end instead of an iron peg.
The best peg tops are made of boxwood. To spin the top a cord
is wound around the metal peg and on the lower part of the body.
The game of Peg-in-Ring is played with the peg top. Other top
games were Chippings, or Chip-Farthing, as it was originally
called. This game is illustrated and described in *The Pretty Little
Pocket Book* printed by John Newbery in London in 1744. The book
was first printed in America by Isaiah Thomas in Worcester,
Massachusetts, in 1787. A verse with a moral was included, for
example:

> Soon as the Ring is once composed,
> The Coin is in the tenter clos'd
> And then the wish'd-for Prize to win,
> The top that drives it out must spin.
> Rule of Life
> Be silent if you doubt your sense
> And always speak with Diffidence.

John Marshall also illustrated games in his Infants Library. An
illustration of Peg-Top is explained thus: "There are two boys playing with a peg-top. One has just made it spin and the other seems
to stand ready to take it up."

Tops made by Gibbs Manufacturing Company of Canton, Ohio, in
the 1890's were of the windup spring type. They whistled and
hummed. A choral top with organ reeds tuned in harmony was
illustrated in *The Youth's Companion* in 1885. A large spinning top
with a harp concealed inside sounded when the air struck it. In an
1880 catalogue of W. Britain & Sons of England, a fountain top was
illustrated. The top was wound in the ordinary way, but spun in a
saucer of water and the spinning threw up a jet of water. A top-
spinning cap pistol was advertised in *Harper's Weekly*, December
21, 1878.

In *The Youth's Companion*, October, 1879, "Duplex Tops" were
advertised. These consisted of two tops held to a rack with a handle,
and the two tops could be released at once. Also in the 1880's
Crandall advertised a spinning-clown top. The National Toy Co. of
New York, manufacturers of novelties in toys, advertised a "Steam
Top" in *Harper's Weekly*, May 25, 1872. Bradley put out a color top,
and a "Magic Figurative and Chromatic Top" was also advertised.
In 1881 Selchow & Richter listed a "Tip Top" that "tips and turns
over."

Outdoor games or sports also included sledding, skating, and skiing, and a history of the sports themselves can be drawn from a collection of these old objects. All these sports were known in colonial times in New England. Judge Sewall wrote in his Diary, November, 1696, of scholars "scating" on Fresh Pond. Early skates were made of bones from reindeer and other animals. Dutch bone skates date from the sixteenth century. Skating was brought to America from Holland, and the Dutch children of New York all skated. The first skates used by William Livingston were made of beef bones. However, wooden skates with iron runners had been invented in Holland and were imported and advertised in eighteenth-century American newspapers: "Best Holland Scates. Different Sizes." Early skates shown in children's books are of wood with a center metal runner that ends at the toes in a thin reversed "C" curve. The Winslow Skate Company of Worcester, Massachusetts, was founded in 1856, and within a few years there were other companies including Coe & Sniffen, Union Hardware, Barney and Berry, and T. A. Williams that met the demand for ice skates. These were usually advertised as "Patented American Skates," but there were other trade names. In 1869 the dealers Bradford & Anthony advertised the following name skates: Florence Skates, Acme Skates, Boston Club Skates, New York Club Skates, American Rink

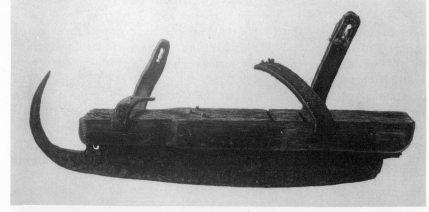

Homemade ice skate. Pine, painted red and black, wrought-iron runner. Made by father of Ralph Eddy, 1870. Index of American Design.

Ice skate, wood with steel runners, early nineteenth century. Index of American Design.

Roller skates, iron frame, hard rubber and wooden wheels. American, 1844–1858. Index of American Design.

Skates, Ladies Rink Skates, and Winslow's Premium Skates. There were also skates labeled "Central Park State Emporium." About this time roller skates also became the craze. Roller skating rinks sprang up all over the country. Roller skates were made by some of the companies that made ice skates, but the best-known roller skates were made by the Crown Roller Skate Company and by Plimpton of Brooklyn.

Children's sleds were popular in America in the nineteenth century, but sleds had been made by individual craftsmen for many years. As might be expected, the earliest manufacturers of sleds were in Massachusetts, Vermont, Connecticut, New York, and New Jersey. By the 1860's there were also makers in Sheboygan, Wisconsin, Grand Rapids, and other midwestern cities. Crandall had made sleds from the 1840's. The Museum of the City of New York owns a child's sled with steel runners that is painted green and bears the date "1841" in gold letters. In 1849 there were eleven makers of coasting sleds listed in the New England Mercantile Union Directory. However, the first factory to specialize in sledmaking was the Paris Manufacturing Company of Paris, Maine. The company was founded by Henry Morton in 1861. The first sleds were of hand-carved wood with wooden runners, and the handpainted decoration was done by Morton's wife. By the 1880's Paris sleds were made in several models. There were two basic styles made with a great variety of design and decoration. The "Paris Cutter" was a low sled with heavy skilike runners, while the "Paris Clipper" was set higher on slender open runners. In the Montgomery Ward catalogue of 1877, sleds on open runners ending in swans' heads are illustrated. They could be had in two sizes—one for 60 cents and one for $1.15. In addition to graceful swans' necks at the ends of front runners, many sleds were decorated with painted landscapes, galloping horses, and bright flowers. There was

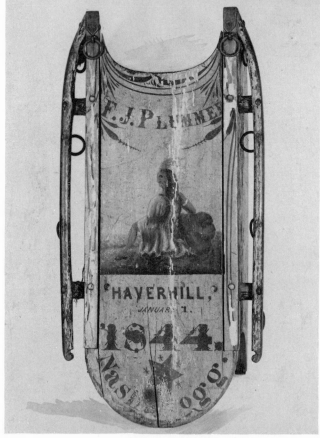

Sled made of pine and poplar by Carpenter Davis in 1874. Painted and decorated with name of owner, Lettie Augusta Davis. Index of American Design.

Painted and decorated sled. Haverhill, Massachusetts, 1844. Index of American Design.

Painted pine sled with iron runners, and loops on handholds. Massachusetts, 1844. Index of American Design.

an oak sled decorated with horses named the "Teaser." "The Boston Clipper," "The Maine Clipper" and "The Snow King" were other popular trade-name sleds. The first steering sled, "The American Flexible Flyer," was made in 1889. In 1896 sleds given as premiums for *Youth's Companion* subscriptions included a "Boys Clipper Sled," "Girls Frame Sled" and "The Ulster Sled." Children also decorated their sleds with names of their own choosing such as "Rover," "General Grant" (*The Nursery,* vol. 13, 1873) ; "Young America," "Tedious," "Old Fogy," "Slowly" (*Demorest's Young America,* vol. 13), "Marquis," "Elite," "Nabob," "Capt. Kidd" (*The Youth's Companion,* 1885).

Children's sleighs which were used instead of a carriage to transport the child in winter were copies of adult sleighs. Provincial European museums have examples of hand-painted children's sleighs decorated with scenes and typical peasant designs. Such sleighs were also made in eighteenth-century America, but few exist today.

Child's cutter painted red with broadcloth upholstery and wickerwork dash. Made by B. LeDoux, Montreal, Canada, 1887. Shelburne Museum.

Child's sleigh made by Asa Poinsett, Wilmington, Delaware, 1784. Index of American Design.

Kites

Kites probably originated in Asia but were known to Greek and Roman children and to all European children. Together with ice skating, hunting, fishing, and bows and arrows, kite flying was one of the earliest outdoor sports of colonial America. The majority of the early kites were homemade, but later they were imported from Asia and continental Europe. Although kites were perishable, and probably few have escaped destruction, if such transitory articles as paper dolls survive, why not kites? I have reproduced the illustrations and quoted from the text of several articles on kite-making by

A. W. Roberts included in *Harper's Young People*, May and June, 1883, and April, 1884.

217

OUTDOOR GAMES

Our first kite will be "mother's kite" for "the boy" (Fig. 1). This kite is made of the common brown straw paper used by grocery men. From this paper a good-sized heart is cut; the paper is then strengthened with numerous broom whisks or splints, which are introduced through small holes that are made with a coarse darning-needle. For a tail several thicknesses of grocery cord is preferable, and for the captive cord linen thread is best.

Fig. 2 is a diamond pinwheel kite. The frame consists of two sticks of well-seasoned white pine; the shorter stick crosses the long upright stick at right angles, and they are tied together where they cross one another. The ends of the sticks contain notches in which the frame cord is secured, giving to the kite its diamond shape. To this kite pinwheels of stiff paper of various colors are attached as shown in the figure. For a tail, strips of old sheeting are best. This kite is a medium high flier, but does not behave well in a strong wind.

Fig. 3 is a shamrock or Patsey kite. The frame (Fig. 3, A) consists of an upright and a cross stick; the three circles which form the outline of the shamrock leaf are of split bamboo or split rattan. These circles are bound together and to the frame sticks with sewing silk or strong linen thread. It is best after the binding is completed to apply hot glue to the parts; this gives greater strength, and holds the binding together. The covering of this kite consists of emerald-green tissue-paper, which is veined with greenish-yellow paint to give the leaf a more artistic and finished look. The stem of the shamrock is formed by winding green paper around the prolonged end of the upright stick of the frame. The Patsey kite is a low flier, and rags are the proper material for the tail.

Fig. 4 is a Union Shield kite, and consists of two slender cross sticks and a stouter upright stick. The outline of this kite is formed around the sticks with curving sections of split bamboo or rattan, which are bound together firmly with silk, and secured with glue. The staffs for the three streamers consist of very thin splinters of bamboo, which are fastened in position with silk to the side strips of bamboo and to the upright centre stick. These streamers and the covering for this kite consist of heavy white tissue-paper, on which the Stars and Stripes are painted with water-colors.

Fig. 5 is the "Evening-Star" kite. The frame is the same as that of the diamond pin-wheel kite. When the frame cord is run around the sticks a diamond kite is formed; but by using four short "gathering-in cords" a star kite is formed. These gathering-in cords are first fastened by their ends where the sticks

Fig. 1.

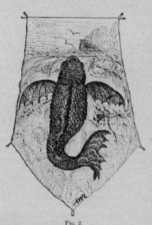

Fig. 2.

Fig. 3.

Fig. 4.

Fig. 5.

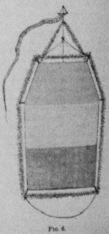

Fig. 6.

store kites. To the outer frame cord red, white, and blue tissue-paper fringing is attached, and on the inner frame cord is pasted the red, white, and blue tissue-paper covering of the kite. The pennant staff consists of a very thin strip of bamboo, and is tied to the cross stick and to the two frame cords. It is also braced with two cords, which are fastened near the pennant and to the upper ends of the long sticks. For this kite face-bands Nos. 1 and 2 are used.

When making and flying kites the following suggestions will be found useful: The tailless Japanese and Chinese kites are for light winds; for strong winds they need tails. For pasting, boiled flour paste is best, and the less paste used on a kite the better. There should be as little pasting-down margin as possible, as a perfect kite should combine great lightness with strength.

The covering of a kite can be made water-proof and transparent by applying cheap furniture varnish that has been thinned down with spirits of turpentine, or by applying a coat of hot paraffine; the paper then becomes the so-called "waxed paper" used by confectioners.

When attaching the captive cord to the face-band, remember that it must be so placed as to hold the kite in the teeth of the wind; also test thoroughly every tie of the face-band, so as to avoid slip-ties and slip-knots. When selecting thread or twine for the captive cord always choose that which is the lightest, strongest, and most closely twisted, as the constant winding and unwinding will soon tell upon any but the best quality. A good way to preserve the cord is to give it a light coat of melted paraffine; this will hold it together and preserve it from dampness. But it must be borne in mind that the kite has to sustain the weight of the captive cord, and that when it becomes too heavy it sags and bears the kite down.

I have found some of the American sewing-machine threads just the thing for medium-sized kites. Some of these threads are to be had on single spools of a length of two thousand four hundred yards. For large kites carpet thread and upholsterers' twine are the best. It is always the safest rule when kite-making to tie with fine silk thread all parts of the frame of a kite that cross one another, and to also apply a small quantity of hot glue to the ties. The covering of a kite will never become baggy if the frame is held together firmly by the ties and the frame cord.

The best parties to apply to for bamboo cane are the dealers and makers of bamboo fishing-rods. From these can be obtained various lengths of bamboo which they have no use for, and any of them will sell for fifty cents an entire but slightly worm-eaten pole, which will make excellent kite sticks. When shaping the sticks for the frame always make them flat, so that when bound together they will not slip, as will round sticks. When using bamboo the projections of the joints should be sand-papered down. The straightness of all sticks should be constantly tested on a level surface.

Kites. Harper's Young People, *June 5, 1883.* Collection of John Mackay Shaw.

These strips are bound together where they cross one another with strong linen thread. The bent piece that forms the head and the sides of the hat can be either willow or split rattan. The dotted lines in the illustration show the positions of the frame cords, and give to the kite the sailor-like form. The hands and feet consist of pieces of cardboard. At all points where the framepieces are fastened with thread plenty of glue should be applied to bind the frame together so firmly that not the least sagging of the paper covering can take place from the loosening of the frame sticks. The best paper for this kite is a moderately heavy white paper, such as the best illustrated newspapers are printed on. Tissue-paper will not do, as it is too thin to receive the painting in water-colors that is required to represent a sailor boy (Fig. 4).

THE RUSSIAN KITE.

The materials of this kite (Fig. 5) are much the same as those of the sailor kite. The arms and legs are made of pink paper-muslin or heavy tissue-paper, and are kept expanded where they join on to the kite by means of circles or rings of split rattan, which are fastened to the frame (Fig. 6) by a number of fine cords. When the kite enters a strong wind-current the arms and legs become inflated, and constantly assume different and comical positions.

TIP-CORDS.

A tip-cord should be made of the strongest and best fishing-line, and fastened to the upper part of the frame of the kite. It was a very delightful experiment the first time we tipped Giant over, head-first, just as he was about to carry us at fearful speed through the water. All we had to do on such occasions was to suddenly let out the captive cord, and then pull hard on the tip-cord, and the result would be to incline the top of the kite toward us, thus reducing the pressure of wind, and, as a result, the pulling or towing strength of the kite.

BALLOONS AND PARACHUTES.

One of the most charming experiments with kites is the releasing of tissue-paper parachutes and rubber balloons (Fig. 7) from the captive cord after the kite has attained its greatest height. This is done by means of what I call a "touch string," which is held in position by a section of looped wires, as shown in the illustration. The best and cheapest wire for this purpose is that used by florists for stemming flowers. After having obtained a hundred yards of this wire, round loops are formed every few yards apart by passing the wire once round a lead-pencil or a smooth and round pen-holder.

This looped wire should be securely fastened by one end to the captive cord at a distance of some fifty feet from the kite, thus becoming a part of the captive cord. For this reason care must be taken when selecting the wire that it is strong enough to bear the pull or strain of

Kites. Harper's Young People, *May 29, 1883.*
Collection of John Mackay Shaw.

cross one another; they are then passed over the frame cord and are drawn tight, and the remaining ends tied in the same place as the first. By this means the frame cord is drawn inward, thus changing the diamond shape of the frame cord into a star having one long and three short arms.

The masses of slender rays which are shown in Fig. 5 spreading out from the angles formed by the gathering-in cords consist of numerous and very slender splints of bamboo; these splints are first glued in radiating positions to a piece of thin card-board, which is known as the "spreader." This spreader is then glued to the kite where the gathering-in cords form the outer (obtuse) angles. The covering of this kite is of light blue tissue-paper be-spangled with gold-leaf. The bamboo rays are also gilded with gold-leaf. In bright sunlight the effect of this kite is very beautiful; it is a medium high flier. Fig. 6 is a combination of star kite and a Greek cross (in open-work). This kite is much the same in its construction as the evening-star kite, the only difference being the two inner circles of split bamboo or rattan and the open-work Greek cross.

The outer and largest circle of bamboo is securely fastened in four places to the two frame sticks, and to this circle are also fastened the gathering-in cords of the star portion of the kite. All that part of the kite which is contained within the arms of the star and the outer circle is covered with light blue tissue-paper, which is bespangled with silver-leaf. The smaller or inner circle is also fastened to the sticks of the kite wherever it crosses them. From the corners of the angles formed by the crossing of the sticks eight strings are fastened; these are again fastened to the inner circle of bamboo at equal distances so as to form the arms of the Greek cross. This cross is covered with brilliant crimson paper bespangled with gold-leaf.

One of the newest styles of Chinese kites that is being offered by toy dealers is known as the tailless fan kite (Fig. 1). The frame of this kite consists of five thin and flat strips of bamboo, the ends of which are shown in the figure as extending beyond the face of the fan. The centre upright strip and the two side strips cross one another at the bottom of the fan, and form a small handle, which acts as a balance weight, and answers the purpose of a tail. The covering is pasted over the entire surface of the fan, and is painted to represent a fan.

The paper covering of this kite is left very loose toward the two upper corners of the fan, so as to form pockets. When flying, the wind fills the pockets and sustains the kite. This style of kite is now selling for from two to five cents each.

Fig. 2 is another new style of Chinese kite, the general shape of which is that of a banner. The frame consists of four very thin and flat pieces of split bamboo, which are glued to the back of the kite. The face of this tailless kite is concave; this concavity is produced by a cord which is tied to the ends of the horizontal strips of bamboo, and then tightened.

The round fan kite (Fig. 3) consists of an ordinary Japanese fan, the bamboo handle of which has been cut away, so as to make it very light. This kite requires a strong wind and plenty of tail.

Fig. 4 is a banneret kite. The frame consists of two sticks, the upright one being the stoutest and the cross stick the thinnest. The frame cord starts from near the right-hand end of the cross stick, and passes through a deep notch in the lower end of the upright stick. It is then brought up, and is securely fastened near the left-hand end of the cross stick.

The upright staff of the banneret is ornamented with a small silver paper star. It is strengthened by two cords, which are fastened just below the star and to the cross stick. To each end of the cross stick is attached a bunch of very narrow tissue-paper streamers. The frame of this kite is covered with white paper, on which is painted with watercolors the Stars and Stripes as shown in the figure. Fig. 5 is a single and very long streamer Union Shield kite.

Fig. 6 is the "champion American kite" in all respects, it being the highest flier and the best behaved when carefully balanced in all its parts, and will remain motionless in the air for hours at a time. Its proportions are graceful, and will admit of a great deal of ornamentation.

The frame of this kite contains two long and one short and light cross stick. The three sticks are so arranged that they cross one another at three different points. In this way greater strength and solidity are obtained in the frame, and the sticks can be much lighter than when they all cross at one point, as is the case with all three-sticked store kites. To the outer frame cord red, white, and blue tissue-paper fringing is attached, and on the inner frame cord is pasted the red, white, and blue tissue-paper covering of the kite. The pennant staff consists of a very thin strip of bamboo, and is tied to the cross stick and to the two frame cords. It is also braced with two cords, which are fastened near the pennant and to the upper ends of the long sticks.

The Sailor-Boy kite is one of the handsomest of all fancy kites, and the most easily made. The frame, as shown in the illustration (Fig. 3), consists of a number of thin and flat strips of well-seasoned white pine. These strips are bound together where they cross one another with strong linen thread. The bent piece that forms the head and the sides of the hat can be either willow or split rattan. The dotted lines in the illustration show the positions of the frame cords, and give to the kite the sailor-like form. The hands and feet consist of pieces of cardboard. At all points where the frame-pieces are fastened with thread plenty of glue should be applied to bind the frame together so firmly that not the least sagging of the paper covering can take place from the loosening of the frame sticks. The best paper for this kite is a moderately heavy white paper, such as the best illustrated newspapers are printed on. Tissue-paper will not do, as it is too thin to receive the painting in water-colors that is required to represent a sailor boy (Fig. 4).

The Russian kite: The materials of this kite (Fig. 5) are much the same as those of the sailor kite. The arms and legs are made of pink paper-muslin or heavy tissue-paper, and are kept expanded where they join on to the kite by means of circles or rings of split rattan, which are fasted to the frame (Fig. 6) by a number of fine cords. When the kite encounters strong wind-current the arms and legs become inflated, and continually assume different and comical positions.

THE TRIAL TRIP.

11

Indoor Games

ndoor games were known and played in America from the earliest times. However, like toys, the average life of a game is short and the chances are against finding an eighteenth-century game intact. But there are many nineteenth-century games available to the collector, and the fascination of collecting children's games is luring more and more collectors each year.

Although there was a strong emphasis on piety, such games as backgammon, checkers, chess, and billiards were known from the early eighteenth century; and dice and card games of one sort or another were also played, as is evidenced by the mention of card tables and billiard tables and the present-day existence of the actual tables. The Dutch settlers played tick-tack, a game similar to backgammon, and trock, a kind of indoor croquet played on a table. Mention of backgammon, chess, and billiards is found in mid-eighteenth-century advertisements. "Baggamon Tables compleat, Chessmen" (*Boston Gazette,* Dec. 5, 1763). Charles Shipman, an ivory and hardwood turner, advertised in *The New York Journal or General Advertiser,* August 6, 1767: "Ivory counters engraved with alphabets and figures (very popular for children) backgammons and chess men."

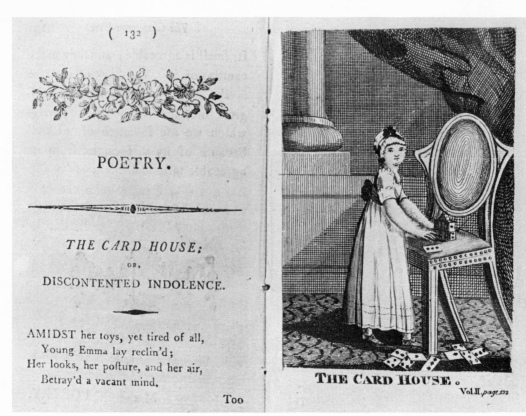

POETRY.

THE CARD HOUSE;
OR,
DISCONTENTED INDOLENCE.

AMIDST her toys, yet tired of all,
    Young Emma lay reclin'd;
Her looks, her posture, and her air,
    Betray'd a vacant mind.

Too

THE CARD HOUSE.

Vol.II. page 132

Child playing with cards. The Children's Magazine, *London, August, 1799.* Collection of John Mackay Shaw.

Cards

Though card playing was considered "an instrument of the devil," it was a popular amusement in the eighteenth century. English and American playing cards were advertised in 1808, and "Eagle Playing Cards" were manufactured in America at that time. The well-known American engraver Alexander Anderson engraved playing cards. Many games using cards of different kinds were invented to teach children and to make learning fun. There were games of travel and history, and geographical games were advertised by Nicholas Brooks in the *Pennsylvania Packet* as early as July 31, 1775. "A journey through Europe or the play of geography invented by Jeffries for the instructive entertainment of young gentlemen and ladies" was an English game, as was "The Don Cossack, a new and interesting Military Game," advertised in a New York paper in 1819. There were also dominoes, Chinese puzzles, solitaire boards, and dissected maps.

An advertisement in the *New York Advertiser*, December 25, 1823 lists "juvenile Pastimes all of which are calculated to improve as well as amuse the youthful mind viz 'Geographical Games: The Travellers Tour through the United States performed with a te-totum and travellers. The Travellers Tour around the world.' " The

games were put up in different ways—on pasteboard and double-
folded cloth with a case, and dissected. There were also dissected
maps of the United States, Europe, North America, South America,
Asia, Africa, and Great Britain. Vernacular cards, geographical
cards, the cabinet of knowledge relative to arts, sciences, and
morality; philosophical cards, astronomical cards, scriptural cards,
botanical cards, and dissected pictures were all popular amusements in the early-nineteenth-century home. In addition to games
of instruction, there were games called "guesses" which included
riddles of various kinds. Conversation Cards was one of the first
card games of this type, and it was advertised early in the nineteenth century. In 1817 T. A. Ronalds advertised "Enigmatical
cards."

Board Games

Games of geography and conversation, historical cards and spelling puzzles continued popular in the 1830's. There was also an
Architectural Game of Transmutation.

In 1831 Munroe & Francis of Philadelphia published *The American Girls Book for Occupations for Play Hours* by Miss Leslie.
The book described the playing of Graces, battledore and shuttlecock, dominoes, checkers, a board game version of Fox and Geese,
jackstraws, Morrice, and numerous card games. Peter Parley's
Games published by Darton & Clark, London, 1842, included the
following instructive games: Royal Victoria Game of Kings and
Queens of England; Game of British and Foreign Animals; an
Instructive Game of Useful Knowledge; the Game of Grecian History; the Game of Roman History; the Nut Game or Necessary
Things. These games undoubtedly found their way to America,
although American companies had begun to make games by this date.

Life in nineteenth-century America was comparatively simple.
The entertainment of children centered about the home, and games
became increasingly popular. Although these games were made for
the instruction and entertainment of children, the whole family
usually joined in and gathered about the center table of an evening.
Dr. Busby, which was published by W. & B. Ives of Salem,
Massachusetts, in 1843, was one of the first card games to sweep the
country. The lithographed cards were colored by hand. In the same
year, Ives issued the board game The Mansion of Happiness. In
1844 The Game of Pope or Pagan or the Missionary Campaign or
the Siege of The Stronghold of Satan by the Christian Army was
advertised. Another game put out by Ives at this time was Master
Rodbury and His Pupils. Also in 1844, L. I. Cohen & Co. of Philadelphia issued The National Game of the Star Spangled Banner or
Geographical & Historical Tour Through the United States &
Canada. In 1846 William Chauncey Langdon published The Game

"Dr. Busby," W. & S. B. Ives, 1843. Reissued by Parker Brothers.

"The Mansion of Happiness," W. & S. B. Ives, 1843. Reissued by Parker Brothers, 1886.

of American Story and Glory. This was a board game with cards representing eleven presidents and twenty-eight states. By mid-century the craze for games had swept the country. Popular games at this time included Oregon; Conversation Cards; Don't Hesitate; The Bohemian Girl; Oracle of Destiny; Kings; The New World; The Young Traveller; The Errand Boy; Heroes; Monkey; Robinson Crusoe; Candle History; American Story and Glory; American Eagle; Reward of Virtue; Busy Bee; Happy Hits; Queen of Beauty; Poor Soldier; Golden Egg; Magic Ring; Yankee Trader; Game of States; Mahomet and Saladin; and Peacock at Home. Such games as Robinson Crusoe and Peacock at Home related to well-known children's books. Others, like Oregon and Mahomet and Saladin, tied in with current news, and the Oracle of Destiny and Magic Ring would appeal because of the great interest in magic and puzzles of all sorts. Around 1850 the well-known game of anagrams was first published. In the 1860's games became big business and the majority of American games were made by four or five large manufacturers including W. & B. Ives, Parker Brothers, McLoughlin Bros., Selhow & Righter, and Milton Bradley. A few were made by S. L. Hill of Williamsburg, New York, and some, especially blocks and puzzles, were made by the Crandalls.

In 1860 Milton Bradley brought out The Checkered Game of Life. The game was so successful that Bradley continued to invent and manufacture games. Up to this time many games had put emphasis on moral lessons, but now Bradley issued games based on current events such as the Civil War. In 1868 four games of war and patriotism were packaged together under the title The Union Games. In 1866 Bradley brought out a game called Croqueterie based on croquet, and in 1867 Richardson & Company, publishers in New York, advertised their version under the name Martelle. This was advertised in *Harper's Weekly*, July 26, 1867, with the claim that it combined the best features of croquet, tenpins and billiards. In 1868 Milton Bradley issued a puzzle called the Smashed Up Locomotive. E. G. Selchow & Co. also made sliced objects including animals, birds, boats, and a church. There were also sliced maps of the United States put out by Milton Bradley. However, Bradley did not confine his interest to games, but in 1868 also put out such optical toys as the Zoetrope, which forecast motion pictures, and panoramas such as the Historiscope and the Myriopticon. Bradley also made painting and crayon sets for children, and building and alphabet blocks called the Kindergarten Alphabet.

"The Checkered Game of Life," 1860. First board game published by Milton Bradley.

THE OLD RELIABLE, CHECKERED GAME OF LIFE.

Game of Ten Pins. The Henry Ford Museum.

Bradley's Historiscope, 1868. Lithographic scenes from Columbus to the Civil War were illustrated on paper rollers and were turned with a handle. Scenes of the Civil War were illustrated in "Myriopticon."

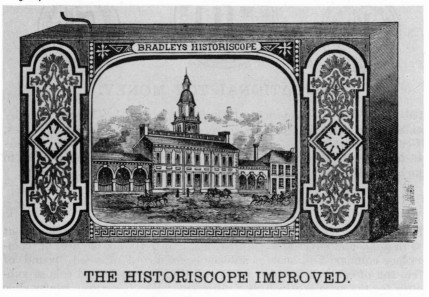

BRADLEYS HISTORISCOPE

THE HISTORISCOPE IMPROVED.

The following is a list of the games illustrated in the Milton Bradley Catalogue of 1900–1901. It includes many of the staple items made by the company between 1860 and 1900.

Five cent series of box games 3x4 inches in size, one game in each box: [The same games were also put up twelve of one kind in a box.] Authors, Stars and Stripes, Peter Coddle, Races, Mimic Ring Toss, The Little Merchants, Toy Shop, Pinch and Hold, Jack Straws, Old Maid, Gem Puzzle Map of the United States, Wild Flowers.

The V Series of Games: The Old Gipsey Fortune Teller is a nice fortune-telling game. The Race for the North Pole is an interesting board game. Toss Target requires some skill to toss the balls through the open mouth of the darkey. Jack O'Lantern represents the trials of a boy attempting to carry a pumpkin lantern to the house of another boy. Gold Hunter is a timely game. The Lively Frog is a board game in which the frog has to keep an eye out for his enemies. The Globe Trotter who first gets round the world, wins, and in Odd and Even the player wins who first reaches the odd space. In Boxing the Compass the moves in the game are determined by the movement of the compass needle, and in Hide and Seek, the players are governed by the spinning of an arrow on a dial. In the game of Canoe Race a counter represents a canoe; the best canoe wins by reaching space 25. The foregoing represent the twelve labels of this series, which are beautifully printed in chromolithography. Each is in a box of 5 by 5 inches, and with the exception of Tip Cat and Toss Target all are board games. Price, each, 5 cents.

The Ten Cent Series: Authors, a good edition of this popular game. Old Maid, a popular edition, with patented matching pictures. Jack Straws: the assortment of straws in this game is very superior and it has met with general approval with the trade. Aesop: of the two cards forming a pair, one contains a fable the other an illustration of it. I don't know: of the two cards forming a pair, one contains a question the other a picture illustrating it. Dickens: the cards are illustrated with characters from his writings. Peter Coddle: a popular edition of this old and interesting game. Animals: an assortment of six dissected lithographed pictures. Birds: an assortment of six dissected lithographed pictures. Donkey Race: the contestants pass over a track, the last one wins as in a real Donkey Race where each rider rides another's donkey. Longfellow contains some of the choicest thoughts from this interesting author. Steeple Chase is a game of the race course style in which the mimic horses and riders contend for the lead.

The Favorite Series: With the exception of Ring Board the following dozen games are all what are called board games. United States Geography furnishes instructions on a very practical subject and in an agreeable manner. Red, White and Blue is a pretty game and gives a good exercise in color. In the Fox and Geese box will be found material for three other popular games, large value for the money. Outing will give a child considerable information about animal life, and at the same time furnish him with wholesome amusement. The label presents an interesting camp scene. Blockade has upon the box cover a vivid representation of a modern battle ship, and the game is supposed to be the attempt of a torpedo boat to run the blockade and enter a harbor guarded by such a ship. Ring Board is a miniature reproduction of the well known hoop games, Pitch-a-ring and Ring Toss. It calls for a good show of skill. The Yacht Race game illustrates a real race, with Stake Boat, Light Ship and Buoy. The game of A Sheaf of Wheat represents the history of a loaf of bread from the wheat field to the bake shop. In My Ship Comes Laden, the names of the common articles in a cargo are introduced, thus furnishing instruction with the amusement. Melodious Mother Goose is a board game, with pictures of the incidents related by the ancient dame in whose memory it is published. Good Luck is an interesting game typical of the name given to it. The Bicycle game is played on a bicycle track and is replete with the usual incidents and accidents of the real race. In the Favorite Series the boxes are seven inches square and the labels covering the entire top are brilliant and attractive. Price, each, 10 cents.

Alaska Series: Sports: a board game illustrating some of the well known sports. Mice and Cheese: a mimic account of how the mice got the cheese. Combat: a board game of merit, giving an opportunity for considerable skill. Dollars and Cents: a board game on which discs are snapped; a good game for teaching the calculating of money. Snap Roulette: an excellent board game; skill and chance combined. The Honey Gatherers: a board game illustrating the journeys of the bees to and from the hive. Game of the Stubborn Pig: a board game showing the troubles in driving a pig to market. The Tourist: a board game of railroad travel. Stock Exchange: a board game with cards to represent different active stocks. Tin Peddler: this board game represents the dealings of a country peddler on his rounds. Conflagration: an exciting board game representing the race of the different pieces of apparatus to the fire. The above games have highly colored labels; the boxes are 8 x 13½ inches. Price, each, 15 cents. Wyhoo: a musical game played with tables; a game of skill and chance combined. Price, 25 cents.

Larger size games included: Sentiment, The Games of Days, Peter Coddle, Old Maid, Colorio, Bible Objects, Words and Sentences; General Literature, Amusement, Royal Jack Straws, Books and Authors, Brother Jonathan, Tossilo, National Standards, Transportation, Funny Fortunes, Budge, Eminent Writers, Game of Centuries, Triumph, Encounter, Shunette (new), Inland to Seaboard, Hustle, Conette, Conette—Popular Edition, Mammoth Conette, Eckha, Genii, Old and New Checkered Game of Life.

The firm of McLoughlin, which was famous as an early publisher of paper dolls, also issued books, games, and toys. They made a

Above: *Little Pets ABC Panorama. McLoughlin Bros., ca. 1870.* Below: *Game of Constantinopel, England, early nineteenth century.* The New-York Historical Society.

fortune selling a game called Chiromagica, and the Whirligig of Life, Jackstraws, and Little Pets ABC Picture Panorama. The following games are from pages in McLoughlin Bros. Catalogue, 1867:

New Games.

In Strong Cases. Put up in doz. Packages of 6 kinds with show bill.

Game of Cinderella, or Hunt The Slipper
      "   Little Red Riding Hood
      "   Cock Robin
      "   House That Jack Built
      "   Mother Hubbard
      "   Where is Johnny   Per gross, $24.00

Games—in Wood Boxes

Varnished covers. Put up in dozen packages of 10 kinds, with show bill.

2 Game, Golden Egg
2   "   Chinese Puzzle
1   "   Hocus Pocus Conurocus
1   "   Visit to Camp
1   "   City Traveller
1   "   Bugle Horn
1   "   Yankee Pedlar
1   "   Happy Family
1   "   Merry Goose
1   "   Six Nations   Per gross, $48.00

Amusing and Instructive Games
 In Strong Cases.
 Rebus Games
 Grandma's Game of Riddles
   "   "   Geography
   "   "   Arithmetic
   "   "   Useful Knowledge
 Old Testament Questions
 New Testament Questions

Game, Dr. Busby
 " Snip, Snap, Snorum (The box cover was designed by
          Ann Anderson Maverick)
 " Old Maid
 " What d'ye Buy
 " Gifts, Uses, and Consequences
 " Speculation
 " Good and Bad Scholars
 " Conundrums
 " of Qualities
 " Hens and Chickens
 " Uncle Sam's History of the United States
            Per gross, $24.00

Conversation Cards
 In Fine sliding Case. 8 different kinds.
 Sybilline Leaves
 "Loves and Likes"
 Ladies' and Gentlemen's Conversation Cards
 Comical Conversation Cards
 Conversations on Marriage
 Quizzical Questions and Quaint Replies
 Conversations on Love
 Madame Morrow's Fortune Telling Cards
            Per gross, $15.00

Cut up Picture
 A Puzzle to put together. Printed in oil colors. In packages
of 1 dozen. 12 kinds.   Per gross, $24.00

Checker Boards
 Two Sizes   Per gross $48.00 and $54.00

Checker Boards
 Black Walnut Frames, Nest of 2   Per gross, $144.00

Card Dominoes   Per gross, $12.00

Alphabet Cards

No. 1.	18mo.	Colored	Per gross,	$1.50	
No. 2.	8vo.	Printed in colors	"	3.00	
No. 3.	8vo.	Large Printed in colors	"	4.50	
No. 4.	4to.	medium "	"	6.00	
No. 5.	4to.	Super Royal Colored	"	9.00	
No. 6.	4to.	Medium Tables	"	6.00	

The Magic Mirror of Wonderland Transformations was published about 1875, The House that Jack Built in 1887, Fish Pond (1890), Yacht Race (1891), and Old Bachelor (1892).

In 1870 Goodwin & Son, Chicago, advertised "The Illustrated Cards of Natural History" in *The Little Corporal*. In *The Youth's Companion*, December 26, 1872, Happy Hours Co., New York, advertised "Games, Puzzles and Novelties; Japanese and Chinese Games; Magic Cards." In *The Youth's Companion*, November 4, 1875, Court—a game with card illustrations of life in the Middle Ages by William Gould of Worcester, Massachusetts—was advertised by the West & Lee Game Co. Logomachy and Go-Bang, the latter a Parker Brothers game, came out in the 1870's and Amusette, a portable billiard game, issued by C. H. Joslin of New York, was also popular in the 1870's. The Lozo Pendulum Board, on which you could play eight games including ring toss, Pockets, Bagatelle and tenpins, with swing ball or cues and balls, was advertised in *Harper's Weekly*, December 24, 1870. Citadelle, by Warner & Co. of Northampton, Massachusetts, was advertised in 1878.

In 1874 *St. Nicholas* published a list of new games for the holiday season. The list which follows includes many old favorites as well as new games.

St. Nicholas expects to be always on the lookout for new games, and playthings, so that our little folk and their parents may be told the latest inventions from Toy-land. But this number goes to press too early for us to speak of all the beautiful and wonderful things that are in store for the coming holidays.

So far, we have been able to examine only a few games, some of which are new, and all good, and well worth recommending to our young friends.

For the older children, one of the new games is "Naval Chess; or, The Admiral's Blockade," a capital entertainment, not complicated, but with all the absorbing interest of chess.

The "Quartette Game of American History," is another. It is historical, amusing and instructive.

The "Lightning Express; or, How to Travel," will set one thinking of what he never thought of before and "Crispino" is one of the best games out.

"Popular Characters from Dickens," is also a new, and a most interesting game.

Another new game is called "Spectrum, or Prismatic Backgammon." It may be played by any number from two to six, and is very exciting. It can be learned by seeing the game played once, and the newest player will often go far ahead of all his competitors.

We must not omit "Totem," a capital little game for the wee ones, with fine pictures of birds and beasts.

And we *must* tell about "Avilude," or the game of birds. It has sixty-four large cards, of unusual beauty. On thirty-two are excellent engravings of birds, and on the others are correct and entertaining descriptions of the same, which players are sure to read. Old and young will be interested in this scientific, yet delightful entertainment.

"The Checkered Game of Life" is not new, but is very captivating—quite as much so as are the new games, "Eskemeo" and "The Lucky Traveler," which last, however, are certainly very entertaining and amusing. The new "Railroad Game," and the games of "Authors," "Poets," "Mythology," and "Popular Quotations," will tend to make young Solomons of the children before they know it; while "Poetical Pot Pie" (a tiptop game), "Silhouette Comicalities" revised, the "Old Curiosity Shop," "The Tickler," "The House that Jack Built" (a Kindergarten game), "Comic Portraitures," and the ever new "Zoetrope," will cause them to laugh and grow fat.

Of puzzles, that are new, we have: "The Blind Abbot and Monks," a mathematical puzzle; "Japanese Pictures," and "Scroll" puzzles; the "Jack-o'-Lantern," and "Star Alphabet" puzzles.

"The Chinese Perforated Target" is an excellent puzzle, which will amuse and delight both old and young.

The "Eureka" puzzle is a mystery, with a string, which is never ending, and always beginning; and the "Centennial" is a wire tease, hard to find out.

The new "Cage" puzzle will put the girls and boys on their mettle. The difficulty is to get the ball out of the cage, without injury to the columns.

"The Magical Trick Box" is a delightful source of amusement. A boy can carry it in his pocket to a party, and delight his friends all the evening, with its help.

"The Spectograph" is a novel invention, by means of which a child may make an accurate drawing without any previous instruction. It would be a precious gift for a little invalid.

Another admirable amusement for the little ones, sick or well, is the "Kindergarten Weaving and Braiding Work." Paper mats, dolls' carpets, tidies, etc., can be woven by their cunning little fingers, with one or two lessons.

"The Kindergarten Alphabet and Building Blocks" is a great invention. The child learns to read while he thinks he is playing.

The "Combination Toy Blocks" are also excellent. Furniture, Buildings, boats, forts—hundreds of objects—can be constructed by these blocks, making of them an endless source of amusement.

There is a new table or carpet game, called, "Lozette," which promises considerable amusement. It is of the same class as the "Trap Game," and "Lozo Pendulum Board."

Of toy picture books, the "Little Folk Series," and "Uncle Ned's Picture Books," are just out. Also, four kinds of gilt-covered picture books; among them, "Dickens' Christmas Story," illustrated by Thomas Nast. The immortal Mother Goose makes her appearance in a new dress; and Dolly Varden paper dolls of large size, have "come out" for the first time this season.

The funniest new steam-engine toy is a colored gentleman, who stands on a platform on top of a little steam engine. Fire up the engine, and he has to dance, whether he wishes to or not.

Of banks, a most useful gift in these hard times, the new one has a race-course on top, to show you where you must *not* put your money. It is a very comical bank, indeed.

Another bank, not so new, but just as good, has a great bull-frog sitting on the top. You pinch his foot, and he opens his mouth, into which you pop the money, when he immediately winks at you—as much as to say, "That was fine! Give me another."

It would be a hopeless task to attempt to enumerate all the delights in preparation for our young friends of *St. Nicholas.*

There are many other games to be found in the shops, not new, but dear to the boy and girl heart, such as "Ring-toss," "Magic Hoops," and "Parlor Croquet." "Smashed up Locomotive," "Dissected Yacht," and "Flag of all Nations," will please the boys. "Uncle Raphael's Puzzle-Chromos," and "Popping the Question," and many others, will delight the girls.

Then there are the mechanical toys and small steam engines, and very curious running rings which tumble, tumble, and yet are never gone; and the centenary gun or cannon, which you can load Monday morning and pop away until Saturday night, in the most perfectly safe and delightful manner.

If we were to go on with all that is made for the delight of children *St. Nicholas* would have to be a book too big for a giant to handle; so we must stop.

Our boys and girls who wish any of these toys, may find them at nearly all the leading toy shops in the United States. Other shops also sell toys and games during the holiday season, but that seems hardly fair.

In *The Youth's Companion,* October 25, 1877, E. G. Selchow & Co.

Jigsaw puzzle, "Les Petit Aéronautes." The New-York Historical Society.

Game of "Banking," 1883. First Parker game.

"Innocence Abroad." Parker Brothers, 1889.

"Christian Endeavor." Parker Brothers, 1890.

of New York advertised the following games: Sliced Objects (animals, birds, boats, churches), Guessing Cards (12 cards of rebus), Vignette Authors, Snap, Parcheesi, Corn & Beans, Crescent, Grand Mother Haphazard's Carnival, Characters from Dickens, Mixed Pickles, Popping the Question, and The Chopped Up Monkey. The U.S. Reed Toy Company of Leominster, Massachusetts, founded in 1875, also made games including The Fortune Teller Game, Parlor Base Ball Game, Jack and Jill Marble Game, Blown-up Fort, Fort Sumpter, The Game of Politics or The Role for the Presidency and the World's Educator.

American children also had French and English games such as Les Anamorphoses first printed in Paris in 1850, and Les Petits Aeronautes, a jigsaw puzzle. Constantinople was an English game of the early nineteenth century. Willie's Walk to See Grandmama, published by A. N. Myers of London in the late nineteenth century, had china pawns and a bone teetotum by which moves on the board were decided.

The games of Parker Brothers reflect the whole American scene and mirror the American way of life over the last eighty years. In 1883 George S. Parker, then sixteen years old, invented his first game, the Game of Banking. Other early Parker games include The Mansion of Happiness published by W. & B. Ives in the 1840's but reissued by Parker in 1885. In 1887 there was The Grocery Store, in 1888 The Yankee Peddler and Country Auction, and in 1899 Innocence Abroad and The Doctors and the Quack. The games brought out in the 1890's included Christian Endeavor (1890), Penny Post (1892), Game of Business (1895), Pike's Peak or Bust (1895), The Battle of Manila (1898), and Klondike. All these games echo events in American history. There were also games of sports such as Athletic Sports, baseball, bicycling, tennis, bowling, football, and golf. There were games and puzzles illustrating popular children's books from Mother Goose nursery rhymes, Cinderella, Dickens, Ivanhoe, and Rip Van Winkle to Robinson Crusoe and The Prisoner of Zenda. The following is a partial list of games made by Parker up to 1900.

Partial List of Parker Brothers Games
Published up to 1900

A.B.C. Blocks	Athletic Sports	Banking
A.B.C. Game	Auction	Barnum's Show
Adventures on a Wheel	Authors	Base Ball
All Aboard for Chicago	Automobile Puzzle	Battle Game
Alphabet		Battledore and Shut
American History	Backgammon	cock
Apple Pie	Baker's Dozen	Battle of Manila
Artists	Ball Pillow-Dex	Battle of Santiago

Battleships Puzzle
Bible
Bicycle
Bicycling
Billy Bumps
Black Cat Fortune Tell-
    ing
Blockade Runner
Bobolink
Boer and Briton
Bo-Peep
Bottle Quoits
Bowling
Boy Blue Puzzle
Brer Rabbit
Brownies
Buffalo Bill
Business

Cake Walk
Captain Kidd
Challenge
Checkers
Chicken Coop Puzzle
Children's Tennis
Chivalry
Christ Before Pilate
Christian Endeavor
Christmas Dinner
Cinderella
Circus
Cities
Climbing the Mountain
Cock Robin
Colors
Conundrums
Corner Grocery
County Fair
Crossing the Ocean
Cube Anagrams
Cut-Up Animals
Cut-Up History
Cut-Up Locomotive
Cut-Up Travel
Cycling

Dark Town Ball
Dark Town Brigade

Dewey's Victory
Dickens Game
Dinner
Doctors and Quack
Dominoes
Donkey Ride
Drawing Teacher
Drummer Boy Picture
    Puzzle
Dr. Busby

Easy Spelling Board
English History

Fairy Tales
Famous Men
Favorite Art
Fighting in the Soudan
Fighting with the Boers
Fire Alarm
Fire Engine Picture
    Puzzle
Fish Pond Game
Flagship
Following the Flag
Foot Ball
Forbidden Fruit
Fortune Telling
French History

Geographical
Go-Bang
Golf
Great Battlefields
Grocery Store

Happy Darkies
Happy Families
Happy Hoppers
Hare and Hounds
Havana
Heads and Tails
Heathen Chinese
Hen That Laid the
    Golden Egg
Hickery, Dickery, Dock
Hold the Fort
Hong Kong

Hop Scotch Tiddledy
    Winks
Horse and Cow Picture
    Puzzle
House That Jack Built

India
Innocence Abroad
International Authors
Italian History
Ivanhoe

Jack and Jill
Jack and the Bean Stalk
Jack Straws
Jack the Giant Killer
Johnny's Historical
Jolly Tars
Jumping Turtles

Kee Poo Kan
Kilkenny Cats
King's Highway
Klondike
Komical Konversation
    Kards
Kringle
Kriss Kringle

Letters
Letters and Anagrams
Life Boat
Limited Mail
Literary Quotations
Literary Salad
Little Corporal
Little Cowboy
Little Folks Picture
    Puzzle
Little Grocer
Little Mother Goose
Little One's Tea Party
Little Pigs
London
Lost in the Forest
Lotto
Luck
Ludo

Mansion of Happiness
Menagerie
Merry Christmas
Military
Motor Carriage
Musical Letters

Napoleon
National Flower
New York
News Boy
Night Before Christmas
Noah's Ark
Nonsense
Nyout

Octo
Office Boy
Old Glory
Old Maid
Oliver Twist
Our Birds
Our Navy

Pat and His Pigs
Penny Post
Peter Coddle
Philippine Dissected Map
Philippine War
Pillow-Dex
Pillow-Dex Golf
Pillow-Dex Tennis
Ports and Commerce
Post Office
Pot of Gold
Prisoner of Zenda
Prisoner's Base
Proverbs
Puppy Dogs Picture Puzzle

Pushkins
Puss in the Corner

Queries from Literature

Race for the Cup
Railroad Game
Railroad Picture Puzzle
Red Riding Hood
Ring Toss
Rip Van Winkle
Robin Hood
Robinson Crusoe
Romany
Roosevelt's Charge
Roses
Rough Riders
Round the World Joe
Royal Arabia
Rubber Bubbles

Sailor Boy Puzzle
Santa Claus
Ship Comes In
Shopping
Snap
Steeple Chase
Story of Liberty Picture Puzzle
Street Car
Sweet William and Marigold

Tadpole Game
Ten Little Niggers
Tether Ball
Three Little Kittens
Tip Cat Puzzle
Tit Tat Toe

Tom, Tom, the Piper's Son
Tommy Town
Tox
Trafalgar
Train for Boston
Travel
Trip Trap
Trolley Came Off

Uncle Sam and Folks
Union Station Picture Puzzle
United States History

Varsity Race

War in Cuba
War in South Africa
War of 1812
Waterloo
Watermelon Puzzle
West Point Cadet
Who
Wide World
Wife and I
Wild and Domestic Animals
Wild Flower
Witchcraft
Wonderland
World's History

Yachts
Yale-Harvard
Yankee Doodle
Young America Target

Zoo

"Chivalry." George S. Parker & Co., 1887.

"The Race for the Cup." Parker Brothers, 1896.

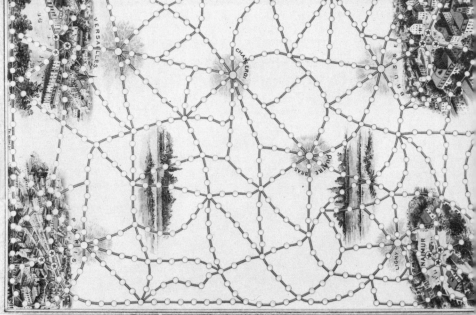

"Waterloo." Parker Brothers, 1895.

Among the articles made by Charles Shipman, ivory and hardwood turner, and listed in his ad in *The New York Journal or The General Advertiser,* August 6, 1767, were "ivory counters engraved with alphabets and figures (very popular for children)." It is not certain whether or not these were blocks, but at any rate the education of children through toys caught on in America at an early age. Alphabet blocks were used in England in the seventeenth century. They were made of bone or wood and marked with the alphabet. In 1820 J. Ruthven of New York, a metal, wood, and ivory turner, made billiard balls, bagatelle, cups and balls, teething rings, whistles, and drum sticks, and undoubtedly made ivory blocks, since such blocks were made by Thomas Anners of Philadelphia, 1822–1829. There were early wooden blocks with stenciled letters, animals, and figures such as stars and anchors, but these must have been made by the local carpenter or cabinetmaker. The first blocks that were made in any quantity were those made by S. L. Hill of Williamsburg, New York. Hill patented his spelling blocks in 1858. They had printed letters, Arabic and Roman numerals, and pictures printed on paper and pasted on. They came in wooden boxes with sliding tops and were best sellers for several decades.

In the 1860's Milton Bradley made building blocks and alphabet blocks. Morton Converse of Rindge, New Hampshire, also made blocks, as did the Embossing Company of Albany, New York, and McLoughlin Bros. A set of blocks picturing a village church with scripture tests on the inside of the blocks was given as a premium for subscriptions to *The Youth's Companion* in October, 1888. And in 1897 Bradley's Bible Panorama and Stratton's Building Blocks were on the market. Other companies that also made small wooden toys were The Tower Toy Guild of South Hingham, Massachusetts, Joy Manufacturing Companies of Weare, New Hampshire, and the Union Turning Works at Claremont, New Hampshire. Blocks were also made by various small wooden toy makers in Vermont, Massachusetts, Connecticut, and New York.

It was the Crandalls, however, makers of children's carriages, velocipedes, horses, and sleds, who were the best-known makers of blocks. They made all sorts of blocks. They invented nested blocks, which were copied by other makers, and Expression Blocks, which had the alphabet on one side and cut-up portraits on the other. Crandall's Sectional Blocks had a part of a letter on each block and the alphabet could be formed by fitting the blocks together correctly. Crandall's Masquerade Blocks had pictures of figures in fancy costumes, and Noah's Dominoes had dots on one side and animal sections to be matched on the other. Crandall's famous building blocks could be used to construct churches, factories, houses, towers, arches, windmills, boxes, bridges, tools, chairs, bicycles, cradles,

Child playing with blocks. Artist unknown. American, ca. 1850. Collection of Mr. E. M. Strauss.

The Domino Girl. Artist unknown. American, ca. 1775. National Gallery of Art, gift of Edgar William and Bernice Chrysler Garbisch. ▶

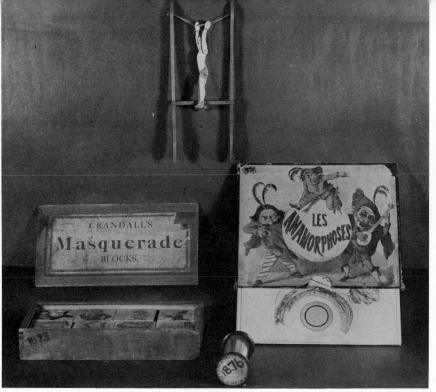

Above: *Man on trapeze.*
Lower left: *Crandall's Mas-
querade Blocks, ca.1873.*
Lower right: *Les Anamor-
phoses, Paris, ca.1870.* The
New-York Historical Society.

Poster, *"Crandall's Building
Blocks," ca.1867.* The New-
York Historical Society.

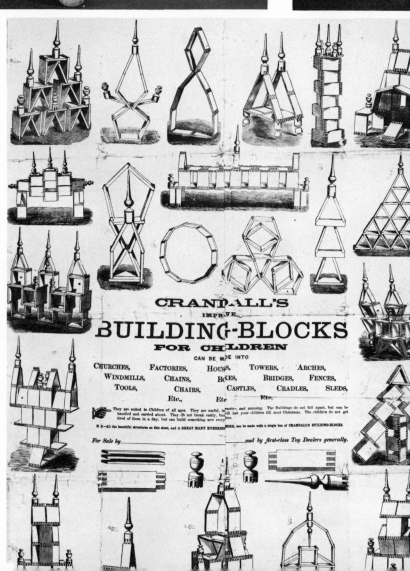

Mr. and Mrs. Ernest Fiedler and their children, ca. 1850. F. Heinrich. Child in foreground is building structure with cards similar to those in "Crandall's Building Blocks." The Museum of the City of New York.

Advertisement of Crandall's blocks and wooden toys. Wide Awake, 1881. Collection of John Mackay Shaw.

DON'T FORGET THE BOYS & GIRLS.

GAMES AND TOYS.

Lawn Tennis.—One of the most delightful games for the family to be found in the market. Sets supplied at from $8 to $60.
Croquet.—Almost any price can be met. Sets at from $1.75 to $14.
Bat and Trap.—Rules accompanying each game, and they are easily learned. Price $2.

CRANDALL'S TREASURE BOX.

This is one of Crandall's latest and best inventions. It is not a single toy, but a dozen in one, comprising a Wagon, Top, Bedstead, 2 Chairs, Wheelbarrow, Mallet, Bench, Table, Puzzle, Set of A B C Blocks, a group of nine Domestic Animals, and a pretty Suburban Village. A most delightful combination for the little folks

Price $1.00. *Too large to go by mail. Expressage to be paid by receiver.*

	Price	By Mail Prepaid
Crandall's Heavy Artillery	$3.00	
Crandall's Happy Family	2.00	
Crandall's Hand Car	1.00	
Crandall's Velocipede and Rider	.50	
Crandall's Trumpet Wheelbarrow	1.00	
The "Æolia" Piano	1.00	
The "Florence' Piano	2.00	

The expressage on the above named toys and games to be paid by the recipient.

	Price.	By Mail Prepaid
Crandall's New Acrobats	$ .50	$ .65
Crandall's Expression Blocks	.50	.65
Crandall's Bridge	.75	1.25
Crandall's Sectional A B C Blocks	.75	1.00
Crandall's Chinese Blocks	1.00	1.25
Crandall's First Reading Blocks	.25	.40
Crandall's Donkey and Rider	.50	.70
Crandall's District School	1.00	1.20
Crandall's Wide Awake Alphabet	1.00	1.30
Crandall's Bo-Peep	.25	.30
Crandall's Toy Horse	.25	.30
Crandall's Lively Horseman	.50	.70
Crandall's Masquerade-Blocks	.75	.90

sleds, castles, etc. Crandall also made movable wooden figures of men and animals set up in compositions such as "The District School" and "The Menagerie." "The District School" included desks and figures of a teacher, pupils, a dunce, and Mary's lamb. It was advertised in *The Youth's Companion* October 31, 1878, Nov. 14, 1878, and Dec. 5, 1878. Other games and toys included in the same advertisement were: Bridge, Chinese Blocks, Acrobats, Expression Blocks, Ye Hero of '76, Wide Awake Alphabet, John Gilpin,* Masquerade Blocks, Happy Family, Jediah, Little All-Right, and Toy House. In December, 1879, advertisements included: Donkey & Rider, Lively Horseman, Two Jolly Blacks, Trained Animals, Merry Lands, Heavy Artillery, and Happy Family. A long list of toys were included in the *Wide Awake Advertiser* in August 1881, and "New Toys" in 1882 included Crandall's Folding Doll House, Folding Dish Cupboard, and Folding Stable, and Noah's Dominoes.

Among the many toys and amusements for children invented by Jesse Crandall in the 1870's and 1880's were games such as The Dude Party, Chinaman Party, Elephant Party, and Barnum's Greatest Show. In November, 1886, a wooden puzzle called Tower of Hannoi was advertised by Haff & Co. of Hartford, Connecticut. It consisted of wooden pegs and blocks on a board and was made in different colors.

Dominoes was also an old game from the East but, together with checkers and chess, it had been popular in America in the eighteenth century. In 1885 Frank H. Richards of Troy, New York, advertised a new domino game, Triangular Dominoes. It is not known how popular these were. Perhaps a box of triangular dominoes would be a rare collector's item.

Any of these games are collector's fun. Their value depends upon their rarity and their condition. Although games get worn and battered, and pieces are lost, there are many on the market and each attic clean-out brings more to light.

---

* This consisted of two figures, Gilpin and his horse, which could be twisted into many positions to illustrate the old English poem, the verses of which were included with the figures.

Mary Caroline and Otis Hubbard Cooley by Joseph Stock, ca. 1850. The Downtown
Gallery, New York City.

12

Push and Pull Toys

ush and pull toys have a long history. Wooden horses and animals on wheels with a string in the nose for pulling were made in early Egypt, and limestone pull toys of Persia date before Christ. One of the most interesting ancient pull toys is the wooden tiger from Thebes, ca. 1000 B.C., which is in the British Museum.

Wood Toys

The horse was a favorite pull toy in America, and one of the earliest existing American pull toys is an eighteenth-century wooden horse on wheels, painted red and green and with a whistle in its tail, once belonging to Robert Livingstone. Such toys were made in Sonneberg, Germany, at this time. The horse pull toys were made in all sizes from a few inches tall to some large enough to ride, and other animals such as dogs, cats, wild animals, and chickens were made as well.

The earliest American wooden pull toys, made in the eighteenth century, consisted of wheels attached to stick handles often ending in a horse's head—the first type of hobbyhorse. These could be pulled, pushed, or straddled for riding, and were often homemade.

The toys of the nineteenth century were generally carved by

Portrait of John F. Anderson in skeleton suit and peaked and tasseled hat. Horse pull toy, ca.1840. The Newark Museum.

Joseph and Anna Raymond with doll and dog pull toy. The Metropolitan Museum of Art, gift of Edgar William and Bernice Chrysler Garbisch, 1966.

The Burnish Sisters with woolly lamb pull toy. William Prior, ca. 1840–1850. Collection of Edgar William and Bernice Chrysler Garbisch.

Birds. Pennsylvania Sunday toy, ca. 1850. Anonymous carver. Index of American Design.

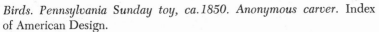

Woolly lamb pull toy. The Henry
Ford Museum.

Painted wooden horse pull toy. The
New-York Historical Society.

itinerant wood-carvers, especially in the Pennsylvania Dutch Country. Their ancestry can be traced back to Switzerland and Germany and the wood-carvers of the Black Forest.

One of the favorite nineteenth-century toys was the woolly lamb, covered with real lamb's wool. There was usually a single lamb set on a platform, but some platforms held as many as six lambs. A rare hide-covered cow with a squeak box that moos when the cow's head is moved was made in the 1890's. It stands on a platform with wheels.

The wood-carvers also made small sleighs and carriages with horses, boats, and, later, toy wooden trains on wheels.

Other wooden toys included villages with houses and figures of men and animals; Christmas scenes of the Nativity, and Noah's Arks.

Although it is difficult to assign any of these small wooden toys to a definite wood-carver, there were two or three known names among the American craftsmen and some of their larger pieces can be identified, especially the eagles of Schimmel and Mountz.

Wilhelm Schimmel (ca. 1817–1890) was the best known among these workmen, and his pieces are treasured by museums and individual collectors today. The articles vary in size from two inches to more than a foot in height. The animals, especially the eagles, are fierce-looking creatures and the carving is bold. One identifying mark is the cross-hatching on wings and body. The wings are made separately and pegged to the body. Some eagles have widespread

Seated squirrel. Wilhelm Schimmel. Philadelphia Museum of Art.

Shepherd and flock. Wilhelm Schimmel, 1865–1890. Philadelphia Museum of Art, Titus C. Geesey Collection.

Child with small horse, wheelbarrow, and other toys, ca. 1850. Artist unknown. American Heritage Collection, Colby College.

wings. The figures were originally painted with bold color, and traces of brown, black, red, green, and yellow can still be seen on most animals. In addition to eagles, Schimmel carved dogs, roosters, lions, and parrots. He also made figures in groups, the best known being the "Garden of Eden," the figures of which were arranged within a picketed fence and tacked to a board. They included an apple tree and the figures of Adam and Eve. Schimmel also carved scenes of the Crucifixion and Noah's Ark. These were known as Sunday toys and were probably made for display rather than for play. He also made Hessian soldiers and flower pieces.

APPLES OF GOLD.

VOL. II.]   *A word fitly spoken is like apples of gold in pictures of silver.*   PROV. XXV. II.   [NO. 50.

THE CHRISTMAS PRESENTS.

I GIVE you on this page a picture of the children
of Mr. Sylvester's family, as they played with their

*The Christmas presents, including hobby-
horse, jumping jack, and Noah's Ark.
Apples of Gold, vol. 2, no. 50. Collection
of John Mackay Shaw.*

*Pair of birds. Wilhelm Schimmel. Phila-
delphia Museum of Art.*

Garden of Eden. Wilhelm Schimmel. Sunday toy. Philadelphia Museum of Art.

Rooster, polychromed wood carving. Wilhelm Schimmel. Philadelphia Museum of Art, Titus C. Geesey Collection.

Giraffe, poly-chromed wood carving. Wilhelm Schimmel. Philadelphia Museum of Art.

Noah's Arks

The Noah's Arks are the most desirable of nineteenth-century wooden toys. The arks range from a simple house set on a block of wood with a group of several dozen animals, to a large ark set on a tugboat structure, similar to medieval representations of the ark. They are usually painted with a decorative border of leaves and flowers or animals and have a figure of a dove painted on the roof. Sometimes there are as many as two or three hundred animals. Noah's Arks were also made in Massachusetts, New Hampshire, and Vermont, where wood was readily available. In the later-nineteenth century Morton E. Converse brought Noah's Arks back into popularity. He also made animals to be packed into freight

Noah's Ark. Polychromed pine. Pennsylvania, ca. 1870–1880. Index of American Design.

cars. These groups are rare and expensive and seldom available, but the smaller individual animals are available. The eagles and roosters are the most desirable and the most expensive.

Aaron Mountz was a pupil of Schimmel who worked in the second half of the nineteenth century. His animals are carved in a smoother style and his favorite subjects were roosters, turkeys, and French poodles.

George Huguenin, also working in the late-nineteenth century, carved barnyard scenes with a stable or barn and domestic animals including sheep, cattle, horses, hens, and roosters. Sheep were his favorites. They were carved of several pieces of wood with legs and tail joined separately to the body which was covered with real pelt. A black sheep was usually included in the group. Huguenin also carved tiny houses which were painted white with the windows outlined in black. He also carved Noah's Arks and circus animals and churches.

There were many other toy carvers whose names are no longer known and whose work is not as desirable. Some are very late and others on the market are from Europe. Only an expert can tell the American folk carving from that of today's Oberammergau.

Although the wooden folk toys of Pennsylvania are the most interesting, there were also other early-nineteenth-century pieces such as hand-carved dolls, ox teams, wagons, cradles, and trains. Later, localities such as South and East Weare and Rindge, New Hampshire, and South Hingham, Massachusetts, became centers for factory-made wooden toys. The Tower Toy Guild, which was formed in the 1830's, made toy wooden boats, toy tools, and especially toy furniture.

Toy wagon. The Henry Ford Museum.

Child in homemade dog cart. Mc-Guffey Second Reader. Collection of John Mackay Shaw.

262

Francis and Charles Cowdry with wagon, ca.1838, Henry Walton. National Gallery of Art, gift of Edgar William and Bernice Chrysler Garbisch.

Wooden carriage. The Henry Ford Museum.

The W. S. Reed Toy Company made wooden trains, toy wooden boats, and wooden circus wagons with lithographed sides. Toy trains with cars that hooked together were also made by Jesse Crandall. Many other toys manufactured by the Crandalls, such as the Lively Horseman and Two Jolly Blacks, were made to pull. In the 1890's wooden push and pull toys were made by Gibbs Manufacturing Company of Canton, Ohio. Some pull toys had figures which moved when the toy was pulled. There was a cat with a head that nodded and an Irishman who danced a jig as the toy was pulled.

Tin Toys

During the 1830's and 1840's tin was also used for toy making. The Pattersons of Berlin and New Britain, Connecticut, had made toys from scrap tin in the late eighteenth century. In 1848 the Philadelphia Tin Toy Manufactory made tin pull toys including horses, dogs, cows, a horse-drawn bus, a locomotive, and boats. These were painted in gay colors. From 1856, George W. Brown of Forestville, Connecticut, also made tin toys, including horses on platforms, horse-drawn street cars, meat and bakers' carts, horses and dogs in hoops, and a whole menagerie of animals on wheels. All were painted in red, green, yellow, and blue, and had stencil decoration.

One of the earliest tin toys, made in the late 1860's by Ives & Blakeslee of Plymouth, Connecticut, was the hot-air toy. This toy consisted of moving figures fitted with pulleys. It was operated by

Mare and colt. George W. Brown, ca. 1860. The New-York Historical Society.

Tin goat cart, red with black goat. The New-York Historical Society.

Fire engine, "Excelsior." Pump handles red, body blue with gold lettering and border. The New-York Historical Society.

Tin toy dancers. The New-York Historical Society.

paper wheels held in shape by little wooden sticks and was supplied with a piece of mounting wire designed to be inserted in the kitchen stove pipe where the current of air was strong enough to move the paper wheel and thus put the toy in motion. The toys would also operate over a lamp, gas burner, or register. A considerable variety of different designs consisting of from one to four figures were manufactured between 1868 and the late 1890's. These included a Cat with Bass Viol, a Man Sawing Wood, and "Good Morning!" figures of a man and a woman. The following advertisement, illustrated by a musical cat, appeared in *The Youth's Companion*, December 2, 1875: "Hot air Toys—Will run over stove, lamp gas jet. Cat Musicians, Grinders, Dancers, etc. Blow gun, Counting Bank, Repeating Canon. W. C. Goodwin Sole Manufacturer, New Haven, Connecticut."

In 1870 Ives moved to Bridgeport and at this date put out his first clockwork toys—a little rowboat that worked on water or on the parlor floor, and also a small velocipede rider with horse's head. These were followed by figures of a boy and girl on a swing, and a trotting horse. In a few years Ives was manufacturing a line of more than twenty clockwork toys which included figures on seesaws, dancing figures, horse trainers, carts with horses, and a hippodrome chariot driven by a woman in a plumed hat. These toys were mostly of tin gaily painted and ornamented with striping, stenciling, and decalcomanias. The clockworks were furnished by the New Haven Clock Company.

The most popular clockwork toy then and today was the little tin locomotive. These miniature engines made in the 1870's and 1880's were painted bright red and decorated with stencils and gilt spread eagles. Since real engines in those days had names, the toy engines bore such fascinating appellations as Tiger, Giant, Lion, Vulcan, and Grand Duke. The Grand Duke was the finest. It had fancy designs on the wheels and cow catcher. These fascinating trackless tin clockwork models were illustrated in the 1870 catalogue. The largest tin locomotive was No. 19–5, an eighteen-inch model. This was replaced by the Grand Duke in the 1880's.

The Stevens & Brown Manufacturing Company's catalogue of tin and Britannia toys, put out in 1870, illustrated tin engines painted

Toy tin locomotive, mid-nineteenth century. Index of American Design.

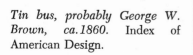

Tin bus, probably George W. Brown, ca. 1860. Index of American Design.

and stenciled with names and scroll patterns. The large "Omaha" was 14 inches long by 9½ inches high; the "New York" was 10 inches long by 7 inches high. The "U.S. Grant" was also large and the "Union" had two passenger cars attached. There was also a tiny five-inch locomotive. These engines were mechanical.

Other early tin toy manufacturers from the 1860's to 1900's were Hull & Stafford (Hull & Wright); Althof, Berman & Co.; American Toy Company; J. N. Bunnell of Farmington, Connecticut; I. F. Crocker, Valley Falls, Rhode Island; James Fallows & Son, Philadelphia; D. T. Knight, Clinton, Connecticut; Merriman Manufacturing Co., Durham, Connecticut; New England Toy Company, Providence, Rhode Island; R. Parry, Wilmington, Delaware; Benjamin T. Roney, Attleborough, Pennsylvania; and Leo Schlesinger, New York City. In the 1860's Musgrove & Son of New York advertised "Tin Goods for Wedding Presents," and a list of such presents included "Toys and Miniatures." Well-known pull toys made by Gibbs of Canton, Ohio, in the late nineteenth century were a butterfly and a rooster set on metal wheels.

Cast-Iron Toys

In the 1880's and 1890's many push and pull toys were made of cast iron. Hubley Manufacturing Company of Lancaster, Pennsylvania, manufactured a variety of fascinating iron toys including a horse-drawn sleigh, a Roman chariot, circus wagons, a Tally-ho, fire engines, and various kinds of carriages with drivers. Cast-iron toys were also made by the Kenton Hardware Company of Kenton, Ohio. A circus bandwagon drawn by two white horses was marked "Overland Circus." The best-known makers were Bevin Brothers, East Hampton, Connecticut; William E. Barton of Chatham, Connecticut; J. L. Watrous & Co. (N. N. Hill Brass Co.) of Cromwell, Connecticut; and J. & E. Stevens also of Cromwell, Connecticut. The toys included figures of fish, alligators, elephants, and other animals doing all kinds of tricks and ringing bells. One called the "Daisy Bell Toy" was the figure of a child in a sleigh driving a horse of which only the head was shown. Some iron toys were very elaborate and had tricky mechanisms. They not only rolled across the floor but they had figures that moved, did tricks, and rang bells. The Baby Quieter rang a bell and bounced the figure on the bell up and down, thus permitting Papa to relax and read his paper. A "Swan Chariot" had moving wings and a whistle; the "Tramp Bell Ringer" swung from side to side pulling chains with clappers that hit a bell. Other iron toys often told a story such as "Jonah and the Whale," or "Ding Dong Bell—Pussy's Not in the Well," or "The Pig." "Columbus Egg" celebrated the Columbian Exposition in Chicago in 1893. Iron toys made by the Gong Bell Company can be identified by the fancy design of the wheels. All these toys were gaily painted in bright colors.

Hook and ladder fire engine, ca. 1888. The New-York Historical Society.

Cast-iron hansom cab. Hubley Mfg. Co., 1890's. The New-York Historical Society.

Left: *The Toonerville Trolley, ca.1920.* Center: *Cast-iron row boat. Early nineteenth century.* Right: *Metal bell ringing toy, ca.1880.* Jerry Smith Collection, Hallmark Gallery, New York.

Bell toy. Doll on velocipede, ca. 1860. Index of American Design.

Trick Pony Bell Ringer No. 39, Gong Bell Mfg. Co., 1880's. Index of American Design.

Metal fire station with horse-drawn wagon. Jerry Smith Collection, Hallmark Gallery, New York.

Trains and horse-drawn vehicles began to be made in cast iron as well. The first iron toys were stiff models copied from the tin models, and the early cast-iron trackless engines and trains were small. In about 1900–1901 the first track trains were made in tin, but soon the iron train took over and Ives was on the way to becoming the largest producer of toy trains. Early toy trains were also made by Wilkins who made a rare scale model of the Boston & Maine. Locomotives were also manufactured by W. B. Carpenter and, in the 1890's, by Hubley of Lancaster, Pennsylvania. The most sought-after iron toys were made by Ives, followed by Carpenter, Wilkins, and Hubley. Any marked or identified pieces are expensive and rare.

As early as 1860, push and pull toys not only rolled but had moving figures with windup motors and bells. There were mechanical windup toys driven by clockwork, and they included mechanical animals such as dogs, bears, and birds in cages. The Automaton Negro Dancer was patented September 27, 1864, and manufactured by Berendsohn brothers in New York. They also made kitchen toys and a magic apple parer. These were advertised in *Harper's Weekly*, December 24, 1864, together with a cut of the Negro dancer. There were also mechanical boats, the first being a row boat with a man moving the oars; this was patented in 1869 and made by Ives of Bridgeport. Mechanical toys were also made in quantity by the Buckman Manufacturing Company of New York, who advertised their toy steamboat "Frolic" in *Harper's Weekly,* 1872. Another patent toy steamboat was advertised by Bramhall, Smith & Co., New York (*Harper's Weekly*, June 22, 1872). A toy steam engine with copper boiler and bottom and called the "Young America" was made by Buckman Manufacturing Company in the 1840's, and steam engines were made by other manufacturers in the 1870's,

Weeden Steam Engine. The Youth's Companion, *1880's.*

1880's, and 1890's as well. The best known of these was the Weeden engine. With a safety valve, whistle, and smokestack, it was an elaborate and well-made engine of nickled tin and brass. It was illustrated in the premium list of the Lothrop Magazine in 1887. Also illustrated were several mechanical toys made to be worked from a belt from the Weeden engine. These included a wood sawyer, a monkey organ grinder, an orchestra of four lithographed figures of cats playing instruments, and a village blacksmith with bellows and hammer. There were undoubtedly many other similar toys.

Toy Pistols

Pistols that shot paper caps were first made by J. & E. Stevens. In their catalogue of 1859 they list "Fire Cracker Pistols." After the Civil War the toy pistol became more popular, and Stevens enlarged their production to include pistols with names and fancy handles. Names included The Gem, Boss of Buffalo, Salute, Triumph, Thunderer, and Safety Supply. There were also novelty pistols. In the 1890's Stevens made a cap pistol in the form of a sea serpent with a cap-exploding jaw. A monkey pistol with a monkey sitting on a tree

Group of cast-iron toy pistols, 1875–1880. From left to right: *Dolphin peashooter, Head of lion, dog, man, and Royal Top Spinning Pistol.* Collection of F. H. Griffith.

trunk holds a coconut. H. M. Quackenbush of Herkimer, New York, also made cap pistols. In the 1880's and 1890's Ives and Blakeslee manufactured many conventional-style cap pistols such as the double-barreled "Crack," but they also made many novelty animated pistols such as Punch and Judy, Humpty Dumpty, Camera, Dolphin, Sailing Ship, and Torpedo. The well-known collector's prize, "Chinese Must Go," and an animated cap pistol marked "Just Out" which was composed of a rooster, egg, and chick that cracked the egg when the trigger was pulled, were made by Ives in the 1880's. Ives also made bombs which were fitted with a paper cap and string. They were dropped on the sidewalk to explode. Bombs were cast in shapes of miniature heads of dogs or other animals. There were also heads of Chinese men and Admiral Dewey. The Devil Bomb was in the shape of a Satan's head. Ives also made toy cannon to explode firecrackers. Some cannon were drawn by horses and driven by the figure of a driver. Cannon also were given names such as Emperor, Swamp Angel, and Yankee, the majority of them relating to the Civil War.

Toy cap pistols. Center: *Bootjack pistol.* Collection of F. H. Griffith.

Animated toy pistols. Top, left to right: *Clown and Mule, The Chinese Must Go, Punch and Judy.* Lower left to right: *Clown on Powder Keg, Sambo, Shoot the Hat.* 1880's. Collection of F. H. Griffith.

Toy cap pistols. Top left: *Monkey and Cocoanut. J. & E. Stevens Co., Cromwell, Connecticut.* Center left: *Lightning Express, Kenton Hardware Co.* Lower left: *Firecracker pistol with open wood handle.* Top right: *Double-barrel cap pistol.* Center right: *King pistol.* Lower right: *Three rare cap pistols.* Collection of F. H. Griffith.

Banks

Tin bank, ca.1860. The Seamen's Bank for Savings, New York City.

One of the most popular collector's items today is the toy bank, both the still, or non-mechanical, and the mechanical type. Tin banks were probably the earliest, made mostly between 1800 and 1860. Early tin pedlars, like the Pattersons of Berlin, Connecticut, however, may have made tin banks around 1770. In the late 1860's the J. E. Stevens Company of Cromwell, Connecticut, put out a still bank shaped like a bank building, and George W. Brown & Company of Forestville, Connecticut, also made many tin banks. In 1868 the two companies went into partnership, and in 1870 the Stevens and Brown Manufacturing Company issued a catalogue of mechanical, tin, and Britannia toys. This catalogue included tin banks shaped like houses and Gothic clocks.

The most common were the house banks, usually small rectangular structures with a center chimney and stenciled windows and center door, but also including octagonal summer houses, Victorian gingerbread houses, and Swiss cottages, all of which were painted and decorated with stencils. One of the most fascinating banks in the catalogue was a church. Later tin house banks had porches and angled eaves ornamented with borders of Victorian gingerbread that was soldered on, and also had lithographed rather than stenciled, decoration. The design of the applied decorations is often the key to the identity of the maker. The house banks made by George W. Brown (1857–1880) and illustrated in the 1870 catalogue have a border trim of vertical rectangular pieces alternating with a leaf form. This and similar borders are found on almost all the larger house banks and also on the church bank. Other tin banks were drums with patriotic symbols of the Civil War, and hats made after the Mexican War.

By the 1890's, beautifully detailed cast-iron banks were being made. They varied from log-cabin houses to modern skyscraper banks. There was a castellated building marked Tower Bank, 1891, and one known as "Castle" bank. It was at this time that the Hubley Manufacturing Company of Lancaster, Pennsylvania, made mailboxes and cash-register banks. Numerous patents between 1883 and 1895 indicate that safe banks were being made as well. Sizes ranged from small, 3½-inch-high, 2½-inch-wide, and 2½-inch-deep banks to larger banks 8½ inches high by 6 inches wide and 5 inches deep. The first safe banks made by J. & E. Stevens were decorated with simple stenciling. In the 1890's the safes were made of embossed cast iron. Some had a door that opened onto an empty interior, others had drawers and separate coin slits for each drawer; some had a lock and key and others had combinations. Many were given names suggesting their purpose, such as State Safe, National Safe, Young America, Royal Safe Deposit, Uncle Sam Security, Columbus Safe Bank of Commerce, The Home Bank, the Globe (shaped like a globe), and Treasure Safe.

Tin Gothic bank. Catalogue, Stevens & Brown Mfg. Co., 1870. The Seamen's Bank for Savings, New York City.

Cottage bank. Catalogue, Stevens & Brown Mfg. Co., 1870. The Seamen's Bank for Savings, New York City.

Tin church bank painted cream color with red roof, brown stencil, inscription, "For Good Little Children," ca. 1860. The Seamen's Bank for Savings, New York City.

Cast-iron "Castle" still bank. The Seamen's Bank for Savings, New York City.

Group of still iron banks. The Henry Ford Museum.

Other still banks can be found in the form of animals and men. The animal banks include a sitting and a standing pig, a cat with ball, a Saint Bernard dog with pack, a puppy on a cushion inscribed "Fido," and a veritable menagerie of lions, elephants, camels, bears, and buffaloes, as well as barnyard animals including donkeys and cows. Humorous banks include those with comic strip figures such as Mutt and Jeff, Little Orphan Annie, Campbell Kids, and Buster Brown and Tige. These were made by A. C. Williams Company of Ravenna, Ohio, one of the largest toy bank manufacturers, and by Wing Manufacturing Company. Although the large tin banks are scarce, especially the church, the large house with gingerbread trim, and the octagonal summer house, many are still to be found in shops and at reasonable prices.

Cast-iron "Royal Safe Deposit" still bank. The Seamen's Bank for Savings, New York City.

The best-known manufacturer of mechanical banks was J. & E. Stevens, who started making them in the 1870's. From then until World War I, Stevens produced more than fifty different figures of mechanical banks. There were buildings of every kind, including banks, animals, well-known individuals, and news events. The animals usually performed an action as indicated by the names given the banks, such as the "Kicking Mule" or the "Eagle Feeding Her Young."

These banks have become so scarce and the prices so inflated that the beginning collector would do well to concentrate on the still banks.

POTTERY BANKS

The earliest were little jug banks of pottery, made in the late eighteenth century. Gray stoneware banks with blue painted and scratched decoration, yellow ware, and red Pennsylvania pottery banks were also made. Some of these have bird finials, and others are shaped like birds, lions, chickens, and other fowl. Banks in the shapes of boats were made, and there is a bureau bank of brown mottled pottery, as well as an organ bank. A rare schoolhouse bank was made of Pennslyvania pottery. These are in many museum collections, but so far they have not caught the fancy of most collectors.

Grey stoneware bank with blue decoration. Early nineteenth century. The New-York Historical Society.

Stoneware cabin bank. American, 1846. The Seamen's Bank for Savings, New York City.

Red Pennsylvania pottery schoolhouse bank. The Seamen's Bank for Savings, New York City.

Child with squeak toy dog.   Painter unknown, ca. 1845.   Shelburne Museum.

Squeak toys, most of them made in Pennsylvania (although originally made in Sonneberg, Germany), were popular in nineteenth-century America. They consisted of a figure, made of wood, papier-mâché, plaster of Paris, or some other composition, fastened to a thin wooden platform with a bellows beneath. The pressure on the bellows produced a squeak, a cat's meow, or a bird's chirp. The eyes, nose, tail, and other features such as spots and stripes, were crudely painted by hand. The colors vary, but red, green, yellow, and brown are the most common. The favorite figures were birds—bluejays, robins, pigeons, and large cranes—and peacocks, which were the rarest. Some birds had twisted wire legs which made the bird twist and sway when the bellows were pressed. There were also dogs, cats, rabbits, and wild animals, including bears. Rare squeak toys include those with more than one animal or figure, such as a bird in a cage, a cat with kittens, a hen with chickens, a girl riding a dog, and a baby in a cradle. Birds and cats were made in the greatest variety. Cats included tiger cats, tabby cats, and yellow cats. Dogs included spaniels, fox terriers, little wooly dogs, and large Newfoundland dogs. Birds and roosters were the favorites. Squeak toys were not made in quantity, and, since they were handmade, there are no two exactly alike.

Squeak toy parrot. Mid-nineteenth century. The Henry Ford Museum.

Peacock, squeak toy. The Henry Ford Museum.

Squeak toy cat. Mid-nineteenth century. The Henry Ford Museum.

Rabbit, squeak toy. The Henry Ford Museum.

Squeak toy cat and kitten. The Henry Ford Museum.

Bear, squeak toy. The Henry Ford Museum.

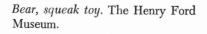

Girl riding on dog, squeak toy. The Henry Ford Museum.

JACK-IN-THE-BOX

Wooden toys, including jumping jacks, dolls on sticks, and Jack-in-the-Box, were made in small factories in New England, New York, and Pennsylvania from the early nineteenth century, and, in the 1840's, toymakers, especially in small towns of New Hampshire, were making small wooden toys such as jump ropes, blocks, wagons, and toy wheelbarrows. From 1872 on, all commercial jumping jacks in America were made by the Toy Manufacturing Company of East Weare, New Hampshire.

The Snake-in-the-Box and Jack-in-the-Box are related to the squeak toy in that they have a folding bellows construction and a papier-mâché or wooden head. The Jack-in-the-Box is an old toy and was originally called Punch Box in Europe. It may have been related to Punch and Judy, since the majority of Jacks are clowns and some have caps and faces similar to those given Punch. There were also women jacks dressed in gowns and caps like Judy. These

Jumping Jacks. Left: *Wooden soldier, American, ca.1920.* Center: *Puss in Boots, color print on carboard, ca.1827.* Right: *Wooden Russian brown bear, ca. 1908.* Museum of the City of New York.

Jumping Jacks. Left to right: *Glass, Austrian. Wooden Santa Claus, Swiss. Large wooden Santa Claus, French, ca.1920. Painted wooden man, Swiss. Chinese clown.* Museum of the City of New York.

Jacks and Snakes were revived in the early nineteenth century. The jumping jack that jumped on a stick when a string was pulled was of Oriental origin. These toys, however, were known in Europe and were illustrated in early prints and universally sold by street pedlars. Although the Jack was the most popular, there were also monkeys on a stick, a dancing skeleton, and numerous animals including deer and horses. An English version was the Admiral-up-

a-Mast. There were also pecking birds and pecking chickens on
sticks. These were popular toys made in Sonneberg and Oberammergau and merchandised and exported through Nuremburg, Germany, and known as Nuremburg toys. In 1888, I. E. Horstman of
New York, importer of dolls, advertised "Revolving Musical Dolls
and Whistling Dolls on sticks." There were also clapping figures on
sticks.

Jack-in-the-Box. John G. Brown, 1831–1913. The Detroit Institute of Arts.

Jack-in-the-Box.   Papier-mâché head, wooden hands, paper-covered box. Nineteenth century. The Henry Ford Museum.

Mary Bumstead Brown, ca.1820, with tiny music box. Mr. and Mrs. Roy R. Bumstead, Jr. Photograph, Old Print Shop, New York City.

Musical toys, which were replicas of adult musical instruments, included the ever popular drums, whistles, trumpets, horns, harmonicas, accordions, music boxes, and later, pianos and phonographs.

Early toy drums were six, eight, and ten inches in diameter and were usually made by the same person who made larger drums. In 1775 Plunkett Fleeson advertised in the *Pennsylvania Gazette* "Toy drums, mahogany and maple eagle or flag (decoration), grape or hazelwood sticks." In 1770 Gilbert Deblois of Boston, Massachusetts, advertised violins, flutes, drums, battledores and shuttlecocks. John Mason of Philadelphia advertised tin drums and Jew's harps in the *Independent Gazetteer*, May 7, 1785. In the mid-nineteenth century tin toy drums were made by tin manufacturers including Benjamin T. Roney of Attleborough, Pennsylvania, and Stevens & Brown Manufacturing Company of Cromwell, Connecticut, who also made tin flutes and horns. Many toy drums were also imported.

Boy and Girl. Artist unknown, ca.1850. Girl wears drop earrings, gold beads and bracelet. Boy carries a dog-headed cane and a toy accordion. National Gallery of Art, gift of Edgar William and Bernice Chrysler Garbisch.

284

Portrait of children with toy accordion. Dress styles mid-nineteenth century. Ginsburg & Levy, Inc., New York City.

Boy with toy drum, ca. 1850. Artist unknown. The New-York Historical Society.

Miniature accordion painted and grained. Mid-nineteenth century. The Henry Ford Museum.

Harmonicas. M. Hohner, Germany. Center left: Round tin and brass harmonica. G. Bruchbauer, pat. 1874. The Henry Ford Museum.

Toy Military Drum.

We offer this year a Drum which is a toy only in size. It has a genuine calf is provided with ebonized drum sticks, hook and sling, and leather ears of app

The shell has a mahogany fini embossed. All metal parts Diameter of Drum 10 inches.

Given for one new subscr cents extra, postage included. postage and packing 30 cents e

Beautiful Gem Stones thirty fine specimens in They are mounted on cardb name of each stone printed u

The complete Collection giv subscription and 10 cents included. Price $1.00, post-p

The Orchestrion. An ingenious musical device for young children, w of producing chords similar to those of a pipe organ. It will make a most interest volume of sound is regulated by the movement of the crank, a rapid turn sound, while a slow movement decreases it. The case is of metal, and 7 x 3 inches

The Orchestrion, as just described, given only to Companion subscribers for one ne and 40 cents extra, postage included. See Conditions, page 404. Price $1.25, posta

Toy drum. Youth's Companion premium, ca. 1880's. Collection of John Mackay Shaw.

The demand for toy drums continued to increase, and in 1854 Noble & Cooley of Granville, Massachusetts, set up a factory solely for the manufacture of toy drums. The Civil War created an added interest in toy drums, and several other companies in Massachusetts began to manufacture toy drums, including B. G. Dikinson of Granville, David Schott of Worcester, and Bush & Spencer of Springfield. In 1890 Noble & Cooley bought out the other toy drum makers, but, at about the same time, Morton E. Converse of Winchendon, Massachusetts, began toy drum manufacture and, by substituting parchment paper for sheepskin drumheads, was able to cut prices. In time, Converse got most of the drum business and became one of the largest manufacturers of toy drums.

Converse also made toy pianos, as did Joel Ellis of the Vermont Novelty Works, and N. P. Cass at Athol, Massachusetts. But the earliest and best-known manufacturer of toy pianos was Schoenhut. Schoenhut set up business in 1872. The smallest Schoenhut toy piano had fifteen keys. Those with two and a half and three octaves cost about twelve dollars and are scarce today. There were both grand and upright toy pianos made between 1870 and 1880. Schoenhut also made toy glockenspiels, xylophones and metallophones. Rare metal-case pianos were made by the Durable Toy and Novelty Company.

The toy music box that played a tune by turning a crank was also a popular nineteenth-century musical toy. First made in about 1835, the little box became so popular that it was introduced into jugs, bottles, miniature houses, carrousels, and other forms. The mechanism was attached to birds that moved, clowns that performed, and

Miniature rosewood piano, ca.1860. The Henry Ford Museum.

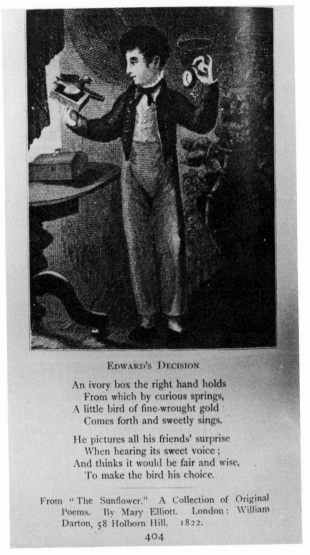

EDWARD'S DECISION

An ivory box the right hand holds
From which by curious springs,
A little bird of fine-wrought gold
Comes forth and sweetly sings.

He pictures all his friends' surprise
When hearing its sweet voice;
And thinks it would be fair and wise,
To make the bird his choice.

From "The Sunflower." A Collection of Original
Poems. By Mary Elliott. London: William
Darton, 58 Holborn Hill. 1822.

404

Music box with bird. The Sunflower, A Collection of Original Poems *by Mary Elliott, London, 1822.* Collection of John Mackay Shaw.

dolls that danced and whistled. The majority of these intricate mechanisms were manufactured in Germany, and only the simple tin and cardboard musical mechanisms were made in America. Many of the items in the "Musical Package for the Little Folks" included in *The Youth's Companion* premium pages, October 29, 1885, were imported. The "Package" included a brass-mounted buffalo horn trumpet, a car starter's whistle, a "French Miriliton which plays like a Kazoo," a Surprise Rooster, a German harmonica, a Jew's harp, a set of rosewood clappers, and a "Nightengale Trill." "The American Songster," a canary whistle, was invented by Jerome B. Secor during the 1870's, and the "Carillon,"

288

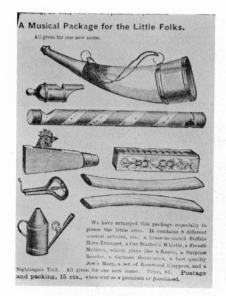

A Musical Package for the Little Folks.

All given for one new name.

We have arranged this package especially to please the little ones. It contains 8 different musical articles, viz.: a brass-mounted Buffalo Horn Trumpet, a Car Starter's Whistle, a French Mirliton, which plays like a Kazoo, a Surprise Rooster, a German Harmonica, a best quality Jew's Harp, a set of Rosewood Clappers, and a Nightingale Trill. All given for one new name. Price, $1. **Postage and packing, 15 cts.,** when sent as a premium or purchased.

Musical toys. Youth's Companion premium, 1885. Collection of John Mackay Shaw.

an automatic music box, was manufactured by Milton Bradley in the 1880's. In the 1890's there were also many small cylinder-shaped toy music boxes. These turned with a crank handle and played from one to three tunes.

All these old toys are in great demand with collectors today. Some, like the squeak and bellows toys, are very scarce and thus very expensive. Others, such as mechanical banks and other mechanical, musical, and bell-ringing toys, are the most popular toy items on the antique market today. Thus prices have soared to the thousands for articles that, when new, sold for a dollar or two. The still banks and the pottery banks are more reasonably priced because they are not in such great demand. However, the little early banks in the shape of birds, and the late-nineteenth-century banks in the shape of a schoolhouse or an organ, are rare and high priced.

13

Dolls

oll-collecting is a highly specialized field with
its own language and terminology. This chap-
ter is not for the seasoned doll collector, for
there are many books on the subject and I
have little new data to add to that already
published; but, since the doll was one of the
most important children's playthings from
earliest days, it is not possible to give a picture of American childhood without knowing something about the
dolls that were owned and played with by children.

Cloth dolls have a long history beginning with Egyptian dolls of
handwoven linen stuffed with papyrus. Homemade rag dolls were
played with by colonial children. Made of linen on unbleached
cotton and stuffed with sawdust or bran, their faces were painted by
hand. Few of the eighteenth- or early-nineteenth-century American
children ever saw any other kind of doll, though there were also
corn-husk dolls with tassel hair and painted faces. The corn-husk
dolls are now scarce (*See* Chapter 16).

The earliest wood dolls seem to have been "fashion" dolls, made
in England as early as the fourteenth century to show French
clothing styles. Prints and portraits show children playing with
these dolls down into the eighteenth century, but some of these
fashion dolls found their way to America early in the seventeenth
century.

English wooden doll.
Queen Anne period,
early eighteenth cen-
tury. Shelburne Mu-
seum.

Mehetable   Hodges
or Salem doll, wood,
ca.1715.   Museum
of the City of New
York.

One of the earliest known American dolls was of this type. She
was brought to America from England in 1699 by William Penn.
The doll, now known as Letitia Penn, is of wood, with a plaster
head. Another doll of this type was "Mehitable Hodges," brought to
Salem, Massachusetts, by Captain Gamaliel Hodges in 1724.

The typical English doll of the Queen Anne period (1700–1750)
had sloping shoulders and a large wooden enameled head with an
extremely high forehead. The eyes were large and long and pointed,
and were forced into the wood, and the real hair was set in a slit in
the top of the head. The head and body were a single piece of wood
and the arms were held in place by a linen strip running through a
hole bored in the wooden body. The legs swung from the hips and
were held by a wooden peg.

Dolls with wasplike waists, full skirts, and fancy lace caps are
shown with little girls in portaits by Sir Joshua Reynolds, John
Wollaston, John Singleton Copley, and other eighteenth-century
painters. There were also wooden dolls with hand-carved wooden
heads, some with high hairdos and combs. These eighteenth-century
dolls have a stiff appearance. Some are entirely of wood, and some
heads have a layer of composition which gives them a glossy
appearance. Although eyes were usually painted, some have fixed

Miss Proctor with parrot and eighteenth-century doll. Artist unknown. The Hammond-Harwood House, Annapolis, Maryland.

Portrait of mother and children. One child holds doll dressed in fashion of era. John Wollaston, mid-eighteenth century. Montclair Museum, Montclair, New Jersey.

Millinery fashion dolls, mid-nineteenth century. Shelburne Museum.

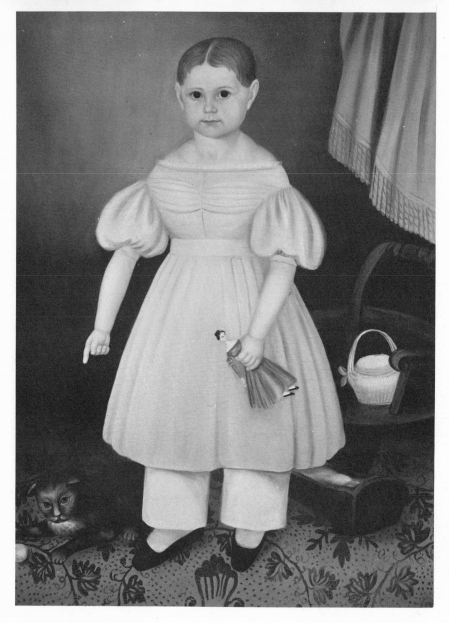

Mary Jane Smith with doll, doll's cradle, and basket. J. W. Stock, 1838. Abby Aldrich Rockefeller Folk Art Collection, Williamsburg, Virginia.

glass eyes composed of a blown glass bead without a pupil. Brown eyes and large heads are generally characteristic of these early dolls.

The painted wooden doll continued in popularity into the nineteenth century, and can be dated by hair styles. The doll of 1800–1810 had glass eyes and real hair or painted and lacquered shadow curls about the face. From 1810 to 1820 the black lacquered hair was arranged in plain waves about the face and held at the back with a comb. From about 1825 to 1840 the hair was molded in large bunlike curls at the side of the head and often had a tall bun on top. An occasional wooden doll of about 1840–1850 had long black lacquered hair.

Small peg dolls, made entirely of wood, were first brought to America from Europe in the early nineteenth century. They are

Top center: *Doll with wooden head, painted black hair, curls and wooden earrings. Jointed body, 1760.* Top left: *Wooden jointed doll with painted shadow curls. Similar dolls seated on right, 1800–1810.* Top right: *Negro boy with composition head, painted face, ca. 1830.* Center: *Undressed wooden jointed doll. Wooden jointed couple. Eighteenth century.* Bottom left: *Doll with porcelain head, arms and legs, 1850.* Bottom center: *Blond Parian type bisque doll holding tiny china doll with bisque hands and cloth body, ca. 1850.* Bottom right: *Small doll with porcelain head, ca. 1850.* Collection of Mrs. Imogene Anderson.

hand-carved, and the hair and face are hand-painted. Since many came from Holland, they are sometimes called Dutch dolls. In the mid-nineteenth century similar small wooden dolls were made in America. Some of these were less than an inch long and others were as long as twelve inches. Some of the first wooden dolls were made of Vermont maple by Joel Ellis. Others were carved in Pennsylvania and had jointed arms. The costumes and faces were painted on. Later, wooden dolls with ball and socket joints were patented in America by Schoenhut and others.

Wax was modeled for crèche figures, and wax portraits and figures of wax saints date from the Middle Ages. In the eighteenth century wax heads were used on fashion dolls and, late in the century, were made for play dolls. Rare wax doll heads date from the Queen Anne period, and wax was used as a medium for dolls' heads throughout the nineteenth century. The finest wax dolls were made by the Montanari, Pierotti, and Marsh families in England from about 1850 to the end of the century. These dolls are modeled with lifelike appearance and have hair, eyebrows, and eyelashes separately inserted into the wax. French wax dolls were similarly made, but a cheaper type was made in Germany.

Although dolls with wax heads were made in the eighteenth century, it was the middle of the nineteenth century before dolls with head and bust of wax and cotton-stuffed kid bodies were generally popular. These dolls had painted or glass eyes, enamel teeth, curly hair, and hands of wood, paste, or kid. Wax dolls were at the height of their popularity in the 1870's and 1880's. The heads were modeled with many styles of hairdos, and the late dolls often

Dolls. Above: *wax head, wooden hands and feet, kid body, real hair.* Below: *Painted wood head, hands, and feet, jointed body. Late eighteenth century.* The Metropolitan Museum of Art, bequest of Mrs. Maria P. James, 1911.

had pierced ears and earrings. Sometimes the hair is in a high pompadour, sometimes it is braided and wound around the head, and again it may be held by a net. As early as 1825 moving eyes had been set within the doll's head. They were fastened on wires and a lever for operation extended to the outside of the head.

The china-headed doll is one of the most popular with collectors. It exceeds all others in number and variety. It is a doll with a cloth or leather body, and a glazed or unglazed china head with painted hair and features. The doll's head was sewn to the cloth body, and holes were put in the doll's neck for this purpose. The earliest dolls had one hole back and front. As with the wooden dolls, the date of the doll can be determined to a certain extent by the hairdo, since the styles followed the times: curls in the 1840's and 1850's, and the chignon about 1860. The ages of these dolls were also indicated by their size and hair style. The matron had her hair parted in the middle and arranged in buns at the side, while the young lady had a curled short bob and the child had a short boy's bob. A tiny china baby doll less than two inches long rocks in a wicker cradle in the doll house at the Museum of the City of New York. These dolls were usually dressed in the printed calicoes of the time, but sometimes have silk dresses.

China portrait dolls were made, modeled after Queen Victoria and other members of the royal family. There was also a Jenny Lind doll and a head known as the Godey with deep top curls. There was a

Sara Louis Spenser with doll with china head, long hair. H. Walton, 1842. Abby Aldrich Rockefeller Folk Art Collection, Williamsburg, Virginia.

The New Doll; or Grandmamma's Gift. *London: R. Ackermann, 1826.* Collection of John Mackay Shaw.

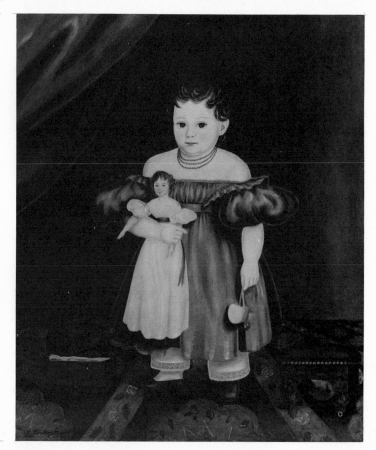

Girl with doll. Artist: Bradley, 1836, Abby Aldrich Rockefeller Folk Art Collection, Williamsburg, Virginia.

Mary Todd Lincoln doll named after Mrs. Lincoln, but it was not a portrait. The doll had a chignon or waterfall hairdo. Some china heads made in the 1840's are of luster. The china doll with brunette hair is the one most often seen in the portraits of children painted by Joseph Stock and other primitive artists in the 1840's and 1850's. The majority of these china-head dolls were made in Germany, in the Dresden and Meissen porcelain factories, and at the Royal Copenhagen factory and the Königliche Porzellan Manufactur in Berlin. Many of these heads were marked.

About this date bisque dolls were perfected by M. Jumeau. These rosy-cheeked dolls with moveable heads were made in all sizes. The hands and feet were also of bisque and the body was cloth. Bisque dolls had real hair wigs or bisque hair made in one mold with the head and shoulders. The hair was painted either blonde or brunette and men dolls often had mustaches painted on. These dolls differed not only in type but in expressions as well. The Jumeau doll was the finest bisque doll made. The bisque has a pinkish cast. Jumeau dolls usually came with a trunkful of costumes and accessories of dress such as jewelry.

Although papier-mâché was in use in the fifteenth century, it was not used for doll heads until the early nineteenth century. Germany took the lead in making papier-mâché doll heads.

German papier-mâché dolls have their hair behind their ears,

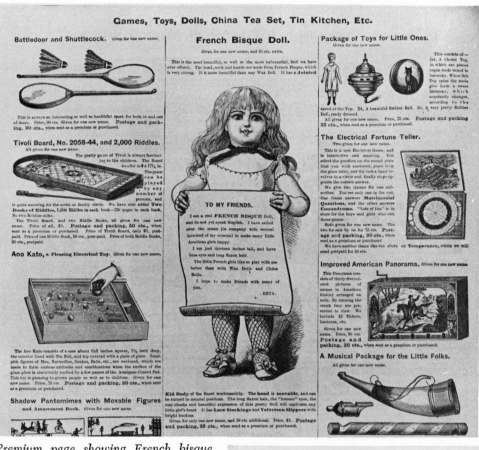

Premium page showing French bisque doll and other toys. The Youth's Companion, *Oct. 29, 1885.* Collection of John Mackay Shaw.

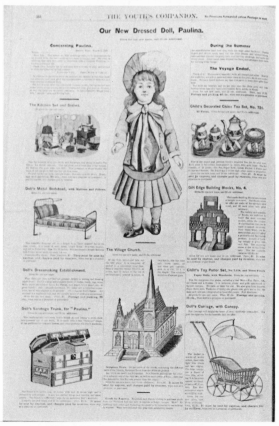

Premium page showing French bisque doll and other toys. The Youth's Companion, *Oct. 31, 1889.* Collection of John Mackay Shaw.

The Herbert children and Doll. ca. 1857. National Gallery of Art, gift of Edgar William and Bernice Chrysler Garbisch.

Doll with papier-mâché head, wooden hands and feet, kid body, ca. 1840–1850. The New-York Historical Society.

leaving the ears exposed. They have blown glass eyes and round faces. Rare heads have long curls. Papier-mâché milliner's models with a kid body and wooden arms and legs were made in sizes from a few inches up to two feet. The hair was dressed in the latest style and the clothes were also the latest. Early heads showed hair parted with high foreheads; later the hair dipped lower and had curls or ringlets on the forehead, and even had naturalistic puffs and curls. Most of these dolls were made in Holland.

Many papier-mâché dolls were made in America in the last half of the nineteenth century. The best known and most sought after by collectors are the Greiner dolls. In 1858 Ludwig Greiner of Philadelphia took out his first patent for papier-mâché doll heads. The two halves of the molded head were joined together with strips of linen, and this feature helps to identify the early Greiner doll. In addition, some early Greiner dolls have imported glass eyes, but most have eyes, hair, and other features painted on.

Another type of doll interesting to collectors is the pedlar doll. Pedlar dolls were popular in the nineteenth century. English pedlar dolls date from the eighteenth century. They are generally made of wood and wear simple cloaks and bonnets, and an apron which holds

the display of tiny wares. Some English dolls have a complete bazaar stall of miniature goods. Later pedlar dolls have been made with all sorts of heads—porcelain, bisque, and papier-mâché. Their clothes were accurate reproductions of the clothes of the working class of the time. Most of these dolls have faces of old women, but there are also some of younger women and men pedlars which are rarer. A related doll, called the Old Woman in the Shoe, with her group of tiny dolls, was shown in *Antiques Magazine* in 1949. A similar doll is in the Essex Institute, Salem, Massachusetts.

Doll's house dolls were made in various sizes in proportion to the sizes of the rooms and furnishings of the dolls' houses. In type, appearance, and materials, they correspond to the other dolls of the period.

The earliest dolls' houses of the sixteenth and seventeenth centuries in Germany, France, and Holland had doll occupants. The dolls were usually not more than five or six inches tall, but they were elaborately dressed in rich brocades styled after the prevailing fashions of the day. Interestingly, they had no underclothes. The early doll heads were of linen. A little later the heads and hands were of carved wood, and many dolls had carefully delineated composition faces and hands, and human hair held in place by wax. In Nuremberg some seventeenth-century doll heads were made of alabaster, although most dolls in the Nuremberg dolls' houses had carved and painted heads and wooden or cloth bodies.

The occupants of eighteenth-century dolls' houses consisted not only of the members of the noble family, but also of a complete staff of servants including maids, butlers, cooks, and housekeepers. In the now famous Ann Sharp doll's house, dating from the reign of Queen Anne, the dolls include Lord Rochett, his lady, their family of children, and servants. Lord Rochett has a wax head, a childish face with blue eyes, and golden hair. He is dressed after the manner of the times in pale blue brocade with lace ruffles, red boots, white stockings, and a large blue silk hat. The daughter of the house is also a wax doll and is dressed in a long brocaded satin yellow and white hoopskirted dress with lace ruffles and a lace apron and cap. She also wears a stiff-boned corset. The child's maid has a head of enameled wood and arms and hands of cardboard, but she wears a silk dress and a cap and apron of lace and a green silk petticoat. The housekeeper and the butler also have large wooden heads with real hair. The butler is dressed in a linen suit with embroidered buttons, while the cook has a dress of printed cotton.

The eighteenth-century English dolls' houses in the Victoria and Albert Museum have typical English dolls of the Queen Anne type. Other English dolls of this period had linen faces with embroidered features. The Dutch eighteenth-century doll was also wooden and dressed in hoopskirts.

From about 1800 many doll's house dolls had heads made of papier-mâché and bodies of leather filled with bran. These papier-mâché heads were popular until about 1840, when porcelain or china heads, arms, and legs came into use, attached to a stuffed cloth body. China dolls had round heads and shiny black hair and they were made in all sizes from the tiny baby doll to the larger adult.

In the mid-nineteenth century the popular bisque dolls of M. Jumeau were also made for dolls' houses in all sizes.

The last half of the nineteenth century was the heyday of the doll's house and its miniature furnishings and tiny doll families. Dolls' houses of all kinds and sizes were available to both rich and poor children, and the dolls themselves were made with the expressions and dressed in clothes that correspond to their station in life. A recent advertisement of doll's house dolls for sale gives an example of the variety:

> five inch Bisque chauffeur, blonde with molded cap
> five inch Chef, brunette moustache
> five inch man, blonde, grey suit
> four inches, two girls, blonde wigs, glass eyes
> three inch girl, blonde wig, bald head.

For the collector, nineteenth-century dolls are the most readily
available because it is this century in which dolls for the first time
became available to children of families with moderate means. It
was still the time when children prized their toys and took good care
of them. Also, there were many dollmakers in the nineteenth century, especially in the Victorian years. As we have stated before, the
hair style of the doll determines its age to a certain degree, and the
earliest eyes were usually brown. Blue eyes were most popular in
Victorian days. Blonde dolls are rarer than brunettes. Naturally, a
doll with a mark or label is more valuable. Hand-sewing is found on
early dolls, machine-stitching later. The style of the dress also
indicates age, but one cannot be sure if the dress was original with
the doll or made from old materials.

Dolls that creep, walk, talk, dance, swim, and sleep offer another
field of doll-collecting. This is necessarily a specialized field. Dolls
with eyes that opened and closed were made as early as the late
1820's, and walking dolls appeared about the same time. Along with
other automatic toys, there was a demand for a doll that moved.
There were many American patents taken out for walking and
creeping dolls in the 1860's and 1870's. One walking doll pushed a
doll carriage. This doll had metal cleats in her feet which enabled
her to walk while the carriage helped her keep her balance. Other
dolls moved by a watch-spring mechanism. There was also a doll
that rode a tricycle. One of the first walking dolls was the "Auto-
peripatetikos," patented in 1862.

Dollmakers often collaborated with specialists in other fields,
such as makers of music boxes. Many Jumeau dolls were set on top
of music boxes. One pair of dolls strummed mandolins in time with
the tune of the music box. There was also a Red Riding Hood, a
flower girl, a girl with a bird cage, a doll with an egg, and one in
Normandy costume. In 1887–1888 Thomas Edison made his famous
talking doll that recited nursery rhymes such as "Jack and Jill" and
"Mary Had a Little Lamb." The dolls that said "Mama" and
"Papa" were first patented by Johann Maelzal.

14

Dolls' Houses

he earliest existing American doll's house is that originally owned by the Homans family. It is now in the collection of the Van Cortlandt Museum, Van Cortlandt Park, New York City. The house is about four feet high by about two feet wide. The roof has the slope of early New York houses and is topped with a center chimney. The house consists of two stories and an attic and has a large drawer below on each side, closed ends, and open front and back. There are metal bale handles on each end of the house. On either side at the front are posts on which are painted in cream the dates 1744 on the left side and 1774 on the right. The interior of the house consists of four rooms—two rooms at the front, with a drawer below, and two at the back with a drawer below. Walls of open slats separate the front rooms from the back rooms so that two children playing with the house at the same time could see each other. Both downstairs rooms have fireplaces with hooded chimneys, and high shelves in the manner of old eighteenth-century kitchen chimneys. Rugs are painted on the floors, and English prints of the late eighteenth century, "Published by C. Carrington Bowles," are pasted on the walls over the fireplaces and on the inside of the attic window. The prints above the fireplace represent figures in costumes of the period, but they

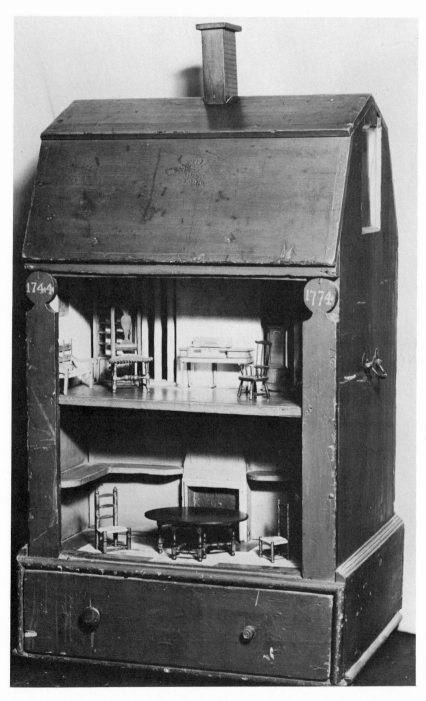

Doll's house of Homans family. American, eighteenth century. Van Courtlandt Museum, Van Courtlandt Park, New York City.

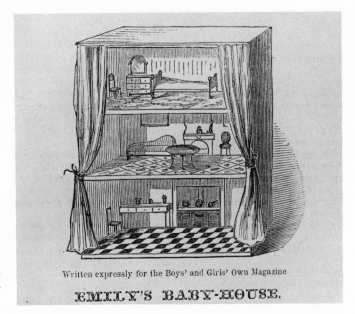

EMILY'S BABY-HOUSE.

Emily's Baby House. Boys' and Girls' Own Magazine, *1861.* Collection of John Mackay Shaw.

are indistinct and the inscription cannot be read. The house is now furnished with furniture of the period, but the only piece of the original furnishing is a small antique basket which was found in the attic. This house is undoubtedly of American workmanship. A dollhouse of the federal period was offered for sale at Parke-Bernet in October 1936. It had six rooms and was furnished with miniature furniture and decorative accessories.

Dolls' houses were called "baby houses" until the mid-nineteenth century. John Pintard of New York City, whose letters and diary tell us so much about early New York life, makes several interesting notations about early nineteenth-century toys. On August 13, 1816, he notes that he had "Eliza's doll's hair Hugganized." (J. R. D. Huggins was a New York hairdresser.) On November 21, 1821, "Another one (shop) has an assortment of German figures which will serve for her baby house." On November 24, 1830, he notes, "Toy shop windows and see endless variety of European toys" and on December 27, 1830, "Arrival of Dutch ship with all sorts of toys." The baby house itself was probably made by a local carpenter or cabinetmaker. T. Homer advertised "furniture for fitting Baby Houses," in the *Philadelphia Public Ledger,* Dec. 23, 1837, and The Tower Toy Guild was making toy furniture in the 1830's. The Brett doll house in the Museum of the City of New York was made in 1840 by the Rev. Dr. Philip Milledoler Brett. A house of 1836 complete with the furnishings of the period is in the Chester County (Pennsylvania) Historical Society. It was made by a Philadelphia cabinetmaker and upholsterer. There are many American dollhouses which date from the 1850's to the end of the century.

In the Museum of the Society for the Preservation of New England Antiquities is a doll's house built in 1860. The furniture which

Old tin kitchen. Early nineteenth century. Collection of Mrs. Imogene Anderson.

Window of toy shop. In foreground mechanical dolls on tricycle and wheeling carriage. Dolls' heads and small toy animals on shelves. The Henry Ford Museum.

it contains dates from the eighteenth century. This furniture was originally contained in a bookcase which served as a doll's house. The Chippendale dining room furniture and the Chinese Chippendale bedroom furniture were made in the eighteenth century and so were the green moiré draperies and the bedspread and tiny blankets. The next furniture was added in 1820 and included an Empire drawing room set upholstered in pink satin, and an Empire bedroom set. Between 1830 and 1860 overstuffed and tufted furniture was added, as were the wax flowers under glass and other Victorian and Louis Philippe accessories. The pictures in the house are photographs of old family portraits. The house itself was built by Paul, a well-known cabinetmaker of Boston in 1860. The contents of this historic doll's house were played with by three generations of children from 1850 to 1908.

Other museums have American dolls' houses and miniature furniture in their collections. These include The Essex Institute, Salem, Massachusetts; The Metropolitan Museum of Art, New York; The Museum of the City of New York; Shelburne Museum, Shelburne, Vermont; The Newark Museum, Newark, New Jersey; The Denver Art Museum, Denver, Colorado.

Although England, Germany, and France supplied most of the toys for American children up until about 1850, toys and miniatures for dolls' houses were made in America before then. By 1850, dolls' houses could be bought ready-made and their furnishings assembled from the stock in the mid-nineteenth-century toy shop, but many dolls' houses continued to be made by a child's father or by local cabinetmakers and architects. Dolls' houses were often made identical with the design of the houses of the children's parents or of some well-known residence in the neighborhood. An example of this custom is the doll's house in the Museum of the City of New York which was a replica of the residence of Peter and Jean B. Goelet at 890 Broadway, New York City, and which was built in 1846 for their nieces, Almy G. Gerry and Jean B. Gerry.

In the Empire period, doll's house furniture had begun to be manufactured in large quantities and was no longer the work of an individual craftsman. Although much was still imported from Europe, it was also made by American manufacturers. There were Empire chairs showing Grecian influence, heavy pedestal tables, sleigh beds, bureaus, secretaries, and many other articles. These doll's house pieces are all available in miniature today and are found in both walnut and better finished mahogany. The Victorian era, as we have said, was the heyday of the doll's house and it was a long day, for the era lasted from the 1840's to 1900. During this time, various styles of furniture were made for the doll's house, from carved rosewood to walnut and golden oak and even iron beadwork and cardboard. There was furniture with French influence and furniture of Gothic influence, and finally tufted uphol-

Doll's house made by Paul of Boston in 1860. The house was played with from 1750 to 1908 and the furniture represents period styles from 1750 to 1860. Society for the Preservation of New England Antiquities, Boston, Massachusetts.

Mother and child with doll and doll's house. The Daisy, J. Adams, Philadelphia, 1808. Collection of John Mackay Shaw.

Doll's furniture. Empire desk, maple and mahogany. Poster bed, pine-stained mahogany. Table with lyre support, plates with food. Sleigh cradle. Doll, porcelain, ca. 1850. Collection Mrs. Imogene Anderson.

Late-nineteenth century toys with large doll's house. New Second Reader McGuffey. Collection of John Mackay Shaw.

stered pieces that had no wood showing at all. When iron bedsteads with brass knobs became popular late in the nineteenth century these were also made in miniature for the doll's house. Iron chairs with backs of Gothic fretwork were made for dolls' houses, and later, wire furniture with no particular style at all was made in miniature for the late-nineteenth-century doll's house.

Doll's house furniture advertised in *The Youth's Companion* in the 1880's included sets of eight pieces with "real marble top tables," a sofa, easy chair, and mirror stand. These were made in "imitation ebony and gold, upholstered in terry."

In the Landauer collection at the New-York Historical Society there are toy catalogues of the late nineteenth century. In a catalogue of 1882, Selchow & Righter, 41 John Street, New York, advertised several sets of doll's house furniture. Under the title of "Little Chamber-maid" they sold bedroom furniture in a box 17" x 8" x 10". "Little Housekeeper Improved" included a house and kitchen with the table set and Black Chloe, the cook, getting dinner.

A country villa with complete furnishings, a cottage and barn, and
a Gothic church were also advertised. A country store complete with
tea, coffee, spices, flour, molasses, canned fruit, patent medicine, toy
money, and a delivery wagon was also available to the children of
1882. "The Girls Delight" included a washtub and wringer, a bed,
table, and tea set. A brick house (probably of cardboard) was 24" x
18" x 9½". The "Doll Mansion" had four rooms with mansard roof
and doors and windows that opened and closed. Besides these, there
were a toy stable and a toy warehouse. In 1885 G. R. Johnston, 43
Barclay St., New York, advertised toy cottage furniture, eight piece
suites, bedsteads, bureaus, commodes, tables, towel racks, and rocking chairs of imitation black walnut or solid walnut. Toy brooms,
pails, bedsteads, and toy willow cradles in a nest were also shown in
the catalogue.

In a catalogue of 1890 "A Fairy Doll House" of two rooms with
lithographed walls was offered for sale, as were toy kitchen sets on
cards. These consisted of molds, spoons, dustpan, grater, etc. Toy
pianos were in the catalogue of 1891 and included the "Gem," 7
inches high; "Princess," 9½ inches high; "Lark," upright 9½
inches; "Orient," 10 inches high; and "Waverly" upright, 11½
inches high. The larger ones were probably not for dolls' houses.

There are many American Victorian dolls' houses. A large size
doll's house in the Museum of the City of New York has eight rooms
and dates from 1860. It is furnished in the typical black walnut
furniture of the era and is carpeted with Victorian floral Brussels
carpets. In the parlor is a square walnut piano, a round table with
lamp, and walnut Empire-type chairs. On the mantel are a clock and
a pair of Staffordshire miniature figures. In one corner of the room
is a tripod stand with a vase of artificial flowers. The chandelier and
wall bracket lighting fixtures are gilt, and colored lithographs of
children and landscapes framed in gilt hang on the walls. The
dining room has a round walnut dining table and chairs. On the
table is a set of white ironstone dishes, and on the mantel are a clock
and a pair of small Staffordshire sheep. The adjoining kitchen has
an iron stove, and iron and tin pots, pans, and kitchen equipment.
There is a wooden washtub, with other woodenware utensils. Off the
kitchen is the servants' room. The house has two bedrooms. One has
a sleigh bed with a patchwork quilt, handmade sheets and a tin bed
warmer between the sheets. A stand with pitcher and bowl, a
basketwork cradle, and an armchair and several side chairs complete the furnishings. The room has a fireplace, and on the mantel
are a pair of Staffordshire figures. The other bedroom is furnished
with a poster bed, a washstand, a towel rack, and chairs upholstered
in horsehair. Between the bedrooms is a bath with bathtub and
pitcher of tin, a washstand, and a large storage chest filled with
dolls' clothes. The sitting room has a horsehair-covered sofa, a
rocking chair, stool, and a walnut secretary. On the mantel are

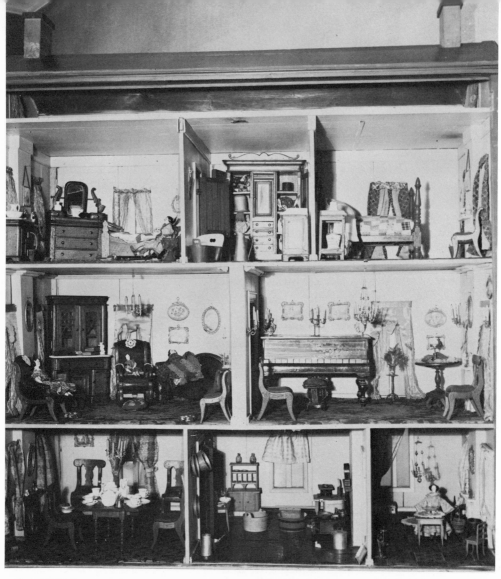

a

(a) *Doll's house, 1860, showing Victorian Empire style furniture and dolls of the period.*
(b) *Parlor showing detail of furniture.* Museum of the City of New York.

b

plaster busts and a clock, and a parrot in a cage hangs in one corner
of the room. Several dolls of the period are included with the house.

The printed inventory of a New York doll's house of 1864 is
owned by the Museum of the City of New York. It gives a complete
picture of the detailed furnishings available in miniature at that
date. Although the house and its furnishings do not exist today, the
inventory is valuable because it lists such unusual articles as a
cuckoo clock, a waffle iron, a coffee mill, a Carcel lamp, a Beebe
range, and a Herring's safe, several of which are articles manufactured on American patents and thus prove the existence of American miniatures for dolls' houses at this date. The following is a
complete copy of the interesting inventory.

Inventory of Furniture, etc., in Fair-y Villa—Belonging to Mr.
Fair-Child, N. Y.—C. O. Jones, Printer, 76 Cedar St.—1864.

Kitchen
1. Beebe's Range in good order
2. Sink
3. Large Table
4. Small Table
5. 4 chairs
6. Dresser
7. Copper Stew Pan
8. Quart Measure
9. Iron Ladle
10. Pail
11. Cuckoo Clock
12. Iron Skimmer
13. Cleaver
14. Dutch Oven
15. Flour Scoop
16. Iron Shovel
17. Frying Pan
18. 2 Skillets
19.
20. Funnel
21. Match Box
22. Broom
23. Firkin
24. Pair Candlesticks
25. Tea Kettle
26. Waffle Iron
27. Dust Pan
28. Dust Brush
29. 2 Market Baskets
30. Swill Tub
31. Sieve
32. 2 Cake Moulds
33. Cullender
34. Tin Skimmer
35. Coffee Mill
36. Bake Pan
37. Wooden Ladle
38. Rolling Pin
39. Tray with Knives, Forks &
      Spoons
40. Japan Tray
41. Smoke Beef Board
42. Grater
43. 3 Stone Jars
44. Castors
45. 3 bottles
46. 2 Tumblers
47. 6 Plates
48. Bowls
49. Iron Pot
Drawing Room
50. Aubusson Carpet
51. 5 Gilt Cornices
52. 5 Pr. Blue Satin Curtains
53. 5 Pr. Lace Curtains
54. Transparencies in Windows
55. Sofa—5 Chairs covered with
      blue satin
56. 2 Jardinieres
57. Mantel & Glass Complete
58. Blue Satin Valence
59. Set Fire Irons
60. Glass Screen
61. Gilt Chair
62. Gilt Camp Stool

63. Clock
64. Pair Vases
65. Pair Statuettes
66. Corner Bracket Gilt
67. Gilt Basket with Flowers
68. Statue of Guardian Angel with velvet cone base
69. Etagère
70. Sofa Table
71. Foot Stool
72. Pier Table & Glass
73. Picture—Copy of Murillo Ascension
74. Pair Side Lights
75. Chandelier
76. Basket of Flowers
76. Jewel Casket
77. Battledore & Shuttlecock
78. Miniature Engine
79. Opera Glass
80. Miniature Cradle
81. Carcel Lamp
82. Pair Silver Candlesticks
83. Snuffers & Tray
84. Chinese Ivory Basket
85. Gilt Inkstand
86. Miniature Chair
87. Gilt Basket
88. Card Plate
89. Pair Candlesticks
90. Ivory Dog

Hall—First Floor

91. Door Mat
92. Herrings Safe
93. Stove
94. Coal Scuttle & Hod
95. Ash Shovel
96. Chandelier
97. Oil Cloth

Dining Room

98. Velvet Carpet
99. 5 pr. Red Silk Curtains
100. 5 pr. Lace Curtains
101. 5 Cornices
102. Mantel & Glass Complete
103. Set Fire Irons
104. Clock
105. Pair Statuettes

106. Fire Screen
107. Engraving black walnut frame
108. Writing Table with blotting book, pair candlesticks, stick sealing wax, pair scissors, knife, seal, pen, inkstand, paper knife
109. Sideboard with Soup Tureen, 6 plates, 2 compotiers, fruit dish, salt cellar, pair candlesticks, liquor stand, Decanter, 2 wine glasses.
110. Six chairs covered with velvet
111. Dinner table with Soup Tureen, 6 plates, Hand-bell, pr. candlesticks, salt cellar, gravy boat, casters, 2 decanters, 6 wine glasses, soup ladle, 6 knives, 6 forks, 6 spoons, 2 wine coolers, with 2 bottles champagne
112. Foot Stool
113. Side Table
114. Tray
115. Tea Set
116. Silver Tête-à-tête set
117. Chandelier

Hall—2nd Floor

118. Oil Cloth
119. Key Safe
120. 2 Armchairs

Bedroom

121. Green Velvet Carpet & Rug
122. 2 Black & Gold Cornices
123. 5 pr. muslin cornices
124. Marble mantel
125. Set Fire irons & stand
126. Pr. Bellows
127. Clock
128. Pr. Vases
129. Mirror
130. Corner Bracket
131. Statuette (Samuel)
132. 2 Chairs

133. Work Table furnished
134. Single wash stand
135. Basin & Pitcher
136. Soap Dish
137. Tumblers
138. Duchess Toilet Table
139. Hand Glass
140. Hair Brush
141. Croton Water Wash Stand
142. Water Bottle
143. Tumbler
144. 2 Toilet Bottles
145. Bed Canopy & Curtains
146. Mattress
147. Pair Pillows
148. Pr. Linen Sheets
149. Pr. Linen Pillow Cases
150. Blanket
151. Marseilles Quilt
152. Afghan
153. Watch Case & Watch
154. Table
155. Candlestick
156. China Figure
157. Tête-à-tête set
158. Fur mat

Nursery

159. Brussels Carpet & Rug
160. 5 pr. Muslin Curtains
161. 5 Cornices
162. Mantel Piece
163. Set Fire Irons with Stand
164. Ash Brush
165. Bellows
166. Bedspread
167. Mattress
168. Pr. Linen sheets
169. Pillow cases
170. Blanket
171. Marseille Quilt
172. Cradle with lace & silk
      curtains
173. Bureau
174. Mirror
175. Cuckoo Clock
176. Pr. Candlesticks
177. Pot Pomade
178. Pr. Scissors

179. Hair brush
180. High Bureau
181. Transparency
182. Bird in cage
183. Table
184. Gold fish globe
185. Basket knitting
186. 4 chairs
187. Rocking Chair
188. Infant's chair
189. Taper
190. Pr. Statuettes
191. Irin Wash Stand with basin
192. Soap dish & Water can
193. Picture framed
194. Piece Oil cloth
195. Infant's Bath tub
196. Infant's Basket
197. Soap Dish
198. Sponge

Cook's Room

199. Bedstead
200. Mattress
201. Pillow & Case
202. Pr. Cotton Sheets
203. Blanket
204. Quilt
205. 4 chairs
206. Dressing Table
207. Wash stand furnished
208. Bureau
209. Wardrobe
210. Carpet

Waiter's Room

211. Bedstead
212. Mattress
213. Pillow & Case
214. Pr. Sheets
215. Blanket
216. Quilt
217. Washstand
218. Basin & Pitcher
219. Bureau
220. Mirror
221. Wardrobe
222. 2 chairs
223. Carpet

Trunk Room

224. Trunks
225. Hat boxes
Bath Room
226. Oil cloth
227. Bath tub
228. Sitz bath
229. Foot tub
230. Water can
231. Shower bath

232. Towels (?)
233. 3 pr. muslin curtains
234. 3 cornices
235. Oil skin cap
Exterior
236. 6 Hanging baskets filled
with choice plants
237. Mat
238. Perambulator

Family Consists of:
Mr. & Mrs. Fair-Child
Elsie & Ida—their two little girls aged 9 & 7 yrs.
Frank aged 5
Willie aged 3½
Bobbie aged 2 yrs.
Minnie, the baby aged 6 months
Adele, the French Nurse
Rose Downing, the Cook
Patrick Mahoney, the Waiter

Made by Mrs. Henry Chauncey and exhibited at her residence, 25 Waverly Place. Sold to Alexander Van Rensselaar for $500 and offered for sale by him at Union Square Fair Building.

There were few dolls' houses as complete or elaborate as the one of this inventory. However, the doll's house was now within the reach of all children for only a small price. The Museum of the City of New York also owns a four-room doll's house made in 1880. In addition to the furniture of the era which is made of golden oak, the interesting accessories include a chafing dish, a chess set, an upright piano, and napkin rings.

One of the most interesting American doll houses—both historically and architecturally—is the Rutherford B. Hayes doll house which was made by a Baltimore carpenter, George C. Brown, in 1878. The exterior of the house is typically Victorian with its mansard roof, cupola, and gingerbread trimming. Another Victorian doll's house is in the Wenham Historical Association. It was built in 1884 by Benjamin H. Chamberlain, a silversmith.

In the Newark Museum is a doll's house of the 1870's. The living room and dining room furnishings of this house are particularly interesting. The set of overstuffed living room side and armchairs have turned bulbous legs and are tufted and finished with long fringe. There are a center table, a tall gilt console mirror, and a screen. The dining room furniture consists of a sideboard stained to represent mahogany, chairs with cane seats, an extension table with two leaves, and a linen chest which contains line tablecloths and fringed napkins. On the table is a decorated milk glass chocolate set of German or English nineteenth-century manufacture. Chairs in

American doll's house, 1880, showing furniture and accessories of the period. Museum of the City of New York.

(a) *Dining room set. Sideboard, extension table, and cane-seated chairs. Milk glass chocolate set, 1870's. The Newark Museum. (b) Sofa and chairs of Directoire period from doll's house of 1870's. The Newark Museum.*

a

b

one of the bedrooms have backs of Gothic design with cushioned seats.

Not long ago a New York antique shop had for sale a doll's house which dated ca. 1898. It was four feet high by three feet wide and two feet deep and was rather crudely made, but with balconies and bay windows with metal trim and two round windows set under the eaves, which held carved roosters. The walls were papered, and the windows were curtained with lace curtains hung from gilt cornices. In the windows were miniature beer steins and potted plants. The furnishings of the house gave a complete picture of the middle-class home of the period and contained many unusual miniature articles. In the upstairs living room were golden oak chairs and a sofa, a center table with gilt centerpiece, and a vase of flowers. A gilt chandelier was of the gaslight variety. On the mantel were a gilt clock and candlesticks, with a picture over the mantel. A pair of gilt busts were set on wall brackets. A metal table and rocking chair, an upright piano, a birdcage, a magazine rack with a miniature copy of the *Chicago Tribune,* and a bear's-head rug and Brussels carpet completed the furnishings.

The bedroom furniture was golden oak and included a bed table and wardrobe as well as a metal washstand, a draped dressing table, and a metal bassinet decorated with lace, pink silk, and flowers. A tall cylinder stove had isinglass windows. The dining room had a golden oak extension table, four chairs, a china closet, a small round table with a phonograph with horn, a wall telephone, a metal magazine rack, and a plaster bust of Goethe on a stand. On the table were gilt candelabra of Gothic design and a glass centerpiece with fruit and flowers. There was a red flowered Brussels carpet on the floor. On the sideboard were a metal castor set and glass decanters. On a desk in the corner stood a calendar and a vase of flowers. Dolls included a nurse, a baby doll in a metal carriage, and a negro butler.

The kitchen was especially interesting. There were an iron stove, iron pots and frying pans, a thermometer on the wall, a bucket, scrub brushes, a coffee pot, a dinner bell, and tin forks and spoons. Of special interest was the complete set of Meissen "onion pattern" jars marked "Barley Vinegar, Oil, Rice, Grit Salt, Sugar, Coffee and Sago" which were held on a wooden wall rack. There was also a kitchen ladder-chair. In the rooms were bisque dolls of the correct scale to suit the furnishings. These included a mother with gray hair, a blonde daughter, and six young children, as well as tiny dogs. The cook was dressed in a red-and-white checked dress with a white apron.

The unique feature of a doll's house at the Children's Museum, Boston, Massachusetts, is a dumb waiter which operates from the kitchen to the three floors above. The furniture in this house includes iron bedsteads, tin bathtubs, a set of willow furniture, a tall clock, a miniature sewing machine, a chafing dish, and a leather traveling case. The dolls are made to scale and include servants, children, and the man and woman of the house.

A popular toy was the Nuremberg kitchen of the time with wide chimney and open grate, and with complete fireplace equipment including andirons, trivets, iron pots and kettles, and candlesticks and snuffers. Above on the chimney hung copper and brass strainers, forks, ladles, and spoons. On a table would be found a set of wooden or pewter dishes sometimes complete with the stamps of the makers. Strainers, meat choppers, irons, mops, brooms, and brushes and many other tiny kitchen articles were also included. On hanging shelves or in cupboards would be dozens of pottery plates, pewter-covered jugs, mugs, and pudding molds all made of the popular German Nuremberg pottery of the time.

In addition to the Nuremberg kitchen, one-room shops were made in Nuremberg in the seventeenth and eighteenth centuries and continued in popularity in the nineteenth century. The butcher shop with miniature meats of many kinds was especially popular. It was hung with clay models of various cuts of meat. The grocery store was complete with tiny packages of foods in tiny glass jars and tins, a cash register, and several clerks. The drygoods store had bolts of material, tablecloths, aprons, pins, pocketbooks, and other merchandise, and the millinery shop had bonnets, hats of leghorn straw, velvet, and felt, hat stands, trimmings, and hatboxes. There were also miniature saddlers', blacksmiths', shoemakers', hatters' and fruiterers' shops. In addition to shops there were "fair booths" complete with stocks of baskets of all types, pottery, or glassware.

Smaller and less elaborate toy shops were made by American toy manufacturers in the late nineteenth century. Some were of wood, but by now cardboard houses had become popular. In 1868 Emily S. Russell took out a patent for a cardboard doll's house complete with paper dolls. However, more than twenty years passed before folding cardboard houses and shops were made by Converse, McLoughlin Brothers and Selchow & Richter, and later still by R. Bliss, and Converse.

The craze for dolls' houses died out with the Victorian era, so that there are fewer dolls' houses after 1900. However, during the last ten or fifteen years, miniature antiques have become collectors' items and the interest in these has created a market for old dolls' houses.

Toy grocery store. American, early twentieth century. Collection of the late James Melton.

Dry goods booth with miniature baskets, materials, and tablecloths. Mid-nineteenth century. The Denver Art Museum.

Toy millinery shop, 1801. The dolls' dresses and hats are of the period. The Denver Art Museum.

In 1924 Queen Mary's Doll House gave impetus to dollhouse-collecting, and since that time the interest has mounted year by year. Information about antique European dolls' houses had been available for some years through the collections of museums such as Germanisches National-Museum at Nuremberg. However, although some American museums owned a few American dolls' houses, the real interest was not widespread until the publication of Flora Gill Jacobs' *A History of Dolls' Houses* in 1953. For several years before this I had been working on such a manuscript, but publishers did not consider the subject of sufficient interest to support another book. Time has proved that they were wrong, since several books have been published both in America and abroad, and the subject is of such interest that no book on toys can omit the doll's house. Through Mrs. Jacobs' interest and efforts many dolls' houses have been discovered in attics, basements, and storage rooms. While the majority of these find their way to museum collections before they are offered to the public, now and then a well-equipped American Victorian doll's house can be found in an antique shop. Small doll's-house dolls, furniture, and bric-a-brac are more available, but there are many collectors for these tiny objects, and prices are mounting, indeed well beyond the worth of the articles.

Fair Tent with miniature china and glassware. Mid-nineteenth century. The Denver Art Museum.

15

Paper Toys

indmills, paper cut-out folded scenes, paper toys mounted in boxes articulated and operated by sand, paper battleships, and the popular paper doll and dollhouse are just a few of the paper toys that were made. As early as the fifteenth century there were paper figures that moved when placed in the draught of warm air made by the heat of a stove. Hand-colored paper toys made to be cut and pasted on cardboard were popular in the eighteenth century when they were made in Germany. Silhouettes cut out of paper had been known in Germany for several centuries. In the Germanisches National-Museum in Nuremberg there is a picture sheet of the seventeenth century with fashion plates intended to be cut out. However, the English were the first to publish cut-out figures with changeable costumes, and these were put on the market in the late eighteenth century. The French adopted the idea to advertise their fashions.

Clockwork pictures and sand toys were also popular. These had originated in Nuremberg in the seventeenth century, and though at first imported, were made in America in the 1870's and 1880's. The sand toy was set in a box and operated by sand falling on a wheel of cardboard or wood, thus moving the figures at the front of the frame. There was a sand toy of the London Exhibition in 1851. There were also scenes with kittens, dogs, and monkeys doing various tricks. They were also made on printed sheets with instructions for cutting and pasting at home. Clockwork pictures of such subjects as dancing kittens were favorites.

English toy books with changeable heads for figures included *The History and Adventures of Little Henry* and *The History of Little Fanny*, published by S. & J. Fuller, London, in 1810. The books were accompanied by a series of painted figures, each with a slot at the back to take the moveable head. Similar books, *Phoebe, the Cottage Maid* and *Hubert, the Cottage Youth*, came out in 1812. In 1814, *Cinderella*, with scenes and six figures, was published by S. & J. Fuller. These books were also published in Boston in about 1812. Between 1810 and 1820 William Charles of Philadelphia reproduced the English toy books, but printed them on sheets of paper ready to cut instead of in book form. In the Museum of the City of New York there are figures from "The Story of Goody Two Shoes" in cut-out form enclosed in a paper envelope. It is marked R. A. Hobbs, Lowell, Mass., and dates ca. 1822.

In 1858–1859 books of picture puzzles to cut out and paste were printed by Frederick Warne and Company. Dean and Son also made cut-out and moveable books. Mother Hubbard consisted of eight pages of color wood-blocks. The figures had moveable heads and arms. *The Old Woman and Her Silver Penny* and *The Old English Farmer and Family* had figures with projecting paper springs that set them out from their background. These books were the overlap between books and pastimes such as paper dolls.

Paper Dolls

Paper dolls. Upper: 1840. Lower: *ca.* 1820. Museum of the City of New York.

The real beginning of the paper doll craze occurred about 1850, although many homemade paper dolls had been made before this time. The first American paper doll was published by Crosby, Nichols & Company of Boston in 1854. The doll was called "Fanny Gray" and she was designed by the commercial artist John Greene Chandler. The doll came in a box with a booklet of verses and six figures and was titled: "Fanny Gray: A History of Her Life, Illustrated by Six Colored Figures. By the author of Cousin Hatty's Hymns and Twilight Stories." The scenes with verses and figures were: The Cottage where Fanny Lived, Fanny with Her Kitten, Fanny Selling Matches, Fanny Feeding Chickens, Fanny a Flower Girl, and Fanny Her Uncle's Pet. There was a wooden base on which the figures could be set up. Chandler later made a series of paper dolls which were published by Brown, Taggard & Chase of Boston. These were sets in envelopes and included a doll with several changes of costume. The envelopes had "Hurrah for the Little Folks" printed at the top and the dolls included Carry, Alice, Charley, Little Fairy Lightfoot, Betty the Milkmaid and Pets, and Jack and his Holiday Companions.

There are a group of small books that give evidence of the popularity of paper dolls at this time. In 1850 Ward, Lock & Co. of

322

Cardboard doll's furniture and directions for making. Godey's Lady's Book, *1870.*

Cardboard church, ca. 1890. Hallmark Gallery, New York.

London published *Children's Fancy Work* which included directions for making perforated cardboard furniture for paper dolls or for dolls' houses. This book circulated in America. In 1856 Anson D. F. Randolph published a book, *Paper Dolls and How to Make Them. A Book for Little Girls.* This was followed by the book *Paper Dolls' Furniture and How to Make It or How to Spend a Cheerful Rainy Day.* In 1857 Anson Randolph also published a group of paper dolls in a box called "The Paper Doll Family." Similar dolls and dolls' furniture were later published in the various children's magazines. There were books and magazine articles giving instructions for making paper dolls, paper doll furniture, and paper dollhouses. In the 1880's Milton Bradley made lithographed paper dollhouses, villages, and trains. In 1892, F. Cairo of Brooklyn, New York, put out a series of rooms for paper dolls. These were labeled "Our Parlor," "Our Dining Room," and "Our Bedroom." The 1894 Montgomery Ward catalogue advertised paper dollhouses printed in bright colors on heavy cardboard ready for the child to put together. Paper doll furniture at ten cents a set was lithographed on sheets of cardboard 15 inches by 17 inches to be cut and bent. In November 1859, *Godey's Lady's Book* published what are often considered the first American paper dolls. There were six figures of boys and girls and a page of costumes for each figure, done in crude colors. Later there were paper dolls in other women's magazines including *Ladies Home Journal, Woman's Home Companion, Pictorial Review,* and *McCalls.*

In the 1860's the three most important paper doll manufacturers were Brown, Taggard & Chase of Boston, Clark, Austin & Smith of New York, and McLoughlin Brothers of New York. Clark, Austin & Smith also made paper furniture for their series of paper dolls. These were sold in envelopes marked "The Girls' Delight." Paper doll number one was called "Florence"; number four was "Nellie, a young lady of the 'upper ten' "; and another was named "Hattie."

McLoughlin Brothers printed dolls, paper soldiers, and toy paper furniture for paper dolls' houses. One series of dolls made by McLoughlin pictured a girl with a basket of flowers, one holding a dog in her arms, one with a cat, and another holding a white rabbit. Other McLoughlin dolls included "The Bride" and "Bridegroom" and "Bridal Party."

a

(a) *Nancy Fancy, box cover.* (b) *Nancy Fancy doll and two costumes. McLoughlin Bros., 1854–1863.* Collection of Barbara Whitton.

b

In the 1867 catalogue of McLoughlin Bros. the following dolls and dolls' paper furniture are listed:

Paper Dolls—Book Form.

Series No. 1.   10 kinds, viz.

Ester Fine   Baby
Flora Fair   Dolly
Minnie Miller   Hattie
Little Pet   Lizzie
Little Fred   May Day
                          Per gross, $3.75

Series No. 1.   6 kinds (new).

Helen   Daisy
Dora   Paul
Bo-Peep   Stella
                          Per gross, $3.75

Series No. 2.   12 kinds, viz.

Kitty Black   Minty Green
Lilly Beers   Emma White
Little Lady   Mary Gray
Fanny Fair   Sarah Brown
Rose Bud   Ruby Rose
Ella Hall   Anna Doll
                          Per gross, $7.50

Series No. 2.   6 kinds (new).

Violet Vernon   Marquis
Eva St. Clair and Topsy   Marchioness
Rose Rustic   Nellie Naylor
                          Per gross, $7.50

Series No. 3.   12 kinds, viz.

Carrie Grant   Susie's Pets
Victoria   Mrs. Tom Thumb
Eugenia   Mr. Tom Thumb
Grace Lee   Minnie Warren
Clara West   Commodore Nutt
Cinderella   Nellie North
                          Per gross, $12.00

Series No. 4.   4 kinds, viz.

Red Riding Hood   Ida May
Goody Two Shoes   Jessie Jones
                          Per gross, $18.00

Paper doll: Hand painted, early-nineteenth century. Museum of the City of New York.

Paper Furniture.

Parlor Set	Bed Room Set
Drawing Room Set	Per gross, $12.00
Bed Room Set, small	Parlor Set, small
	Per gross, $7.50

Beautiful Play House, —2 Room, Parlor

Per doz. $4.00

Beautiful Play House, —1 Room, Parlor and Outside

Per doz. $6.00

Beautiful Play House, —2 Rooms, Parlor, Bed Room

Per doz. $8.00

In 1900 McLoughlin issued a series of "Dolls of All Nations." Most of these were sold in boxes or envelopes.

Paper dolls were also manufactured by Kimmel and Foster, The Chromatic Printing Company of Philadelphia, Peter G. Thomson of Cincinnati, Selchow & Richter, Frederick A. Stokes & Co., Samuel Gabriel Sons, and Dennison & Co. In 1866 Kimmel & Foster brought out a boxed set of dolls, "The American Lady and Her Children," with twenty-five changes of the latest costumes.

Raphael Tuck of England, an early maker of paper dolls, later had offices in New York, and in the 1890's was the leader in the paper doll field. Tuck's dolls ranged in size from five and one-half inches to thirteen inches tall. They stood by means of a cardboard easel. The subjects included an Artistic Series with dolls representing Dick Whittington, Prince Charming, Red Riding Hood, Mother Goose, Bopeep, and others. In 1894 there was a Fairy Tale Series. There was also a Prince and Princess series and a series of the Kings of England printed in relief on embossed cardboard.

By the end of the century commercial paper dolls were lithographed on shiny cardboard. Many of them were large, jointed dolls. However, jointed paper dolls had been printed by Dennison on the 1874 patent of W. H. Hart, including one of "an Indian and a Darkey."

Advertising paper dolls along with advertising puzzles were popular in the 1880's and 1890's. Worth, the Paris couturier, had brought out paper dolls showing his costumes. One of the earliest paper doll advertisements in America was Willimatic Thread, published in 1885. The Palmer Cox Brownies advertising Lion Coffee were published in 1892. Hood's preparations brought out paper dolls in 1894, and MacLaughlin's Coffee gave away paper doll queens in 1894. In 1895 Columbia Bicycle Company put out a paper doll of Miss Georgia Cayvan wearing a cycle costume of Eton Jacket, trousers, leggings, and sailor cap. The paper doll giveaway of Prescott Piano Company had movable head and arms. Other companies that used paper dolls for advertising included Aunt Jemima, Diamond

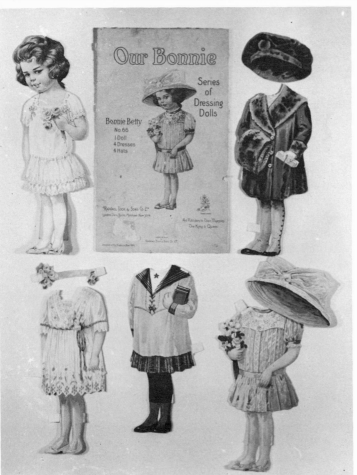

Paper dolls. The American Lady and Her Children. Kimmel & Foster, ca. 1866. Museum of the City of New York.

Bonnie Betty. Cover, doll, four dresses, three hats. Raphael Tuck & Sons, Ltd. Designed at Studios in New York. Collection of Barbara Whitton.

Dyes, Clark's O.N.T. Spool Thread, Wilson Sewing Machine, Dennison's Paper Co., New England Mince Meat, and Duplex Corsets. Worcester Salt gave away a paper doll "Little Jack Horner." There were also paper dolls printed in newspapers and magazines. The Lettie Lane Paper Family and their house and Betty Bonnet appeared in *Ladies Home Journal* intermittently from October 1908 to 1918. Dotty Dingle was created by *Pictorial Review;* Adele was the *Delineator* paper doll, and *Woman's Home Companion* dolls were Kewpie, Punch and Judy, and Twins that Grow Older. The Little Colonel Series was printed by L. C. Page & Company in 1910, and in 1916 *Little Folks' Magazine* printed paper dolls from famous paintings. If you have any of these old magazines, these dolls would make a good beginning for a collection.

Among the most popular of the early paper toys were the quaint dancers or pantines that were moved with strings. These toys were first made in France and were imported to America at the beginning of the nineteenth century. The early pantine was a cardboard figure with dress of gauze and ribbon and moveable arms and legs. The early ones were hand colored; later they were printed and lithographed. These figures were first made for the amusement of adults. They were a cross between a puppet and a paper toy. It was an easy step from the pantine to the dancing paper doll.

During the 1840's, when ballerinas were the vogue, manufacturers of paper dolls brought out boxes of the popular dancers with costumes illustrating their dances. The dolls included Fanny Elssler in her dance "The Cachucha," and five more of her costumes and headdresses. "Taglioni, First Dancer of Paris" also had six costumes and matching headdresses. The doll is posed on her toes with her arms in dance position. These are hand tinted and glazed. Other dancers were Carlotta Grisi and Fanny Cerrito. In 1850 the singer Jenny Lind was printed in paper doll form in Germany. The doll is boxed and has costumes illustrating her roles in *Don Juan, Vielka, Norma, The Huguenots, The Daughter of the Regiment,* and *Robert the Devil.* The doll is a small, hand-colored lithograph.

Little Fairy Lightfoot, one of the series of paper dolls published by John Greene Chandler in 1857, was another of the paper dancers. She stands on her toes and has costumes for offstage as well as two costumes and headdresses for dancing. There were also homemade dancers made of tissue paper and lace, embossed paper, valentine bits, and wallpaper. In June 1861 *Godey's Lady's Book* gave directions for making a dancing doll. Elaborate handmade paper dolls of the 1880's were made with tissue paper, colored crepe paper, bits of tarlatan, ribbon, and cloth flowers. There were also later paper dolls of the actress Maude Adams and the opera singer Geraldine Farrar. Directions for cardboard fairy dancers for children to make were given in *The Youth's Companion,* December 4, 1884.

Anyone who collects paper dolls must have patience and determination. Paper dolls are seldom found in perfect condition, nor are the sets found complete. Sometimes a hat or hand or foot is missing and may not be found at all, or the pieces may turn up in an old scrap book mixed with bits of decalcomanias. Hand-painted dolls are sometimes repainted. This of course reduces the value but does not exclude them from a collection. Paper toys generally are still comparatively inexpensive.

Painted paper dancing doll, ca. 1860. Museum of the City of New York.

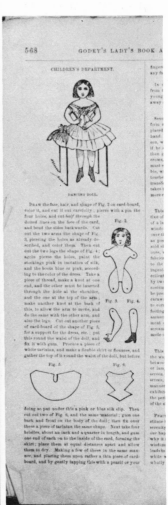

Directions for making a dancing doll. Godey's Lady's Book, *June, 1861.*

16

Cloth Toys

Children's Printed Kerchiefs

inen and cotton materials were printed in America in the eighteenth century. As early as 1712, newspaper advertisements in Boston newspapers referred to printed linens, calicoes, and silks. In 1735 Francis Gray, calico printer from Scotland, "Prints all sorts of callicoes of several colors." There was also a group of calico printers near Philadelphia. Of these John Hewson (ca. 1774) is the best known, since some of his existing materials have been identified. Hewson is recorded as making a kerchief showing Washington on horseback, and an advertisement in the *Pennsylvania Packet,* November 9, 1779, states: "The branch . . . they mean to carry on is the printing of blue handkerchiefs with deep blue grounds and white spots: Hewson and Lang." In 1822 the Merrimack Manufacturing Company printed materials at a large works in Lowell, Massachusetts. The Germantown Print Works printed historical kerchiefs in 1824. Fall River was also an important textile manufacturing and printing center, and in 1831 the American Print Works was established there. There were also several other print works in that vicinity in the early nineteenth century. Dyers' receipt books and swatches from the American Printing Company are in the Textile Depart-

Printed cotton. American Printing Co., 1876. The Cooper Union Museum, New York.

ment of the Cooper Union Museum. Besides the usual floral, leaf, and moss designs, there are designs with pictorial subject matter. One swatch marked 1869 has an American shield with alternating stripes of the word "Peace" and bars of music. There are designs of clasped hands inscribed "Union Forever"; a design of repeating roosters in brown and white (1876); a chick emerging from an egg stamped 1776; a repeat design of dogs (1882); a repeat of small cranes; an underwater repeat of fish and coral; a red and white repeat of bowling pins; and several designs of jockey caps, horseshoes, and horse's hooves (1887). A larger sample of material has a repeat of a boy riding an eagle alternating with the phrase "To Philadelphia." This is on a seaweed background and is printed in black on a white ground and was made in 1876. Since several of these designs, such as the dogs and cranes, would be of interest to children, it is possible that they were made in kerchief squares, but no handkerchiefs as such have been attributed to the American Print Works. Samples of prints from the Dover Manufacturing Company, later Cocheo Manufacturing Company, are in the Rhode Island Historical Society, as are the records of Phillip Allen and Sons of Providence, Rhode Island. The Rhode Island School of Design has pattern books of Woonsocket and Company and Harvey Arnold and Company, 1862, which in 1876 became the Arnold Print Works. Prints from Manchester Mills are found in their pattern books in the Metropolitan Museum of Art.

Cotton kerchiefs depicting events in American life and history were printed at the Germantown Print Works in 1824 and perhaps earlier. However, the first kerchiefs that may have been designed for children are those with illustrations from "Poor Richard's Almanack," and scenes depicting American sports. Both of these groups were printed in France or England. Other kerchiefs have verses and vignettes of autumn and winter. Later there were kerchiefs with printed scenes designed especially for children. A kerchief with verses and cuts taken from early-nineteenth-century children's books was printed in America in about 1820. The verses

Cotton kerchief printed with Christmas scenes. American, Oriental Print Works, late-nineteenth century. The New-York Historical Society.

Children's kerchief with Sabbath School Hymn. Printed at Henry Bowen's Chemical Print Works, Boston, Massachusetts, ca.1831. The Cooper Union Museum, New York.

Printed cotton kerchief with verses for children. American, ca.1820. The New-York Historical Society.

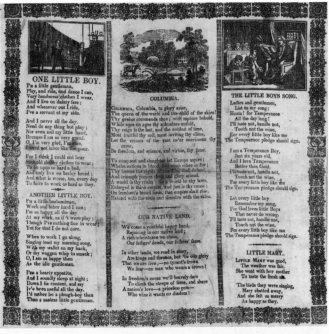

speak of industry, temperance, patriotism, and good children—subjects considered most important in those days. Kerchiefs with picture alphabets and Sunday-school lessons were printed at the Boston Chemical Printing Company in the 1830's. Sunday Lesson No. I has printed prayers and poems for children. It is stamped in gray ink on white cotton. Since the kerchief is marked No. I, there was probably a series of such kerchiefs. Sunday Lesson No. VI is in the collection of the Rhode Island School of Design. One kerchief is inscribed "Sabbath Schools first instituted by Robert Raikes in Gloucester, England, in A.D. 1782." There is a small cut of a teacher and children and this is followed by a few bars of music and the six verses of the Sabbath school hymn, the Golden Rule, and the maker's name, Henry Bowen's Chemical Print, 19 Water Street, Boston. The design and verses are enclosed in a leaf-bordered circle, and this is set within a diaper-bordered square. The kerchief measures ten inches square. Sabbath School Hymns No. 3 has music and words for the hymn and Mary's Lamb. A kerchief with a schoolmaster instructing his class set within a border of ABC's was printed in Germany in the mid-nineteenth century. The Picture Alphabet with pictures of birds and animals in gray ink on a white cotton ground was printed by the Boston Chemical Printing Company at about this time. A kerchief with scenes of children playing

Printed kerchief with center scene of children playing soldiers. English, ca. 1830. The Cooper Union Museum, New York.

Cotton kerchief printed with scenes of Uncle Tom's Cabin. English, ca. 1870. The Cooper Union Museum, New York.

at soldiers was printed in England from early wood blocks, and one with shadow pictures, which were popular in the mid- and late nineteenth century, illustrates hand shadows of the camel, the goose, the dog, the goat, and the bunny. These two kerchiefs are English, of the early nineteenth century. In the 1870's a kerchief with scenes from the book *Uncle Tom's Cabin* was printed by the yard with lines for cutting into separate kerchiefs. Also in the 1870's, "The House that Jack Built" was printed in pink on a white ground. This kerchief was printed in New England and was one of a series of kerchiefs with Mother Goose Tales. Also printed in red on white at about this date was a kerchief with the multiplication table. This was ornamented with bees and flowers. In the late 1880's a cotton kerchief with a Thomas Nast figure of St. Nicholas in the center and four small scenes, one in each corner, was printed by Oriental Print Works and is so stamped. Such children's kerchiefs continued to be printed up to the end of the nineteenth century, and some are still manufactured. In 1941 a kerchief printed in red, white, blue, and yellow on a white ground pictured dolls of various kinds. Another kerchief was stamped with scenes from the poems "Little Bo Peep" and "Baa, Baa Black Sheep." There was also a "Red Riding Hood" kerchief and one of George Washington and the cherry tree.

Printed children's kerchief with story of "The House That Jack Built," American, mid-nineteenth century. The New-York Historical Society.

Books were also first printed on cotton or linen in the 1820's, but they did not become popular until the 1850's. Dean's of London were the first to advertise cut-out and untearable books. A rare cloth book, "Dame Fortune's Magic Wheel," was printed by W. F. Wheeler and Co., London, in 1852.

In 1857, Darton's of London advertised the following "Indestructible Books":

Study Books	*Pleasure Books*
Alphabet	Little Bo Peep
Primer	Mother Goose
Reader	Wedding of Cock Robin
Multiplication	Death of Cock Robin
Spelling	Old Mother Hubbard
	The Cat and Mouse
	Jenny Wren
	Old Woman and Pig
	Little Man and Little Maid

In 1860 "The Child's Own Alphabet" with twenty-four pictures was advertised by Low and Son of London, together with a list of other "Indestructible books" which included the same titles as the Darton list. The printers were Thompson and Vincent.

Cloth books were printed in America by McLoughlin Bros., who started business in 1854. In their catalogue of 1867 the following cloth books are listed:

Dame Dingle's Series—Linen
    Square 12mo. 18 pages. Printed in oil colors. 6 kinds.
                             Per gross, $36.00

Joyful Tales—Linen
    Square 12mo. 18 pages. Printed in oil colors. 6 kinds.

Printed cotton ker-chiefs, English and American, late nineteenth century. From the top: *Santa Claus. Boy with whistle and dog. Dog with basket. Boy and girl blowing bubbles.* Index of American Design.

Linen—Susie Sunshine's Series
    A Series of Large 18mo. Toys. 6 kinds. Printed in oil. Covers gilt.
    The Three Little Kittens
    Sad Fate of Poor Robin   The Robber Kitten
    The Little Old Woman   Little Bo-Peep
    Story of Simple Simon   Per gross, $24.00

Linen—Fairy Moonbeam's Series
    A Series of Large 18mo. Toys. 6 kinds. Printed in oil.

Covers gilt.
  The Frog Who Would a Wooing Go
  Cinderella; or, The Little Glass Slipper
  Aladdin and The Wonderful Lamp
  The Three Bears
  Hop O' My Thumb
  Sleeping Beauty   Per gross, $24.00

Linen—Peter Prim's Series
  A Series of Large 18mo. Toys. 6 kinds. Printed in oil.
Covers gilt.
  Pauline and the Matches   Cruel Frederick
  Heedless Johnny   Truant Peter
  Lazy Charlotte   Inky Boys
                             Per gross, $24.00

Linen—Little Slovenly Peter
  A Series of Large 18mo. Toys. 6 kinds. Printed in oil.
Covers gilt.
  Carrie and The Candle   Tim the Thief
  Johnny Sliderlegs   The Dirty Child
  Sammy Tickletooth   Little Jacob
                             Per gross, $24.00

Printed cotton kerchiefs, English and American, late nineteenth century. Above: Grace Darling. Below: The Pet Donkey. Lower left: Twelve Funny Little Travelers. Lower Center: A B C's, marked Boston Chemical Printing Company. Lower right: Children in goat cart. Index of American Design.

An 1890 catalogue of Dean's of London lists the following untearable toy books: "All the Alphabets and many others are mounted on cloth as Untearable Toy Books. 1 s. each." These included the following books: *Bessy and Jessy Picture Alphabet; Military Alphabet; Alphabet of Birds and Beast; Alphabet of Birds; Alderman's Feast-Alphabet; Alphabet of Flowers and Fruit; Alphabet of Nouns and Objects; Alphabet of Horses, Dogs and Ships; Alphabet of Trades and Industry; Comic Alphabet; Historical Alphabet; Steam Boat Alphabet; Railway Alphabet; Scripture Ball;* and *My Aunt's Ball.*

Cloth dolls have a long history beginning with Egyptian dolls of handwoven linen stuffed with papyrus. In America, homemade rag dolls were played with by colonial children. They were made of linen or unbleached cotton sewed and stuffed with sawdust or bran. Their faces were painted by hand. Few of the eighteenth- or early-nineteenth-century American children ever saw any other kind of doll but the homemade rag doll. There were also early stuffed animals. A rare stuffed cloth elephant made in 1829 is on exhibit at the Museum of the City of New York. Such animals and cloth dolls continued to be made and played with by children for many years.

The first commercial cloth dolls were those made by Izannah Walker of Rhode Island in 1870. It is not known in what quantity these dolls were made. There are a few existing today, but they are rare. *The Delineator* printed directions for making rag dolls in December 1882. In 1889 Lawrence and Company of Boston put out a rag doll and a tabby cat which were designed by Celia and Charity Smith. The Columbian Doll was designed by Marietta and Emma Adam of Oswego, New York, in 1890. Mrs. Martha Chase of Pawtucket, Rhode Island, made dolls of stockinette. These dolls were stuffed and their features were painted. Chase stockinette dolls were popular for several decades. The Arnold Print Works of North Adams, Massachusetts, made material for cloth dolls and animals in the 1890's, and the Art Fabric Mills of New Haven, Connecticut,

Cotton doll dressed as Dutch boy. Late nineteenth century. Collection of Mrs. Margaret Whitton.

also printed cloth for stuffed dolls and Brownie tenpins. The cotton material with the printed figures, front and back, was sold at ten cents the half yard at dry goods and country stores. According to the advertisement in *The Youth's Companion* in 1893, the Tabby Cat and Kittens and Bow-Wow, a pug dog with puppies, were the first figures that were printed by Arnold Print Works in 1892 when the company took out the patent. Tabby was thirteen inches tall, and the kittens, half that height. They were marked to cut, sew, and stuff with cotton. A pasteboard was used at the base to make them stand. Other figures which were patented in 1892 included Uncle Sam and the Palmer Cox Brownies. There were twelve Brownie figures on one yard of cloth for twenty cents. The directions read: "Cut, sew, stuff with cotton, bran or sawdust." Our Soldier Boys; Rooster hen and chicks; Little Red Riding Hood; Pitti Sing; ??? the Owl; Bunny; Jocko, the Monkey; Floss, the Spaniel Dog; and Pickaninny were also put out in 1892. Pickaninny was registered in England in August 23, 1893, as was Tatters, the Skye Terrier. Columbian Sailor Boy was patented in 1893 as a souvenir of the Columbian Exposition. Dollie, a jointed rag doll, is shown sitting in a chair. She was patented September 26, 1893. There was also a Baa-Lamb. In December, 1893, the Cocheco Manufacturing Company advertised their cloth figures in *The Youth's Companion*. These figures included the Doll Baby, Brownie Doll, Japanese Doll, Baby

Cloth Animals and Dolls. Arnold Print Works. The Youth's Companion, *October 25, 1894.* Collection of John Mackay Shaw.

Printed cotton "Brownies," Collection of Mrs. Margaret Whitton.

Printed Christmas stocking. Patented by S. Howe, New York City, 1889. The New-York Historical Society.

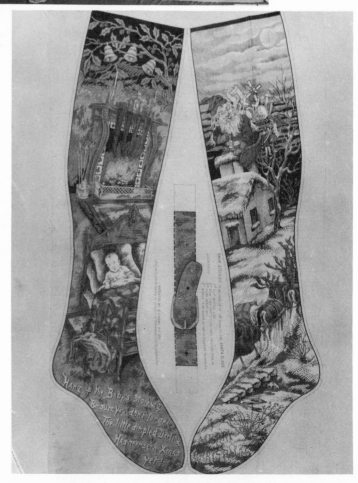

Elephant, Darkey Doll, and Doll and Clothing. The last two were

patented August 15, 1893. The features were prominent, not flat-faced. Lawrence & Co. were the selling agents in Boston, New York, Philadelphia, and Chicago. Shepard, Norwell & Co. of Boston also sold these dolls.

In 1886 a muslin St. Nicholas doll was printed by E. S. Peek. The figure was copied from the Thomas Nast drawing and was sold by the New York Stationery and Envelope Company. The Art Fabric Mills put out a rag doll called "Cry-Baby" which was given away for ten cents plus the names of three friends. This was advertised in *The Youth's Companion,* November 7, 1901. In September 1901 Punch and Judy dolls were used to promote the sale of blueing for the Textile Blueing Company whose New York address was next door to the Art Fabric Mills. So it is safe to say that Art Fabric Mills also made the Punch and Judy, which was printed on sateen. Between 1905 and 1910 Art Fabric Mills put out sheets of rag dolls including Diana, Bridget, Billy, Uncle, The Newly Wed Kid, Baby, and a French doll. Aunt Jemima, Uncle Mose, Little Diana, and Little Wade were printed on muslin by the Grennell Lithograph Company, New York City and advertised in 1896. These were given away in exchange for one Aunt Jemima box top. Sunny Jim and the Cream of Wheat Chef were also used as advertising. There were also cloth beanbags printed with ABC's and other subjects suitable for children. A Christmas stocking patented by S. H. Howe, 1889, is printed with a scene of St. Nicholas on the house top and an indoor scene of stockings hanging at the fireside and the verse "Hang up the baby's stocking / Be sure you don't forget / The little dimpled Darling / Has ne'er seen Xmas yet!"

Linen books and printed cotton children's kerchiefs and dolls are available, although they are not in every antique shop. When found, they are not always in good condition, and one can expect stains and faded colors, with the doll's face perhaps worn threadbare. However, this is a little-explored field of collecting and prices are not high; since there are few collectors, the demand is not great. The cloth dolls and animals are being reissued and are on sale in toy shops.

Chapters 1 and 2

Dwight, Timothy. *Travels in New England and New York*. 4 vols. London: Baynes, 1823.

Earle, Alice Morse. *Child Life in Colonial Days*. New York: Macmillan Co., 1953.

Goodrich, Samuel G. *Peter Parley's Own Story*. New York: Sheldon and Co., 1864.

Hone, Philip. *Diary. 1828–1851*. Edited by Allan Nevins. New York: Dodd, Mead & Co., 1927.

Larcom, Lucy. *A New England Girlhood*. Boston: Houghton Mifflin Co., 1889.

Mather, Cotton. *The Diary of Cotton Mather*. Edited by William R. Manierrett, II. Charlottesville: University of Virginia Press, 1964.

McClinton, Katharine Morrison. *Collecting American Nineteenth Century Silver*. New York: Charles Scribner's Sons, Inc., 1968.

Newell, W. W. *Games and Songs of American Children*. New York: Dover Publications, Inc., 1961.

Pintard, John. *Diary and Letters*. 4 vols. New York: The New-York Historical Society, 1937–1940.

Seybolt, Robert Francis. *The Public Schools of Colonial Boston*. Cambridge: Harvard University Press, 1934.

————. *The Private Schools of Colonial Boston*. Cambridge: Harvard University Press, 1935.

Wilson, Emily. *The Forgotten Girl*. New York: Alphabet Press, 1937.

Winslow, Anna Green. *Diary*. Edited by Alice Morse Earle. Boston: Houghton Mifflin Co., 1899.

Chapter 3

Earle, Alice Morse. *Costume of Colonial Times*. New York: Charles Scribner's Sons, 1894.

————. *Two Centuries of Costume in America*. 2 vols. New York: Macmillan Co., 1903.

Pitz, Henry C.; Warwick, Edward; and Wyckoff, Alexander. *Early American Children's Dress*. New York: Benjamin Blom, Inc., 1965.

Chapter 4

Luscomb, Sally C. *The Collector's Encyclopedia of Buttons*. New York: Crown Publishers, Inc., 1967.

Chapter 5

Bickham, George. *The Universal Penman*. New York: Dover Publications, Inc., 1954.

Bobbitt, Mary Reed. *A Bibliography of Etiquette Books Published in America before 1900*. New York: New York Public Library, 1947.

Carpenter, Charles. *History of American School Books*. Philadelphia: University of Pennsylvania Press, 1963.

Drepperd, Carl W. *American Drawing Books*. New York: New York Public Library, 1946.

Ford, Paul Leister. *The New England Primer*. New York: Dodd, Mead & Co., 1897.

Minnich, Harvey C. *William Holmes McGuffey and His Readers*. New York: American Book Company, 1936.

Nash, Ray. *American Writing Masters*. Boston: Newbury Library, Harvard University, 1959.

Nietz, John A. *Old Text Books*. Pittsburgh: University of Pittsburgh Press, 1961.

Plimpton, George A. *The Hornbook and Its Use in America*. Worcester, Mass.: American Antiquarian Society, 1936.

Tuer, A. W. *History of the Hornbook*. New York: Charles Scribner's Sons, 1896.

Chapter 6

Darton, Frederick Joseph Henry. *Children's Books in England*. Cambridge: Cambridge University Press, 1932.

Field, Mrs. E. M. *The Child and His Book*. London, 1891. (Reprint, Detroit: Singing Tree Press, n.d.)

Haviland, Virginia. *Children's Literature. A Guide to Reference Sources*. Washington, D.C.: Library of Congress, 1966.

James, Philip Brutton. *Children's Books of Yesterday*. London: Studio Publications, 1933.

Mahony, Bertha E.; Latimer, Louise Payson; and Folmsbee, Beulah. *Illustrators of Children's Books, 1744–1945*. Boston: Horn Book, Inc., 1947.

Opie, Iona and Peter. *Oxford Dictionary of Nursery Rhymes*. New York: Oxford University Press, 1951.

Tuer, Andrew White. *Pages and Pictures from Forgotten Children's Books*. London: Leadenhall; New York: Charles Scribner's Sons, 1898–1899.

————. *Stories from Old-fashioned Children's Books*. London: Leadenhall, 1899–1900.

Catalogues of Collections

The Osborne collection of early children's books 1566–1910. A catalogue prepared for the Boys and Girls House by Judith St. John. Toronto Public Library, 1958.

The Kerlan collection. A brief guide to the manuscripts, original art, and letters from authors and artists in the Kerlan collection of children's literature. University of Minnesota, 1963.

Early American children's books. A compilation by Abraham Simon Wolf Rosenbach, with bibliographical descriptions of the books in his private collection. Foreword by A. Edward Newton. Portland, Maine, 1933. (This and other interesting collections are now in the rare book room of the Free Library of Philadelphia, which, on request, will furnish a pamphlet describing its holdings.

Childhood in poetry, by John Mackay Shaw. A catalogue, with biographical and critical annotations of the books of English and American poets that are in the Shaw Childhood in Poetry collection, in the Library of Florida State University. 5 vols. Detroit: Gale Research Co., 1967–1968.

A bibliography of American children's books prior to 1821, by d'Alte A. Welch. American Antiquarian Society, Worcester, Massachusetts, 1963–1968.

Chapter 7

(no references)

Chapter 8

McClinton, Katharine Morrison. *Antique Collecting for Everyone*. New York: McGraw-Hill Book Co., Inc., 1951.

Chapter 9

McClinton, Katharine Morrison. *Antique Collecting for Everyone.* New York: McGraw-Hill Book Co., Inc., 1951.
————. *The Complete Book of Small Antiques Collecting.* New York: Coward-McCann, Inc., 1965.

Chapter 10

Bolton, Ethel S., and Coe, Eva J. *American Samplers.* Society of Colonial Dames, 1921.
Harbeson, Georgina Brown. *American Needlework.* New York: Coward-McCann, Inc., 1938.
Little, Francis. *Early American Textiles.* D. Appleton-Century Co., Inc., 1931.
McClinton, Katharine Morrison. *Antique Collecting for Everyone.* New York: McGraw-Hill Book Co., Inc., 1951.
————. *Collecting American Victorian Antiques.* New York: Charles Scribner's Sons, 1966.

Chapters 11–16

Ackley, Edith Flack. *Paper Dolls.* New York: Frederick A. Stokes Co., 1939.
Anson, D. F. Randolph. *Paper Dolls and How to Make Them.* New York, 1856.
Coleman, Dorothy S., Elizabeth A., and Evelyn J. *Encyclopedia of Dolls.* New York: Crown Publishers, Inc., 1968.
Daiken, Leslie. *Children's Toys Throughout the Ages.* London: Batsford, 1955.
Fraser, Antonia. *The History of Toys.* New York: Delacorte Press Book, 1966.
Jacobs, Flora Gill. *A History of Doll Houses.* New York: Charles Scribner's Sons, 1965.
Jacobs, Flora Gill, and Faurholt, Estrid. *A Book of Dolls and Doll Houses.* Rutland, Vt.: The Charles E. Tuttle Company, 1967.
McClintock, Inez and Marshall. *Toys in America.* Washington, D.C.: Public Affairs Press, 1961.
Price list of Mechanical, Tin, and Britannia Toys manufactured by The Stevens and Brown Mfg. Co., Cromwell, Connecticut, 1870. (Reprinted by Margaret Whitton.)
von Boehn, Max. *Dolls and Puppets.* London: George C. Harrap & Co., Ltd., 1932.

Aunt Judy's Magazine. 1866–1885.

Boy's Own Magazine. 1855–1874 (magazine published by Beeton in London under various titles, 1855–1874).

Chatterbox. 1866–1943.

Children's Friend. 1866–1875.

Demorest's Young America. 1866–1875.

Harper's Round Table. 1879–1897. Combined with *Harper's Young People* in 1895.

Little Corporal. 1865–1875.

Little Folks. 1897–1926.

Merry's Museum. 1841–1872.

Our Little Ones. 1880–1899.

Our Young Folks. 1865–1873.

Peter Parley's Magazine and *Peter Parley's Annual.* 1833–1844.

St. Nicholas. 1873–1940.

The Nursery. 1867–1881.

Wide Awake. 1875–1893.

The Youth's Companion. 1827–1929.

Other Magazines Consulted

American Agriculturist. 1842–1880.

Chronicle of Early American Industries. 1933 to the present.

Godey's Lady's Book. 1830–1898.

Peterson's Magazine. 1842–1898.

Harper's Weekly. 1857–1916.

Harper's Bazar. 1860's and 1870's.

Index

Page numbers in italics refer to illustrations.

345

Cup and ball (game), 202–3
Cyphers; *see* Alphabets

D

Davenport, pottery of, 171, 178
David, John, 25
Delft; *see also* Cradles
  cradles, 36
  shoes in, 49
Dining rooms, doll house, 309, 314
Dinner sets, 166, 169, 171
Dishes, 166–83; *see also* Papboats; Porrin-
    gers; Specific entries
  doll house, 309, 314
  for children, 168–79, *168–79*
Dodge, Mary Mapes, 114
Dog carts, *10*, 261
Doll carriages, *165*
Doll clothes, *196*, 198, *201*, 300
Doll houses
  late 19th cent., *305, 307, 308, 310, 315*
  advertisements for, 304, 308
  books on, 319
  cardboard, 317
  country store, 309
  dolls for, 299–301, *303*, 314
  furniture, 304–17
  makers of, 306, 314
  paper, 322
  Queen Mary's, 319
  Rutherford B. Hayes, 314, 316
Dolls; *see also* Specific entries
  18th cent., *290–91*
  mid-19th cent., *293, 294, 295, 296, 297,
    298, 299*
  bisque, *293*, 296, *297*, 299, 300
  carriages for, 153
  cloth, 336, *337*, 338–39
  doll house, 299–300, 314, 316–17
  kid, 294
  makers, 296, 298, 300
  moving, 301
  musical, 281
  paper, *321–24, 326, 328*
  pedlar, 298–99
  portrait, 294, 296
  wax, 294
  wood, 292–94
Dominoes, *245*, 249
Drawing; *see also* Art; Books; Painting
  directions for, *92*
  lessons in, *95*
  17th cent., *43*
  18th cent., 45, 53, 55, 64
  late 19th cent., *58, 59, 60, 61*
  christening, 38
Drums, 283, *285*, 286
Dupuy, John and Daniel, 25

Dutch dolls; *see* Peg dolls
Dutch settlers, clothing of, 49

E

Earrings, 62; *see also* Jewelry
Earthenware, cradles, 35–36
Education
  17th cent., 96
  18th cent., 84–89
  19th cent., 15–18, 79, 90–93, 95–96
  colonial, 12–15, 75–76, 84–85
Emeries, 197
England
  buttons from, 66, 70, 74
  dolls from, 289–90
  games from, 202, 211, 238
  hornbooks from, 75
  toys from, 280
Evans, Edmund (engraver and printer), 110

F

Fables, 107
Fabrics, 18th cent., 52
Fairy tales, collectors of, 106–7
Fairy tricycle; *see* Tricycles
Fashions; *see also* Clothing; Costumes;
    Dresses
  18th cent., 30, 45, 48–53
  late-19th cent., *60, 61*
Fauntleroy suit, 56, *57*
Fire engines, *264, 267, 269*
Food-pushers, 32
Franks, Elizabeth, *50*
Franks, Samuel and Sarah, *63*
Furniture; *see also* Specific entries
  17th cent., *136*
  18th cent., *138*
  advertisements for, 145, 153
  collecting, 135
  doll house, 304–17
  paper doll, 322

G

Game books, 206, 208, 211, 225; *see also*
    Books
Games, 19–20, 202–4, 223; *see also* Toys;
    Specific games
  advertisements for, 224–25, 227, 238, 249
  geographical, 224–25
  historical, 225–27
  lists of, 227, 235, 238–40
Gaudy Welch mugs, 178; *see also* Mugs
Geographical games, 224–25
Germany
  dolls from, 296
  dolls' houses from, 299

hornbooks from, 76, 78
sampler patterns from, 194
toys from, 159, 250, 255, 277, 287
Gibbs, Margaret, *41*
Gilt buttons, 68, 69; *see also* Buttons
Girls
  18th cent., *50, 51*
  19th cent., *29*
  clothing, 39, 42, 45, 48–49, 53, 56, 61, 64, 69–70
  education of, 89, 184–88
Gloves, 42
Goat carts, toy, *264*
Gold
  buttons, 69
  rattles, 24
  whistles, 26
Goodrich, Samuel, 14
Grammar books, 80–82; *see also* Books
Greatcoats, buttons for, 66; *see also* Coats
Greenaway, Kate, 70, 74, 115, 177
  drawings by, *72, 73*
Greiner, Ludwig, 298
Grilley, Henry, 68
Grocery stores, toy, *317*

H

Hair album; *see* Albums
Hamilton, Sinclair, 110
Handwriting; *see* Penmanship
Hanson cabs, toy, *267*
Harmonicas, *285*
Hatch family, *17*
Hats, children's
  18th cent., 52–53
  mid-19th cent., *56*
Hayes, Rutherford B.
  doll house, 314, 316
Hieroglyphic books; *see* Books; Riddle books
High chairs, *144, 145, 146–48,* 153; *see also* Chairs
Historical games, 225–27
Hobbyhorses, 156, 157, 159, 162, 250; *see also* Rocking Horses
  advertisements for, 156, 159
Holidays, 19–20, *21*
Homespun, clothing of, 38–39, 42
Hoops, 204–6
Hornbooks, 75–78, *76–78; see also* Books
Hot-air toys, 263–64, 320–21; *see also* Toys
Huguenin, George, 260
Humphreys, Richard, 25
Hutchinson, Thomas, 38

I

Ice skates, *212,* 212–13
Infants; *see also* Christening
  clothing, 37–38, 53, 56, 59

furniture, 153
jewelry, 62
Iron; *see* Cast iron
Ironstone, mugs, 178; *see also* Mugs

J

Jackets
  18th cent., 45
  Norfolk, 56
  Zouave, 59
Jack-in-the-Box, 279–80, *281*
Jenny Lind dolls, 294, 327
Jewelry, 62; *see also* Beads; Earrings; Necklaces
  18th cent., 42
  advertisements for, 62
  buttons as, 69
Jumeau, M., 296, 300
Jumping jack, *78, 280, 281*
Jumping ropes, 205, *205*

K

Kerchiefs, 329–33, *330–35*
Kid, dolls of, 294; *see also* Dolls
Kipling, Rudyard, 114
Kitchens, doll house, 309, 316–17
Kites, 216–17, *219, 220,* 221–22
Knee buckles, 45, 62–63, *63*

L

Lang, Andrew, 106
Larcom, Lucy (*New England Girlhood*), 18
Leacock, John (silversmith), 24
Leeds, pottery from, 36, 169, 171, 183
Lithography, invention of, 110
Little Folks (magazine), *111*
Living rooms, doll house, 314
Locomotives, toy, *265; see also* Trains
Lodge, Thomas, *47*

M

Mackay, George, 114
Magazines
  toys noted in, 18, 21, 53–54, 59, 95–97, 112, 121–22, 193–98, 201, 211, 233, 235, 327
Manufacturers
  of blocks, 243
  of buttons, 69–70
  of cloth dolls, 336, 339
  of furniture, 153, 155
  of games, 227, 232, 243
  of marbles, 208

of paper dolls, 322, 325, 327
of skates, 212–13
of sleds, 213, 215
of tops, 209, 211
of toys, 260, 263–74, 283, 286
Marbles, 206, *207*, 208, *209*
Mary Todd Lincoln dolls, 296
Mason, Alice, *40*
Mather, Cotton, 11, 12, 42, 81, 89, 135
Maypole dance, *21*
McGuffey's Readers, 82, *83*
McLoughlin Brothers
  games of, 231–33
  list of paper dolls of, 324
  paper dolls of, 322, 325
  paper dolls' houses of, 322
Mechanical banks, 288; *see also* Banks
Mechanical toys, 270; *see also* Toys
Memorial samplers, 190; *see also* Samplers
Metal; *see also* Specific metals
  buttons, 68, 71, 72
  toys, 308
Millinery store, toy, *318*
Milne, Edmond (silversmith), 24, 30, 66
Moravian
  children, *63*
  schools, 189
Mother Goose; *see also* Buttons; Nursery
  rhymes
  books of, 106
  buttons from, 74
Mountz, Aaron, 260
Mouth-organs, *285*
Mugs, 177–79
Music boxes, 286–88; *see also* Toys
Musical dolls, 301; *see also* Dolls
Musical toys, *282–88*, 283–88

N

Name, Emma van, *23*
Napoleon, 24
Necklaces, 12, 30, 42, 62; *see also* Jewelry
Needlebooks, 197
Needlework, 184, 186, *188, 189, 191*, 193; *see also* Samplers
Nelson, William, 52
New England Primer, 79, 108; *see also* Books
Nicholson, Mrs. John, *44*
Noah's Arks, 259–60; *see also* Toys; Individual makers
Norfolk jackets, 56
Nursery rhymes; *see also* Mother Goose
  buttons from, 70
  collecting of, 106
  in books, 82, 106
  in primers, 80
Nursing bottles, *30*

O

Ogden (William), children, *54*

P

Painting; *see also* Art instruction; Books
  books on, 89, *93–95*
  fashions in, 49–52
Pantines, 327
Pants, 18th cent., 64
Papboats, 30, *31*
Paper
  doll house, 317
  dolls, *321–24, 326, 328*
    advertisements for, 325, 327
Paper
  perforated work on, 195
  toys, 321–28
Papier-mâché, dolls of, 296, 298, 300
Parker Brothers, list of games, 238–40
Pedal toys, 164; *see also* Velocipedes
Peg dolls, 293
Peg tops, 211
Pencil boxes, 97–98
Penmanship, 84–89
  books on, 85–89
  samples of, *88*
  teaching of, 84–87
Pennefeather, John (goldsmith), 24
Pens
  making of, 85
Periodicals; *see* Magazines; Specific entries
Pewter
  buttons of, *67*, 68–69
Pianos, toy, 286, *286*
Pictures, in schoolbooks, 87
Pincushions, *197–99*
  christening, 38
Pistols, *270–72*
Plates, 179–83, *179–82*; *see also* Dishes; Specific entries
Pocket rolling slates, 97; *see also* Slates
Porringers, 31–32
Porter, Abel (pewter), 69
Portrait painters
  listed, 45
Portraits
  17th cent., *40, 41*
  18th cent., *23, 25, 43, 44, 46, 47, 48, 50, 51, 63, 245, 291, 296*
  19th cent., *17, 28, 29, 54, 57, 59, 137, 148, 149, 155, 161, 175, 206, 244, 247, 248, 251, 252, 253, 256, 262, 276, 281–84, 292, 295, 298*
  jewelry illustrated in, *43, 59,* 69–70
  pottery shown in, 174, *175*
Post, Catalynje, *43*
Potteries, 169–71, 174, 179–80

351